MANAGING COAL

SUNY Series on Administrative Systems
Mariann Jelinek, General Editor

MANAGING COAL

A Challenge in Adaptation

Balaji S. Chakravarthy

State University of New York Press

ALBANY

Published by
State University of New York Press, Albany

©1981 State University of New York

For information, address State University of New York
Press, State University Plaza, Albany, N.Y., 12246

Library of Congress Cataloging in Publication Data

Chakravarthy, Balaji S
  Managing coal.

  Bibliography: p. 235
  Includes index.
  1. Coal trade—United States—Management.
I. Title.
HD9545.C43   622'.334'068   80-24891
ISBN 0-87395-467-X
ISBN 0-87395-468-8 (pbk.)

Dedicated to the memory of my father, V. S. Vijayaraghavan

Contents

Contents

Figures

Tables

Preface

This book is based on my doctoral research at the Harvard Business School. It represents a synthesis of two parallel interests of mine: energy management and the theory of adaptation. Professors Robert Stobaugh and Mel Horwitch introduced me to the energy project at Harvard. My interest in the coal industry grew out of my association with that project. My interest in the theory of adaptation was largely shaped by Professors Charles J. Christenson, Paul R. Lawrence, Alfred D. Chandler, and Chris Argyris at Harvard. I am deeply indebted to all of them.

The in-depth field research conducted for this study would not have been possible without the unstinting cooperation of executives in the coal companies that were my research sites. I acknowledge with gratitude their help and guidance. I must thank in particular Mr. Otes Bennett, Jr., President and Chief Executive Officer of the North American Coal Corporation; Mr. Bradlee V. B. Postell, Vice President (Planning and Projects) of Island Creek Coal Company; Mr. Jarvis B. Cecil, Executive Vice President of Consolidation Coal Company; and Mr. Don E. Lee, Manager (Public Affairs) of Exxon Coal, U.S.A. While the content of the case studies included in this book has been cleared with the respective companies, the interpretations and conceptualizations that have been drawn from the cases are solely my own and are not intended to represent in any way the views of executives in these coal companies.

Deans Walter O. Spencer and James T. Murphy at Tulane gave me both encouragement and administrative support to write this book. Professor Mariann Jelinek of McGill University reviewed drafts of this book and gave me some valuable feedback. I also received constructive comments from the editors and outside reviewers engaged by the SUNY Press. Mrs. Mary Lyell cheerfully did all of the typing and secretarial work on the manuscript. I express my sincere thanks to all of them.

My parents inspired me to choose a career of scholarship and research. Unfortunately, my father is not alive today to share my accomplishments. I have dedicated this book to his memory. My wife Kiran cheerfully provided me encouragement and moral support despite the several sacrifices that this project has demanded of her. My warmest thanks go to my family.

For whatever errors of omission or commission that occur in the book in spite.of the excellent support and encouragement that I have received, I am solely responsible.

Balaji S. Chakravarthy

1. Introduction

Coal has been hailed in recent times as "America's ace in the hole," an energy source of abundant supply. The United States is estimated to have about 30 percent of the recoverable coal reserves in the world.[1] Even with liberal mining allowances, these deposits represent a far larger energy reservoir than the known oil deposits in the Middle East. The importance of coal as an energy source for the United States, therefore, needs no further emphasis. Federal energy planners have proposed several measures to expand the conventional use of coal as a fuel for power plants, and also hope to stimulate the early birth of a synthetics-from-coal business. For purposes of this study, the coal industry is defined to include all companies engaged in the conversion of coal to a source of energy, in the solid, liquid, or gaseous form.

The role of the coal industry in the nation's energy future has been looked at from several macro viewpoints (Stobaugh & Yergin, 1979; Wilson, 1980). However, an industry's response is but an aggregate of the responses of the companies that form the industry. Each coal company may be expected to respond to the challenges and opportunities posed by the industry, in keeping with its own objectives and resources. How have individual companies responded to the coal challenge? How are they likely to contribute to the energy future? Important as these questions are, answers to them are sketchy because coal companies and their strategies have been of little interest to researchers. This study is devoted to the understanding of strategic management in coal companies. Its primary focus is to examine how coal is managed.

Mining and processing enterprises such as coal have historically produced relatively few types of products for a well-defined market. Consequently, they have been under less pressure to concern themselves with organizational matters. Their only administrative challenges have been in the

1

improvement of the administrative control of the departmental headquarters and the central office. (Chandler, 1962, p.328)

However, in the two decades since Chandler's study, there have been several major changes in the coal industry. The Arab oil embargo of 1973 in
particular gave the coal industry a new look. More recently, utility markets
for coal are planned to be strengthened, some of the industrial consumers
that coal had lost to oil and gas are being induced to revert back to coal, and
new markets for coal are expected to be created through the synthetics-
from-coal business. While progress on all these fronts may not be rapid,
coal-company managers now have a broader range of product-market options to choose from. Organizational matters have also demanded the increased attention of coal-company managers because of several other
changes in the coal industry. Since the mid-1960s, coal companies have had
to cope with strict regulations in the area of safety and environmental protection. Besides the direct administrative challenge posed by these regulations, there are secondary effects that have been of equal concern to coal-
company managers. Labor productivity in the nation's coal mines has been
on the decline since 1969, the year that the Federal Coal Mine Health and
Safety Act came into effect. Though the Act was responsible in part for the
lowering of productivity, a major factor has been the growing militancy of
the nation's coal miners. The 1970s have been an era of chaotic labor conditions, caused in part by leadership problems in the United Mine Workers of
America (UMW), the largest union of coal miners. Managing human resources has consequently become a major challenge to coal companies. The
Clean Air Act of 1970 and its subsequent amendment in 1977 have had a
destabilizing influence on the long-term plans of coal's utility customers.
The expansion plans of coal companies have also been affected.

To summarize, the recent euphoria of new business opportunities, the
various uncertainties associated with them, restrictive legislations, and a severe human-resource-management problem present a complex set of environmental changes in the coal industry. The industry's long history of poor
financial resources and limited management skills further accentuates the
challenge faced by coal companies. The taxing environment of the industry
makes it an ideal setting for understanding the internal working of coal companies, especially "those aspects of the internal structure that were chiefly
instrumental in limiting performance" (Simon, 1969). The challenge facing
the manager of a coal company is in transforming such limiting aspects of
the company's "internal structure" so as to fit it more particularly for existence under the conditions of its changing industry environment. The challenge is one of managing adaptation.

This study attempts to ascertain, using the concept of adaptation, how coal companies are managed. However, adaptation is in itself a partially developed concept in management literature. A model of adaptation is, therefore, proposed, building on existing concepts in the field. By demonstrating the descriptive power of the model in the coal industry, this book makes a simultaneous contribution to the theory of adaptation. No claim as to the general validity of the model is made by its mere illustration in the coal industry. However, the model does offer a succinct language system to describe comprehensively a rather complex management process. Some of the findings of this study are also supported by recent research in the field, most notably by Miles and Cameron (1977) and Miles and Snow (1978).

The major objectives of the book are (1) To propose a comprehensive model of adaptation, building on existing concepts in the field; (2) to describe the managerial responses of select coal companies to challenges posed by a rapidly changing environment; (3) to explore whether the proposed model of adaptation can help describe the responses of these companies and to offer reasonable explanations for the distinctions in their responses; and (4) to examine the implications of the study for management theory, management practice, and managing coal.

SITE SELECTION

For an exploratory study such as this, in-depth case studies are recommended as the appropriate research method (Roethlisberger, 1978). After a careful survey of the coal industry, four companies were selected for detailed study. The basis of their selection is explained in the following paragraphs.

The coal industry may be classified broadly into three types of companies:

Independents are old coal companies that continue to rely exclusively on coal and coal-based products for their financial well-being, e.g., North American Coal (predominantly in steam coal), Pittston (predominantly in metallurgical coal).

Diversified companies include metal companies like Amax, engineering companies like Utah International, energy companies like Conoco, and natural-resource companies like Occidental Petroleum (Oxy), all of which have major coal companies as their subsidiaries. These coal subsidiaries derive substantial financial leverage through their parents and have a broader management base to work from. This category may be further subdivided into those companies that acquired ongoing coal companies, and those that entered the coal industry de novo.

Captive coal producers include companies like U.S. Steel and Bethlehem Steel which have captive coal mines. Among captive producers of steam coal, Pacific Power and Light is the largest, ranking among the top ten producers of coal in the United States.

The strategic responses of captive producers are mostly shaped by the needs of their captor parents. Since they comprise a special category, captive producers were excluded from this study. The top ten coal companies are arranged in the remaining three categories in Table 1−1.

Table 1−1. A Classification of the Top Ten Coal Companies

	Top ten coal producers	Top ten coal reserve holders
1. Independent	Peabody Pittston North American Coal	Peabody North American Coal
2. Diversified (through acquisition)	Consolidation Coal (Conoco[2]) Amax Island Creek (Oxy[2]) Arch Minerals (Ashland Oil [2])	Consolidation Coal (Conoco[2]) Amax Island Creek (Oxy[2]) Pittsburgh[2] & Midway (Gulf Oil [2])
3. Diversified (de novo entrants)	−	Carter Oil Co. (Exxon [3])

The coal companies sought for the study were successful and seemed a priori to have a long-term commitment to the coal industry. Several coal companies in Table 1−1 were contacted, and from among those to which access was available, the North American Coal Corporation (NACCO), Island Creek Coal Company, Consolidation Coal Company (Consol), and the Carter Oil Company[4] were selected for detailed study (see Table 1−2). Together these companies cover all three industry categories discussed above. NACCO, Island Creek, and Consol have a long history of prominence in the industry, and Carter Oil Company is the most ambitious of the new entrants to the coal industry.

It must be emphasized that only coal companies that are predominantly in the steam-coal business (over 50 percent of sales) were considered for the study, since the major new opportunities for coal are in the energy sector. The team coal "company" as used in this study includes those divisions and subsidiaries of diversified corporations that are exclusively associated with the coal business. Except for the North American Coal Corporation, the sites

Table 1–2. Site Selection

Criteria	North American Coal	Island Creek Coal	Consolidation Coal	Carter Oil
Must represent each industry category	Independent	Diversified parent, Oxy, acquired Island Creek in 1968	Diversified parent, Conoco, acquired Consol in 1966	Diversified parent, Exxon, entered the coal industry de novo in 1965
Must be among the major coal firms in the industry				
a) Industry rank in reserves, 1976	6	8	1	5
b) Industry rank in production, 1976	9	4	2	-
c) Planned production in mid-1980s (million tons)	25	23	91	33
Must be predominantly a major steam-coal producer	yes	yes	yes	yes

chosen for in-depth field study are not really "companies" even though they are described as such: they are divisions or subsidiaries. Nonetheless, the term "company" will be used for all.

A MODEL OF ADAPTATION

The essence of management is the "creation, adaptation, and coping with change." (Ansoff, 1979, p. 30). Ansoff distinguishes between two types of change: one that leaves the nature of the firm intact, and another, strategic change, which "transforms the firm: its products, its markets, its technology, its culture, its system, its structure, its relationships with governmental bodies." The process of strategy helps the firm cope with strategic change.

Strategy is an insightful managerial synthesis of what the company can do, what it ought to do, what it wants to do, and what it must do, into a coherent stream of decisions (Andrews, 1971). Chandler (1962) describes how strategy results from an awareness of the opportunities and needs of environment, and why strategy needs to be matched with a "new or at least re-fashioned" structure if the enterprise is to operate efficiently. When a manager is able to modify the strategy and structure of his firm to match its environment, he has led it to a state of "fit."

However, as Ansoff observes, this fit cannot be an enduring one. Strategy is not the solution to a single problem. Even as the firm transforms itself to meet the needs of the original problem, the underlying problem can undergo enormous changes. The solution may be inappropriate to the new problem. The process of strategy must now be managed to solve the new problem. Such a task is called strategic management (Schendel & Hofer, 1979). Strategic management is needed not only because the firm's environment is changing constantly, but also because of firm-centered "revolutions" (Greiner, 1972), or addition of activities (Scott, 1971). It would seem that the surplus or "slack" (Cyert & March, 1963) created by a successful strategy would itself be a destabilizing influence on that strategy. The firm has more resources as a consequence and can, therefore, seek new activities. Strategic management incorporates simultaneously the notions of fit and evolution. It represents the attempt of a manager to manage the adaptation of his firm to its environment.

Both the notions of fit and evolution, as they relate to organizational adaptation, have been researched extensively. But very few attempts have been made to reconcile the two, which are contradictory at first glance. Christenson (1973) offers one reconciliation by suggesting that there is a hierarchy of fits that a firm must go through as it evolves in its capability to manage more environmental complexity. Clearly a higher-level fit has more long-term survival value than a lower-level fit. The latter has to be disturbed as the firm seeks better assurance for its future. By building on Christenson's work and related research, a compact model of adaptation is proposed in Chapter 2.

The model has three distinct components: (1) adaptive ability, or what the manager has by way of internal resources; (2) adaptive process, or what the manager does to both exploit and enhance these resources; and (3) a hierarchy of adaptive states that a manager must lead the firm through.

Each level of fit presumes a given level of adaptive ability. The process of strategic management is to constantly enhance and exploit the adaptive ability of the firm, taking it to a higher-level fit. The adaptive ability of the firm is in turn determined by its material capacity and organizational capacity.

This model, summarized in Figure $1-1$, offers a succinct language system for studying adaptation in the four coal companies.

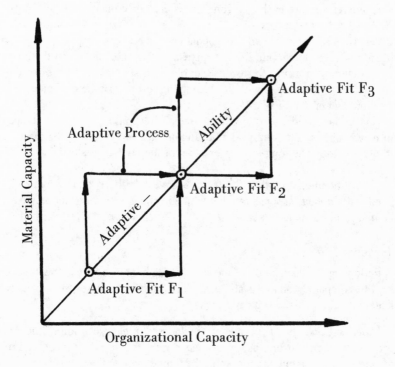

Figure 1−1. A Model of Adaptation

The Case Studies

The four case studies are an important contribution of this book. They provide rich data on distinct adaptations within the same industry. The fact that an archaic industry like coal can show a spectrum of adaptations is by itself an interesting finding.

The data for the cases were collected through field interviews and study of company records and public documents. In order to ensure the integrity of the cases, they were cleared with the respective companies. The author's analysis and interpretation of the case data are presented separately (see Chapter 8), mainly to disassociate the coal companies from any responsibility for his interpretations. However, to help the reader link the cases to the model of adaptation, the cases have all been structured in a standard format, which is described in the following paragraphs.

State of Adaptation

The strategic response of a firm is indicative of its state of adaptation. The strategic response of each coal company is described under three headings:

(1) The Early History: The North American Coal Corporation, Island Creek Coal Company, and Consolidation Coal Company all have a long history of association with the coal industry. The case studies on these companies start with a brief history, describing the strategic responses of these companies as they coped with the fluctuating fortunes of the coal industry up until the end of World War II.

(2) Product-Market Posture: The strategic response of the coal company to new business opportunities and changing business conditions is discussed in this section. The long-term orientation of the company is also briefly presented.

(3) Responding to Other Strategic Changes: If the company had articulated a significant response to other strategic changes, such as in the areas of human-resource management or regulation, such a response is described.

Adaptive Ability

Following the description of the state of adaptation, each case next discusses the company's adaptive abilities. This module discusses the company's material and organizational capacities.

Material Capacity: This category includes a brief discussion of the company's financial strengths; a discussion of the coal reserves and the resource-management practices of the company; and a consideration of technology.

Finance is an important material resource. Discussion of this resource is rather cursory in the cases, because three of the four coal companies are subsidiaries or divisions of a parent oil company. Finances do not appear to be a significant constraint for these companies. Moreover, managers of coal companies were sensitive to probing in the finance area. In the analysis of the cases (Chapter 8) finance is discussed on the basis of external information from public sources.

Coal reserves, unlike other energy resources, are extensively mapped and quite accurately documented.[5] The bulk of the U.S. coal reserves have already been acquired. It is only in the West[6] that some new coal leases may be available, if the federal government lifts its moratorium or if a satisfactory arrangement can be worked out with the Indian tribes that own coal. Most coal companies are, therefore, constrained in their strategies by the extent and nature of their current reserves. Buying or leasing new reserves is not feasible, except from other coal companies. In this context it is important to repeat what a coal sales executive emphasized:

> Coal is a variety of products. For example, for steam coals, variety is determined by location of the reserves and its size, BTU [British Thermal Unit, a measure of the heating value of coal], its sulfur and ash content. Its marketability is influenced by the type of combustion equipment that customers have and the reliability and cost of transportation to get the coal to these customers.[7]

Competitiveness of a coal company is, therefore, shaped to a large extent by the size, location, rank, and grade of its reserve holdings.[8]

However, reserves by themselves do not provide a strategic advantage. In addition, the company must have a good resource-management capability, one that can translate reserve tonnages into production tonnages. The case study describes both the reserve holdings and resource-management practices of each coal company.

The case studies do not provide a separate discussion of technology, normally an important material resource, because the technology of coal mining is fairly standard.[9] Innovations made by one company quickly get incorporated by equipment suppliers into mining machines and are available to other companies soon thereafter. The use of a new mining technology is often constrained not by lack of access to that technology, but by the limited financial resources available to a coal company for investment in the necessary capital equipment. Furthermore, some mining technologies, for example longwall mining, are suited only to certain seam conditions. Thus, access to a superior mining technology is not of significant strategic advantage to a coal company.

Even in the case of synthetics, where research is afoot to develop new technologies, the currently popular technologies (Lurgi, Koppers-Totzek, and Winkler) are available to all coal companies. The experimentation with these technologies is more to establish suitability of a given coal or to establish commercial viability of the process. However, to the extent that coal companies are involved with such research they have a definite competitive edge. The case studies on Carter Oil and Consol describe their endeavors in the synthetics field.

Organizational Capacity: The organizational capacity of a firm is determined by the nature of its administrative arrangements. These include its organizational structure, as well as other administrative systems such as planning-and-control systems, resource-allocation systems, and reward systems.

The case studies describe the organizational structures of the four companies in some detail. The other administrative systems in use are described briefly, mentioning only their high points.

Adaptive Process

This is the process through which a manager enhances and exploits the adaptive ability of the firm. There is no separate section of the case study devoted to the discussion of this process. Its description has been woven through several sections, especially the ones on management of coal resources, and reorientation of the company's organizational structure and administrative systems.

CONTENTS

This book has four major objectives. Part I serves the objective of proposing a model of adaptation, building on existing concepts in the field.

Part II introduces the reader to the history of adaptation in the coal industry and describes the new challenges that coal companies must respond to. Part III presents the case studies. Each case is structured in such a way that the reader can readily identify case data with the key components of the model of adaptation proposed in Part I. Parts II and III together describe the managerial responses of a representative sample of major coal companies to the challenges posed by the coal industry.

Part IV presents an analysis of the four cases, and explores the broader implications of the study. In Chapter 8, the distinct managerial responses of the four coal companies are analyzed, using the proposed model of adaptation. Chapter 9 discusses the contribution of the model to management theory and practice, and explores the implications of the study for managing coal. The latter discussion includes implications both for coal-company managers and federal energy planners. The monolithic public-policy orientation to the coal industry is questioned in view of the spectrum of adaptations exhibited by the industry. Adaptive abilities and adaptive processes (both firm-centered characteristics) are highlighted as factors that shape the coal industry's response, besides the governmental carrot-and-stick.

This book is addressed to several audiences. Managers would find Parts I and IV particularly useful. Coal-company managers will, in addition, find the case studies in Part III interesting. Federal energy-policy administrators may find Parts II and IV of special interest. The academic reader is advised to read all parts in order to appreciate the relationship between the model and data described in this book.

An appendix on coal and coal mining is provided at the end of the book to provide a quick overview.

Part I
Adaptation: A Promising Metaphor

2. Toward a Model of Adaptation

Adaptation deals with the interaction between the firm and its environment. Adaptation was described earlier as the transformation of a firm, so as to fit it more particularly for existence under the conditions of its changing environment. Both corporate strategy and business strategy address this process (Schendel & Hofer, 1979). However, the former looks at environment rather broadly, dealing with the question: What industries should the firm compete in? Business strategy, in contrast, deals with the question: How should the firm compete in a given industry? Since this study is about a single industry, coal, adaptation within a given industry will be the focus of this chapter.

ADAPTATION: SOME PREVAILING CONCEPTS

Under the business-policy framework (Andrews, 1971), a manager seeks to match the material and organizational resources available to the firm with its environmental opportunities. His choice is influenced by his personal values and the social obligations accepted by the firm. Such a process of relating the firm to its environment, called strategy, must be followed by a matching transformation of the firm's organizational structure. Following Chandler's (1962) seminal work in this area, several researchers have studied the relationship between strategy and structure (Rumelt, 1974; Salter, 1970; Scott 1971; Wrigley, 1970). This line of research showed conclusively that a change in structure follows a change in strategy.

At the level of the firm, the normative implication of the above line of research is that a manager seeking to adapt the firm to its environment must formulate an appropriate strategy and design a structure to match that strategy. In a state of adaptation, the environment, strategy, and structure of the firm are matched. Case studies in business policy suggest that there are several distinct strategies and structures that firms use to compete in a given industry (e.g., The World Wrist Watch Industry case series in Learned, Christensen, & Andrews [1961]; cases on the Farm Equipment Industry in Learned, Christensen, Andrews, & Guth [1969]; cases on Mechanical Writing Instrument Industry in Christensen, Berg, & Salter [1976]). These cases suggest that there can be several states of adaptation within a given industry environment. However, apart from providing a framework for understanding adaptation on a case-by-case basis, business policy does not offer any coherent framework for distinguishing these states of adaptation. In contrast, contingency theory offers one such framework for understanding adaptation in an industry.

Contingency theory views firm−environment interaction in systemic terms: many internal aspects of the firm are treated as dependent variables whose form is largely determined by forces originating in the firm's environment (Burns & Stalker, 1961; Lawrence & Lorsch, 1967; Woodward, 1965). In a study representative of this school (Lawrence & Lorsch, 1967), the environmental complexity of an industry is classified in a continuum ranging from highly dynamic to relatively stable. Given the environmental complexity of an industry, it is postulated that a high-performing firm in that industry has to have appropriate "differentiation" and "integration," two firm-centered organizational properties (Lawrence & Lorsch). Interpreting these two properties broadly, Christenson (1973) defines differentiation as the richness of the firm's communication links with the external environment, and integration as the richness of the internal communication links of the firm. The two together determine the information-processing ability of the firm (Galbraith, 1973). In a condition of fit the information-processing ability of the firm must match the environmental complexity of its environment. The Lawrence and Lorsch study would seem to suggest that there is but one such fit for each industry environment. There are two definitional issues that need resolution before such a suggestion can be accepted.

The first issue is the definition of an industry. Industry can be defined very precisely by the product−market combinations it represents, using the Standard Industry Classification (SIC) code. At a fine level of detail a single product−market combination can define an industry. However, managers are urged to avoid precisely this type of myopic thinking. "Management must think of itself not as producing products but as providing customer-creating value satisfactions" (Levitt, 1975). An industry can also be correspondingly defined in functional terms. The coal industry, for example, was defined in this study as performing the function of converting the fossil "coal" to a source of energy. Coal gasification and liquefaction were, therefore, considered activities belonging to the coal industry. Such a definition clearly offers a wide range of product—market options within an industry and, consequently, perhaps a wider choice of adaptive fits. Moreover, product—market complexity is not the sole determinant of the adaptation challenge in an industry. The sociopolitical, ecological, and resource environments of that industry are other determinants (Ansoff, 1979). It is possible that these determinants allow for a wide range of adaptive responses.

The second definitional issue relates to fits. The Lawrence and Lorsch measure of organizational performance includes growth in sales volume, growth in profits, and number of products introduced over a five-year period. The better the showing of the firm along these growth parameters, relative to its competition, the higher its performance. In other words, fit, as equated with high performance, presumes an orientation to growth. Ansoff suggests that "the assumption of search for growth . . . needs to be modified to accommodate conditions of limited and zero growth." In other words, the notion of fit should not necessarily be linked to growth. Growth, limited growth, and no growth may all be viable strategies for successfully surviving the conditions of a firm's environment. A firm following any of these strategies could be in a state of adaptation.

The previous two paragraphs suggest that a theory of adaptation should accommodate more than one state of adaptation. Christenson (1973) provides one such framework. Not only are multiple states of adaptation recognized in that framework, they are further arranged in a hierarchy, ascending from an adaptation to lower level of environmental complexity to a more complex adaptation. Christenson argues that managers and organizational designers must consciously seek to increase the capability for more complex adaptation of a firm which has adapted at a low level of complexity, i.e., they may have to disturb a state of adaptation for the sake of new and higher states of adaptation.

The discussion on adaptation in the previous paragraphs points to several gaps in the literature and raises many questions: (1) If an industry can accommodate multiple states of adaptation, how are these states defined? (2) What does a hierarchy of adaptations mean? (3) How does a manager lead his firm to a state of adaptation? (4) Why should he seek the next higher state of adaptation? (5) How does he get there? (6) What resources are crucial to the process of adaptation?

Questions 1 and 2 refer to the states of adaptation. Questions 3, 4, and 5 deal with the process of adaptation. Question 6 is concerned with the resources on which adaptation is predicated, or the adaptive ability of that organization.

Existing literature has addressed itself only partially to the above questions. The present study describes a model of adaptation, built on three basic components: states of adaptation, process of adaptation, and adaptive ability (see Figure 2−1).

The dotted arrows in the model are suggestive of the transition a firm makes from one state of adaptation to the next higher state. In a state of adaptation, the firm can generate a surplus, or "slack" (Cyert & March, 1963). This slack can be either stored as excess of inducements over contributions with the stakeholders (Barnard, 1938) or reinvested in increased adaptive abilities with a view to move the firm to the next higher level of adaptation. The basic model will be elaborated in the sections that follow.

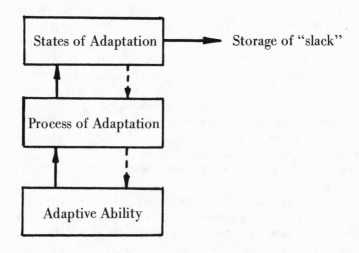

Figure 2−1. The Basic Model of Adaptation

STATES OF ADAPTATION

A state of adaptation, in a biological sense, describes a state of survival for an organism. Analogously, a state of adaptation for business organizations is one in which they can survive the conditions of their environment. In a given industry there may be several niches available to a firm for surviving the conditions of its environment. These niches can be further arranged in a hierarchy based on the extent of environmental complexity the firm attempts to handle. The higher the environmental complexity that can be handled by a firm, the better are the chances of its long-term survival and thus the higher is its level of adaptation. Three such levels are proposed in this study (see

Figure 2−2). The proposition derives from Simon's (1969) parallel definition of the three modes that are open to a system for coping with its environment: passive insulation, reactive negative feedback, and predictive
adaptation.

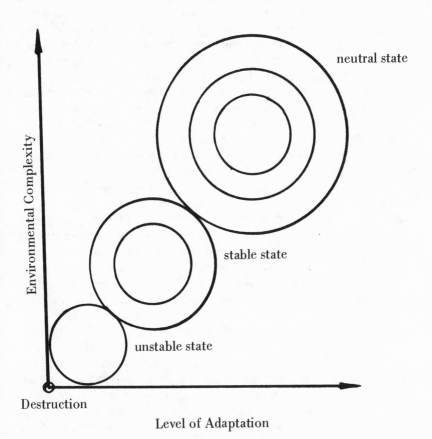

Figure 2−2. A Hierarchy of States of Adaptation

Each level of adaptation represents a cluster of niches that have a common
characteristic, and that correspond to a state of adaptation. Three such states
are defined: unstable, stable, and neutral state. The terminology, borrowed
from mechanics, aptly describes the distinguishing characteristics of the
three states. The unstable state is the most vulnerable to changes in the

firm's environment; a neutral state is the least vulnerable; and a stable state is vulnerable only to certain environmental changes.

In the unstable state, a firm tries to buffer itself from its environment, as it is extremely susceptible to environmental changes. The manager of such a firm, concerned with the fragility of his firm's adaptation, is continuously on the lookout for new buffering arrangements. It is possible for a firm in this state of adaptation to show good financial results in the short run. However, its long-term viability is severely constrained and vulnerable. Called defenders, such firms have "narrow product–market domains—they seldom need to make major adjustments in their technology, structure, or methods of operation" (Miles and Snow, 1978, p. 29). "Defenders deliberately create stability through a series of decisions and actions which lessen the organization's vulnerability to environmental change and uncertainty" (p. 37). "While perfectly capable of responding to today's world, a defender is ideally suited for its environment only to the extent that the world of tomorrow is similar to that of today" (p. 47). Or as Miles and Cameron (1977) state, such an organization adapts by simply ignoring environmental events or demands.

A stable state is a state of adaptation where instead of buffering itself from the environment, the firm is open to it and in fact offers a reactive move in keeping with every move of the environment. The firm reacts to environmental changes and complies with environmental mandates (Miles & Cameron, 1977). While the response of the firm lags environmental change, the response time is extremely short. Called an analyzer, such a firm has a buffered core like the defender, but unlike the defender it also has "extensive market surveillance mechanisms" (Miles and Snow, p. 47), that enable it to imitate the best of products and markets developed by others.

In a neutral state, a firm can withstand most environmental changes because they have been anticipated before their occurrence and the firm has invested in the requisite adaptive ability. The environment may even have been modified to suit the organization's needs. Miles and Snow refer to a type of organization that offers a parallel behavior. Called prospectors, these organizations are continuously searching for market opportunities. They often create changes in their environment, to which their competitors must respond. "A true Prospector is almost immune from the pressures of a changing environment since this type of organization is continually keeping pace with change, and . . . frequently creating change itself" (p. 57). Miles and Cameron describe three different strategic choices that seem open to a firm in a neutral state: (1) Forecasting or anticipating environmental events so as to either restructure for them in advance or prevent their occurrence; (2) absorbing noxious or threatening environmental elements; and (3) adapting the environment to the firm's preferred goals and modes of operation.

The properties of the three states of adaptation described in the previous pages can be summarized as per Table 2–1.

Table 2–1. Three States of Adaptation

Proposed in this model	The nature of coping exhibited in this state (Simon)	Nomenclature used by Miles and Snow for firms in this state	Nature of interaction with environment
Unstable state	Passive insulation	Defenders	Defensive
Stable state	Reactive negative feedback	Analyzers	Reaction
Neutral state	Predictive adaptation	Prospectors	Proaction

All the three states of adaptation are viable ways of coping with the environment. The defender, analyzer, and prospector are all "stable" forms of organization. "If management chooses to pursue one of these strategies, and designs the organization accordingly, then the organization may be an effective competition in the particular industry over a considerable period of time" (Miles and Snow, 1978, p. 14).

However, all states of adaptation do not have the same immunity from environmental changes. The neutral state has the highest immunity, followed by the stable and unstable states. A firm seeking to ensure its future should prefer a neutral state of adaptation over the other two states. As to the question why all firms do not show such a preference, the answer has two parts: (1) the state of adaptation for which a firm aspires is predicated on the resources that it commands, i.e., its adaptive ability; and (2) further, the nature of management processes within these firms (broadly called the process of adaptation) influences the state of adaptation sought.

Both these contingencies will be examined in the pages that follow.

ADAPTIVE ABILITY

As mentioned earlier, the three states of adaptation lie in a hierarchy ascending from an unstable state and progressing to a neutral state of adaptation. The higher the level of adaptation the higher the environmental complexity that can be handled by the firm. A firm can be made to handle higher environmental complexity if its repertoire of information is continuously expanded and its ability to exploit such repertoire correspondingly improved, by improving, respectively, its differentiation and integration. Christenson (1973) defined a property of the firm called level of organization, which is a composite of its differentiation and integration. The level of organization of a firm, relabeled as organizational capacity in this study, is thus directly related to the state of adaptation that can be sought by a firm.

Organizational capacity, which measures the information-processing ability of the firm, is an aggregate measure of the human resources of that firm. However, as business-policy literature (for instance, Andrews, 1971) would suggest, adaptation is also determined by the extent and nature of the firm's material resources. Miles and Cameron (1977) make a similar suggestion and define an "environmental receptiveness cluster" which influences the state of adaptation. Under this cluster, they include resource scarcity, or the extent to which elements in the input environment of an organization are lean in needed resources, and internal resources, defined as the generalizability of a firm's core technology and expertise, and the extent of its slack.

Material resources of a firm include input materials, finance, and technology. The extent of these resources is not measured in absolute terms, but by their relative abundance for that industry. The latitude available to managers in the exploitation of these material resources is another important determinant of a firm's material capacity. For example, a manager pressed for short-term profits is unlikely to devote his attention to resources that require a long lead time for exploitation. The extent of material resources and the latitude available for their exploitation together determine the range of strategies open to a manager.

Summarizing the discussion thus far, it would appear that the human and material resources available to a firm influence its state of adaptation. In both cases, the extent of the resource and the latitude available for its exploitation define the strategic capacity provided by that resource (see Table 2−2). Adaptive ability is shaped by the firm's organizational capacity (ORGCAP) and material capacity (MATCAP).

Organizational Capacity (ORGCAP)

There have been several studies that have examined the information-processing ability of different organizational arrangements. Two ideal types that emerge from these studies are the "mechanistic" arrangement and the "organic" arrangement (see Table 2−3). A mechanistic arrangement is excellently suited to stable environments. A firm in such an environment has fairly stable goals, and its strategic response can be shaped by systematic

Table 2−2. Determinants of Adaptive Ability

Resource	Extent	Usability	Composite Measure
1. Human	Differentiation	Integration	Organizational capacity (ORGCAP)
2. Material			
i. Input materials	Relative	Latitude for	Material capacity
ii. Finance	abundance	exploitation	(MATCAP)
iii. Technology			

optimization models. In contrast, for a more complex and unstable environment, an organic arrangement is the best suited. Strategic response in such an environment involves a constant revision of goals and is characterized by heuristic, disjointed incrementalism. The organic arrangement can process a greater variety of environmental information than can a mechanistic arrangement.

Organizational capacity was defined earlier as the information-processing ability of a firm. To the extent that an organic arrangement processes more varied information, its ORGCAP is higher than that of a mechanistic arrangement. In a mechanistic arrangement, top management alone is involved in the shaping of the firm's strategic response. It is characterized by a highly boss-centered leadership style. Important strategic signals from the lower levels of management are often ignored because authority in the firm is based on one's position in the organization. Such an arrangement limits access to external information, and the firm can consequently deal only with an environmental complexity lower than that possible under an organic arrangement. An organic arrangement is more open to external information. Authority in the firm derives from expertise, regardless of one's position in the organization. The arrangement is characterized by a subordinate-centered leadership style.

In between the two ideal types of organizational arrangements lies another, which provides neither a predominantly position-based authority like a mechanistic arrangement, nor an expertise-based authority like an organic arrangement. For want of a better term, such an arrangement is called bureaucratic. In a bureaucratic firm, strategic response is largely shaped by formal planning systems, whereby subordinates are allowed to participate in the evaluation and elaboration of a strategy, identified by top management. The firm is neither boss-centered nor subordinate-centered: it is closest to being systems-centered.

Table 2–3. Contrasting Mechanistic and Organic Arrangements

Subsystems	'Mechanistic' system characteristics	'Organic' system characteristics
1. Environmental scanning	routine, standardized procedures	nonroutine, flexible arrangement
2. Formal organization	high specificity of tasks, functions, and roles	low specificity of tasks, functions, and roles
	authority based on position	authority based on knowledge
	power concentrated at the top	equalization of power, flat organization structure
	conflicts not normally surfaced, but resolved by superior, compromise, or smoothing	conflicts resolved by group (situational ethics), and open confrontation
3. Reward system	emphasis on extrinsic rewards, security, and lower-level needs	emphasis on intrinsic rewards, esteem and self-actualization
	finite supply of rewards; zero-sum game	supply of rewards dependent on environment, plus sum game
	influence based on manipulation of income and economic security	influence based on linking individual to organizational goals
4. Planning, control, and information system	problem-solving characterized by algorithmic, systematic optimization models	problem-solving characterized by heuristic, disjointed incrementalism, satisficing models
	take goals as given	concerned with revision of social-system boundaries
	uses standard information taxonomies and standard sources of information	uses special-purpose information and open to information exchange with other systems
5. Leadership style	boss-centered	subordinate-centered

Sources: Kast and Rosenzweig, 1973; Dunn, 1971; Normann, 1976.

The information-processing abilities of the three organizational arrangements described above can be classified as per Table 2—4.

The three organizational arrangements identified here correspond to the three states of adaptation described earlier (see Table 2—5).

Table 2–4. Three Levels of ORGCAP

Organizational arrangement	Basis of authority	Organizational capacity
Mechanistic	Position	Lean
Bureaucratic	A combination of both position and expertise	Moderate
Organic	Expertise	Rich

Table 2–5. Relating ORGCAP with States of Adaptation

Organizational arrangement	ORGCAP	The state of adaptation most appropriate, given ORGCAP
Mechanistic	Lean	Unstable
Bureaucratic	Moderate	Stable
Organic	Rich	Neutral

The relationship suggested parallels that described by Miles and Snow (1978). For a defender, they recommend an organizational arrangement characterized by a functional structure, centralized control, long-looped vertical information systems, and conflict resolution through hierarchical channels—in sum, an arrangement ideally suited to maintain stability and efficiency, but not well suited to locating and responding to new product or market opportunities. Their description corresponds closely to the definition of a mechanistic organizational arrangement.

For a prospector, Miles and Snow recommend a product structure with low division of labor, a low degree of formalization, decentralized control, short-looped horizontal information systems, and resolution of conflicts through integrators—in sum, an arrangement ideally suited to maintain flexibility and effectiveness. This fits the description of an organic organizational arrangement.

The analyzer, a hybrid of mechanistic and organic arrangements, aims at balancing stability and flexibility. Its coordinating mechanisms are necessarily extremely complex and expensive. Systems play an important role. The analyzer's organization resembles a bureaucratic arrangement.

Material Capacity (MATCAP)

When material capacity of a firm is poor, the firm is preoccupied with conserving its limited resources. The strategic choices open to the firm tend to be limited because of the scanty material resources available to it. Moreover, given the extremely limited latitude available to its managers for experimentation, their choices tend to be conservative. In contrast, a firm with unlimited material resources and a larger latitude for experimentation can explore several strategic options.

The latitude for experimentation is infulenced by two factors: (1) the importance of the firm's short-term performance to its financial viability—constant pressure for short-term results can divert a manager's attention from strategic goals; and (2) the extent of financial risk that a manager is allowed to take—the greater the risk, the more proactive the strategies that can be explored. In anticipating the environment there is always the danger that a manager may guess wrong. But such risk-seeking behavior may have to be encouraged if proactive strategies are desired.

There is an obvious relationship between the material capacity of a firm and the type of strategy that it can pursue. A firm poorly endowed with material capacity is preoccupied with the conservation of its limited resources, and is likely to prefer defensive strategies. In contrast, a firm richly endowed with material capacity is likely to seek proactive strategies. A firm endowed with rich material resources but constrained in its latitude to exploit these resources is likely to opt for low-risk reactive strategies, which tend to be imitative. The three distinct strategic responses described above are associated with the three states of adaptation proposed in this study (see Table 2–6).

Table 2–6. Relating MATCAP with States of Adaptation

Strategy	Material resources		MATCAP	The state of adaptation associated with MATCAP
	Relative abundance	Latitude for exploitation		
Defensive	Low	Low	Lean	Unstable
Reactive	High	Low	Moderate	Stable
Proactive	High	High	Rich	Neutral

ADAPTIVE ABILITY AND STATES OF ADAPTATION

In the previous section a definite relationship was shown to exist among organizational capacity, material capacity, and states of adaptation. Figure 2−3 summarizes this relationship.

Three types of adaptive fits can be identified in Figure 2−3: Unstable Fit, Stable Fit, and Neutral Fit.

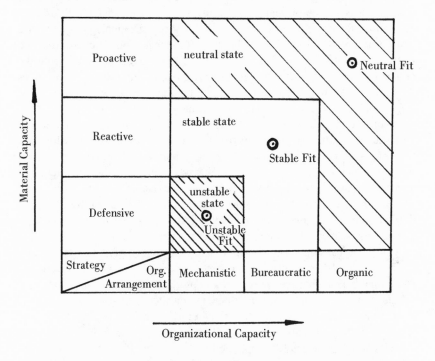

Figure 2−3. Relationship between Adaptive Ability and States of Adaptation

Unstable Fit is the equilibrium condition that exists when a defensive strategy and a mechanistic organizational arrangement are matched. The firm tries to buffer itself from the environment, as it is extremely susceptible to environmental changes.

Stable Fit is the equilibrium condition that exists when a reactive strategy and a bureaucratic organizational arrangement are matched. The firm has enough material capacity to respond to several environmental changes. However, given the limited latitude for exploitation available to its managers, decision−making is often reactive.

Neutral Fit is the highest equilibrium condition, in which a proactive strategy and an organic organizational arrangement are matched. The firm has an ideal match of both material and organizational capacities for its managers to make innovative decisions. The firm's vulnerability to environmental changes is likely to be the least since its managers can anticipate most environmental changes before they occur.

It is important to distinguish between states of adaptation and adaptive fits. Whereas a state of adaptation ensures survival, an adaptive fit ensures *in addition* the optimal use of the material and organizational capacities of a firm. Survival of a firm requires that its effectiveness and efficiency must be kept within desired limits (Ashby, 1971).[1] Effectiveness has to do with the choice of a purpose acceptable to the environment, and efficiency presumes that the "contributions" generated by the firm in meeting its purpose are at least equal to or greater than the "inducements" it has to provide to ensure the cooperation of its stakeholders (Barnard, 1938). Effectiveness requires a constant reexamination of purpose and the selection of alternate purposes—an innovative activity. Efficiency requires, in contrast, a productivity orientation. Clearly the degree of innovation or productivity required of a firm varies from industry to industry. For example, the auto industry until recently is described as having tolerated more of a productivity orientation with minimal demands on innovation (Abernathy, 1978). The computer industry has perhaps demanded the exact opposite emphasis. Whereas a state of adaptation can represent varying emphasis on creativity and productivity (within the limits for survival in a given industry), an adaptive fit represents an optimal balance between creativity and productivity (see Figure 2−4).

It is important to note that a defender, analyzer, or prospector need not necessarily be adaptively fitted. As shown in Figure 2−4, P, P_1, P_2, P_3, P_4, and P_5 are all prospectors, but only P_3 is adaptively fitted. Thus, one can conceive of a prospector having moderate or even low organizational or material capacities, depending on the industry. In fact, the curve P A$_2$ D may trace the path of one such prospector P, that chose to ride the entire product life cycle. While such a firm is adapted to its environment at all times, it is adaptively fitted only at A$_2$. However, instead of moving the firm from a totally creative orientation to a totally productive orientation as the life cycle implies, managers may choose instead to keep creativity and productivity in relatively better balance. As described earlier, adaptive fits—D_1, A_2, P_3—are points of such balance.

Firms outside of these adaptive fits can move to a point of fit through the process of adaptation, to be discussed in the next section. In general, a defender, analyzer, or prospector is distinguished by the highest fit that it can aspire for. Thus a defender can at best seek an Unstable Fit, an analyzer a

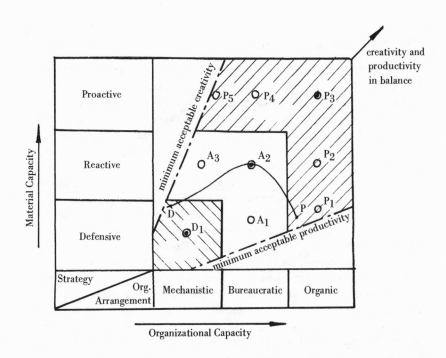

Figure 2−4. Adaptive Fits and States of Adaptation

Stable Fit, and a prospector a Neutral Fit. In the process of such a transition, these firms may be misfitted temporarily. It is in the nature of adaptation to transcend misfits before achieving an adpative fit. Firms under such a transition should be distinguished from firms, called reactors, whose pattern of adjustment to the environment is "both inconsistent and unstable" (Miles & Snow, 1978, p. 81). The inconsistency stems from three sources: (1) failure to articulate a viable strategy; (2) inappropriate linkage of strategy to technology, structure, and process; and (3) pursuit of a strategy−structure fit no longer relevant to the environment. A reactor cannot adapt to its environment. It is important to note that a firm in a state of adaptation can at times show inappropriate linkages or misfits similar to those a reactor would. It is not the misfits per se that make a firm classifiable as a reactor. A firm in a state of adaptation is misfitted with a purpose; it may be in transition to a point of fit. At any rate, such a firm has the ability to manage misfits, while a reactor is incapable of managing misfits.

THE PROCESS OF ADAPTATION

The process of adaptation includes two subprocesses. Dunn (1971) called these adaptative specialization and adaptive generalization. Adaptive specialization is the process of improving the goodness of fit in a given state of adaptation. It refers to the rationalization of processes and structure using available MATCAP and ORGCAP for moving to the nearest adaptive fit. Adaptive generalization refers to the process which improves the survival potential of the organization. It is the aim of adaptive generalization to enhance the material and/or organizational capacity of a firm as required to move it to the next higher state of adaptation.

Adaptive specialization has been discussed at great length in business-policy literature. It involves the choice of a strategy appropriate to the environment and resources of the firm, and the design of a matching structure. Adaptive generalization, in contrast, is a little-understood process.

In order to understand adaptive generalization let us consider a successful firm, adaptively fitted with its environment. In such a condition of fit, the firm generates a surplus of contributions over the inducements that it provides. This surplus is called slack (Cyert & March, 1963). Slack is normally identifiable in monetary terms. It can be paid back to stakeholders as added inducements, advance payments to secure their sacrifices in times of future adversity for the firm. Alternatively, the slack can be used to build the material and organizational capacities of the firm. Managing slack is the key to adaptive generalization. Christenson (1973, p. 46) describes how slack should be managed:

> The manager or designer of an organization who wishes to increase its capability for the long run should "invest" any capacity his system has to do work in excess of its current maintenance requirements to create conflict-resolution mechanisms of the preferred kind. That is, he should *overintegrate* the system relative to what a "fit" theory would call for. Then he should seek to provide as much cognitive conflict as his system can handle effectively, by increasing the flow of environmental information. That is, he should *overdifferentiate* the system relative to the subjective environment. The natural tendency of the system, then, as it seeks to restore its internal equilibrium will be to increase the complexity and sophistication with which it perceives the environment.

The process of adaptive generalization thus requires that an old fit be consciously disturbed for the sake of a new and higher fit. However, the process not only requires an improvement in the organizational capacity of a firm as suggested by Christenson, but also an improvement in the firm's material capacity. Furthermore, once the firm acquires these additional capacities mere "natural tendencies" will not make it adaptively fitted once again, as suggested by Christenson. The process of fitting a firm at its new and higher state of adaptation was defined earlier as adaptive specialization. This is a consciously managed process.

The process of adaptation includes both of the above subprocesses: adaptive generalization or *managing misfits* and adaptive specialization or *managing for fits* (see Figure 2−5).

A MODEL OF ADAPTATION

The discussion in the previous sections may be summarized as follows:

(1) Adaptation is influenced both by the organizational capacity and material capacity of a firm.

(2) Organizational capacity of a firm is measured by its information-processing ability. Firms are classified in their increasing order of organizational capacity, based on whether they have mechanistic, bureaucratic, or organic organizational arrangements.

(3) Material capacity of a firm allows for defensive, reactive, or proactive strategies. Such a capacity is determined by the relative abundance of material resources that the firm has and the latitude available to its managers for exploiting these resources. Material resources include input raw material, finances, and technology.

(4) Each level of material and organizational capacity is associated with a corresponding state of adaptation. Three such states of adaptation were defined: unstable state, stable state, and neutral state.

(5) When organizational and material capacity are perfectly matched, a firm is said to be in an adaptive fit. One such adaptive fit can be identified in each state of adaptation.

(6) The subprocess of improving the goodness of fit in a given state of adaptation is called adaptive specialization, and the subprocess of disturbing an adaptive fit so as to lead the firm to a higher state of adaptation is called adaptive generalization. The process of adaptation includes both these subprocesses.

The basic model of adaptation suggested in Figure 2−1 can now be elaborated (see Figure 2−6).

The firm's strategy evolves in the amount of environmental complexity that it can handle through the process of adaptation. Managing the evolution

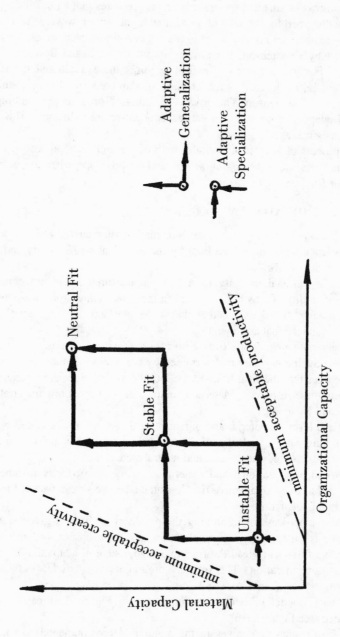

Figure 2-5. The Process of Adaptation

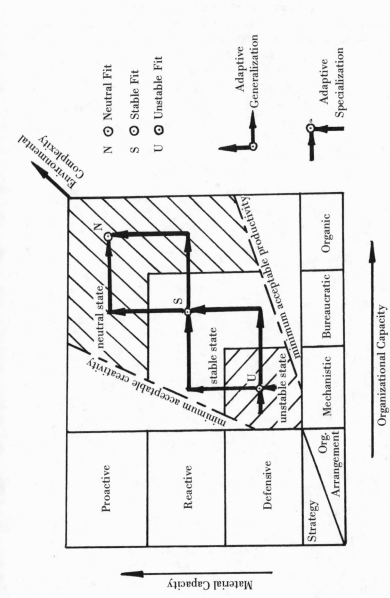

Figure 2–6. An Expanded Model of Adaptation

of strategies is strategic management (Schendel & Hofer, 1979). Managing adaptation and strategic management are identical concepts.

The model of adaptation proposed here will be used to study strategic management in the four selected coal companies.

Part II
Adaptation in the Coal Industry

3. Historical Patterns and New Challenges

Coal companies have experienced great adversity since the 1920s, making mere survival a major accomplishment. The expanding use of the internal-combustion engine, the clean-burning properties and convenience of oil and gas for other uses, and above all, the lowering of the average price of energy through the use of oil and gas have displaced coal as a major fuel source (see Figure 3–1). Except for brief periods of profitability spurred by extraneous factors such as World War II or the Arab oil embargo of 1973, the industry has earned very poor returns on its equity (see Table 3–1). Poor financial resources have constrained the strategic choices available to coal companies. In recent years, mushrooming legislation and militant labor have added to the woes of the industry. Coal companies must cope with these challenges and simultaneously find ways of exploiting the new business opportunities that are apparently emerging given the newfound importance of coal. As we shall see, even these new opportunities are nebulous and uncertain.

ADAPTING TO CHANGING MARKETS

The markets for coal have changed radically through this century. In the first two decades of the current century, railroads and home heating were the major markets for coal. The railroad markets were lost to diesel oil, a cleaner and more convenient fuel. The home-heating markets were also captured by oil and gas. Changes in the markets for coal are shown in Table 3–2.

The declining markets for steam coal up to World War II made cost of mining an important competitive factor. Wages were depressed and working conditions were allowed to deteriorate as coal companies tried frantically to

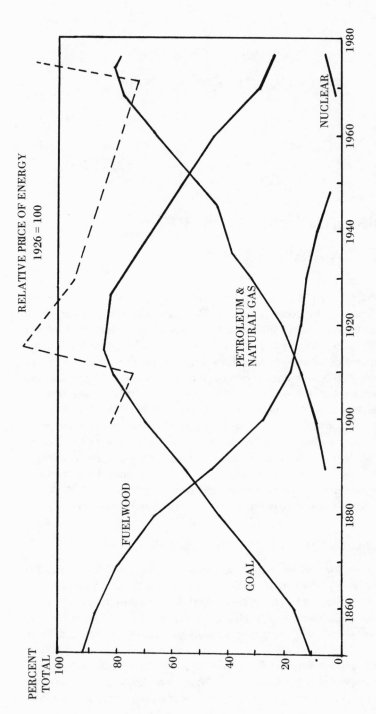

RELATIVE PRICE OF ENERGY
1926 = 100

PETROLEUM &
NATURAL GAS

NUCLEAR

FUELWOOD

COAL

PERCENT
TOTAL

100

80

60

40

20

0

1860   1880   1900   1920   1940   1960   1980

SOURCE: Bureau of the Census Bureau of Mines, *Historical Statistics of the United States, 1974.*

Figure 3–1. U.S. Energy Consumption Patterns

Table 3–1. Profitability Trends

Year	Coal industry net income after tax ($ million)	Return on average equity (%)	
	approximately		
1930	-50	-	
1935	-15	-	
1940	10	-	
1945	40	3.5 ⎱	World War II era
1948	200	12.5 ⎰	
1950	90	5.0	
1955	34	2.4	
1960	9	0.6 ⎱	Growth in utility
1965	70	4.2 ⎬	markets
1970	157	11.2 ⎰	
1972	22	1.1	

Source: Tomimatsu, *The State of the U.S. Coal Industry: A Financial Analysis of Selected Coal-Producing Companies*, 1976.

cut costs in order to remain profitable. However, the growing power of the UMW made that a short-lived strategy. Operating economies had to be sought in larger mine sizes and in increased mechanization. The more enlightened coal companies acquired smaller coal companies and/or merged with other coal companies in an effort to increase their financial base and to preempt competition. North American Coal (NACCO), Island Creek, and Consolidation Coal (Consol) all went through a phase of acquisitions and mergers as they sought to attain a dominant position in the coal markets.

Metallurgical or coking coal did not suffer the declining fortunes of steam coal in the period 1920–1950. However, representing a relatively smaller market segment, it could not become an alternative of major importance either. Nevertheless, coal companies that had earlier ignored metallurgical-coal markets sought a presence in that segment. NACCO and Consol, for example, stepped up their metallurgical-coal activities. Coal companies sought joint ventures with steel companies not only to guarantee demand, but also to help them cut down on the capital expenditures required for the development of their metallurgical-coal reserves. Companies like Island Creek and Consol used the joint-venture strategy effectively, making metallurgical coal an important product in their portfolios. While metallurgical coal did provide a useful hedge against the generally declining markets for coal, a strategy built around metallurgical coal presumed adequate availability of acceptable-quality metallurgical-coal reserves. Companies not en-

Table 3–2. Changes in Markets for Coal

	Distribution (Millions of Tons)						Percent share of distribution			
	1920	1940	1950	1960	1970	1974	1920	1940	1960	1974
Railroads	135	85	61	2	*	*	24.7	19.9	0.5	—
Utilities	37	49	88	174	319	390	6.8	11.4	43.4	63.6
Coke	76	81	104	81	96	90	13.9	18.9	20.2	14.7
Retail deliveries	260†	85	84	30	12	9	47.5†	19.9	7.5	1.5
Other manufacturing & mining		111	98	77	88	64		25.9	19.2	10.4
Exports	39	17	25	37	71	60	7.1	4.0	9.2	9.8
Total	547	428	460	401	586	613	100.0	100.0	100.0	100.0

*The railroad tonnage is included under other manufacturing for 1970 and 1974.
†Includes steel-rolling mills and cement mills.
Sources: Booz-Allen and Hamilton, Inc., *Survey of Opportunities to Stimulate Coal Utilization*, 1962.
Tomimatsu, *The State of the U.S. Coal Industry: A Financial Analysis of Selected Coal-Producing Companies*, 1976.

dowed with or financially incapable of acquiring metallurgical-coal reserves were denied this mode of adaptation.

Apart from diversification into metallurgical coal, coal companies also sought diversification into other product areas through research and development. NACCO and Consol, for example, tried diversifying into the chemical business. Consol also set up an R&D program in 1946 to explore the feasibility of converting coal into synthetic fuels. NACCO's R&D efforts were, however, unsuccessful and the company disbanded its research department in 1963. By and large the experience of other coal companies was similar to NACCO's, with the exception of Consol. Diversification outside of coal did not occur to any significant degree.

While the above efforts helped coal companies to cope modestly with the changes in the markets for coal, the fast-growing utility segment proved to be the biggest benefactor. Coal consumption by utilities expanded dramatically from 6.8 percent of all coal produced in 1920 to 63.6 percent of the coal produced in 1974. Coal had finally found a new market segment that was large and growing. Not surprisingly, all the major steam-coal companies aspired for a share in this market segment. Price, reliability, and continuity of supply became competitive factors. Coal companies like NACCO and Consol that already had large operations and were diversified geographically became natural contenders. These were among the first companies to establish long-term contractual relationships with utilities. Both were cosigners in 1953 with the Ohio Valley Electric Corporation of the first long-term contract in the coal industry. Since then both companies have looked into long-term contracts for protecting their production of steam coal. Long-term contracts ranging from two to thirty years accounted for approximately 80 percent of the 25 million tons that Consol sold to utilities in 1965. In the case of NACCO, 76 percent of its production of nearly 6 million tons was under long-term contract with utilities as of 1965. Long-term contracting soon became an industrywide phenomenon; coal companies tried to buffer themselves from the uncertainity of demand through this instrument.

However, the growth in utility markets did not help improve the profitability of all companies in the industry. Many utilities exploited their position as customers who had a large sustained demand by extractinng very favorable supply contracts from coal comapnies. The average price of coal at power-generating plants actually declined by 6 percent in the period 1948–1959, while the price of its chief competitor, natural gas, more than doubled. Only the large coal companies could make use of the new opportunity for their financial well-being. As a consequence, the industry became more concentrated in the period 1950–1965 (see Table 3–3), and the size of mines increased (see Table 3–4).

Table 3–3. National Coal-Production Concentration Ratios

Year	4-Firm	8-Firm	20-Firm
1950	13.6	19.4	30.4
1955	17.8	25.5	39.6
1960	21.4	30.5	44.5
1965	26.6	36.3	50.1

Source: General Accounting Office, *The State of Competition in the Coal Industry*, 1977.

Table 3–4. Percentages of Coal Output by Tonnage Class

Tonnage Range	1949	1960	1965
Million tons and over	50.5	64.9	68.1
100,000–999,999 tons	31.7	22.1	22.5
Less than 100,000 tons	17.8	13.0	9.4
Total	100.0	100.0	100.0
Total million tons	438	415	512

Source: 1977 Keystone Coal Industry Manual.

COPING WITH REGULATION

Safety

The coal industry has traditionally been a notoriously unsafe one. While the safety record of the industry has steadily improved with increased mechanization (see Figure 3–2), even as late as in the 1950s there were nearly 450 mine disasters in which nearly 400 men were killed. In an effort to improve the safety of the nation's mines, Congress enacted Public Law 91–173 of 1969. This law is commonly known as the Federal Coal Mine Health and Safety Act (Safety Act).

The Safety Act has definitely had an impact on the safety performance of the industry. Table 3–5 compares the fatalities for two seven-year periods, one prior to the Act and one subsequent to the Act. In acknowledging the beneficial contribution of the Act, the National Coal Association[1] and the Bituminous Coal Operators Association[2] mention in their joint report:

The two most dramatic reductions—in fatalities caused by roof and rib falls and by gas or dust explosions—were undoubtedly due to the combined efforts of vigilant enforcement of the Act and hundreds of

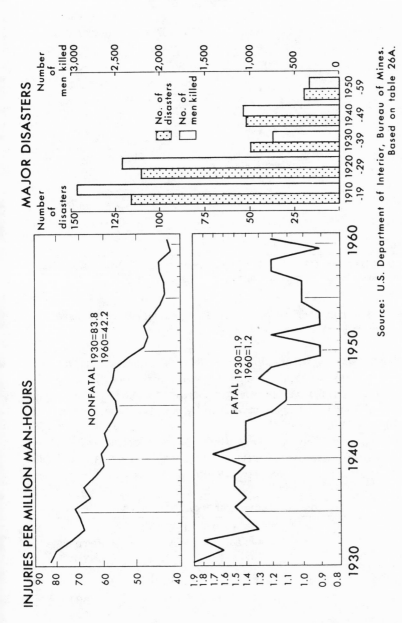

Figure 3–2. Injury Rates, 1930–1960, and Major Disasters, 1910–1959 in Bituminous Coal Mining

Table 3−5. Fatality Comparison

Cause	1961−1967 period	1970−1976 period	Percent reduction or increase
Roof/rib fall	807	381	−53%
Explosion	153	73	−52%
Haulage	256	208	−19%
Surface	255	238	− 7%
Explosives	17	7	−59%
Other	58	38	−34%
Machinery	99	127	+22%
Electrical	44	56	+11%
Total	1,699	1,139	−33%

Source: NCA and BCOA, "Federal Coal Mine Health and Safety Act of 1969. A Constructive Analysis with Recommendations for Improvements," 1977.

thousands of man-hours spent by industry operating and safety personnel controlling the working environment in the mines.[3]

During the seven-year period of 1961−1967, the average fatality rate per million man-hours was 1.05. During the seven-year period following the passage of the Act, the average fatality rate dropped to 0.58, a 44.8 percent reduction. The total disabling-injury-frequency rate also dropped subsequent to the Act (see Table 3−6).

These improved safety conditions were, however, achieved with an associated loss of productivity, especially in underground mines (see Table 3−7). Without suggesting that the trade-off was not desirable, it must be

Table 3−6. Total Disabling-Injury Rates

	1967−1969 Average rate	1975−1976 Average rate	Percentage Reduction
Underground	48.60	40.07	−17.6
Surface	23.11	17.77	−23.1
All bituminous operations	42.30	31.80	−24.8

Source: NCA and BCOA joint report, op. cit.

Table 3-7. Productivity Trends in U.S. Coal Mines

Year	Labor productivity tons/man-day Underground	Strip
1960	10.64	22.93
1965	14.00	31.98
1970	13.76	35.96
1975	8.50	26.00

Source: U.S. Bureau of Mines.
Note: The productivity decline is only partly attributable to the Safety Act.

pointed out that the Act did significantly alter or restrict the permissible production techniques in a mine. Illustrative of such provisions are:

(1) Every twenty minutes the continuous miner must be shut down to sample the air for its methane content.

(2) Formerly, continuous miners tunneled distances of 100−400 feet before the roof was bolted and the walls coated with limestone. They are currently restricted to twenty feet before this work must be done.

(3) Only equipment items smaller than a mine car can be moved while other employees are working nearby. Consequently, all significant equipment must be moved either during idle shifts or by completely stopping production and removing the personnel who are working nearby.

(4) Mine superintendents cannot alter the mine-ventilation system or move a high-voltage cable without prior federal approval.

Further, the disruption of work caused by frequent federal and state inspections of mines contributed to the loss in productivity.

In an earlier section it was pointed out that coal companies had aggressively sought long-term contracts with utilities since the late 1950s. The long-term commitments posed a special problem. The drop in productivity associated with the Act required coal companies to expand their work force even to maintain contracted production. For an industry which until then was accustomed to the luxury of a surplus labor market, the sudden pressure to recruit under a tightening labor supply came close to being a traumatic experience.

There were important organizational changes that took place in coal companies in response to the pressures brought on by the Safety Act. Firstly, the administration of the Act itself required a central liaison group, which could keep the chief executive fully apprised of the progress of implementation. Another major central function was recruitment. Coal-company management

at the highest level began worrying about recruiting workers and supervisors. The administration of the Safety Act had created a number of new
jobs with the government as mine inspectors. Many experienced supervisors
from the coal industry filled up these openings, thus creating, in addition to
the manpower shortage, a supervisory vacuum in the coal mines. Companies
like Consol set up a central recruitment department to cope with the problem. With the elevation of the recruitment function from the mines to the
corporate office, the foundations for the establishment of a corporate personnel department had been laid. A related development was the growth of
the training function. The Safety Act mandated safety-related training for the
miners. However, the real impetus for training came from the tough recruitment situation. Coal-company managers realized that many of the miners recruited in the early 1970s were inexperienced. They had to be trained before
they could become productive miners. Coal companies like Island Creek and
Consol set up a central training department to address that problem.

In summary, two distinct organizational developments occurred in the
panies grew in scope from its hitherto industrial-relations orientation.
Recruitment and training were recognized as important functions. In con-
junction with these, employee-welfare activities began expanding as coal-
company managers tried to cope with the increasing militancy of their coal
miners. The makings of a full-blown personnel function could be identified
in major coal companies. The other development was the elevation of personnel management beyond the level of the mine foreman. In some coal
companies like NACCO the function was elevated to divisional jurisdiction.
In others, like Consol and Island Creek, the personnel function was elevated
to corporate jurisdiction. As a corollary, the job of the mine manager became increasingly production-focused. He had his hands full coping with requirements under the Safety Act, the associated drop in productivity, the
larger number of men required to mine the same tonnage of coal, and the
higher level of inexperience in many of the new recruits.

Environment

In the late 1960s a nationwide consciousness emerged for environmental
protection. The Clean Air Act of 1970 sprung out of this public consciousness. The Environmental Protection Agency (EPA) established air-quality
standards that in effect prohibited the use of coal with more than 0.7 percent
sulfur in any new power plants. After July 1, 1975, the prohibition applied
to old power plants as well. In reporting the impact of the Act, *Forbes*
stated:

At the 1975 deadline, according to one estimate, 300 million tons of high sulfur coal will no longer be acceptable for power plant use. To replace half the coal industry's output in less than three years might seem impossible if not unthinkable.[4]

Stack-gas cleaning was supposed to do the job. But the Flue Gas Desulfurization (FGD) technology, as it was called, was not only unreliable but expensive. As late as 1977, both the capital investments and operating costs of alternate FGD technologies were prohibitive (see Table 3−8).

Reacting to the pressure on high-sulfur coal, many coal companies expanded their reserves of low-sulfur Western coal, but that strategy was almost short-lived since, in response to the growing clamor of environmentalists, the federal government (owner of 70 percent of the coal reserves in the five southwestern states) imposed a moratorium in 1971 on leasing its Western coal lands. The state governments and Indian tribes, who each hold 13 percent of the coal lands, are equally reluctant to lease coal lands, and if they do at all, it is at a healthy leasing fee.

The major coal companies of the 1960s had traditionally concentrated on the Eastern coal fields. The new entrants to the industry had, in contrast, focused on reserve acquisition in the West. This was primarily because Eastern coal reserves were difficult to obtain. Moreover, the Western subbituminous and lignitic coals were considered more suited for conversion to gas and oil—an important consideration for many large oil companies that entered the coal industry in the 1960s. With the exception of Consol, the then major coal companies largely ignored this westward move. The Clean Air Act of 1970 pointed to the shortsightedness of these coal companies. The low-sulfur Western coals became an important reserve to seek. The federal moratorium on coal leases, however, made the acquisition of Western reserves a difficult task. Coal companies established a central-reserve-acquisition department to cope with the challenge.

This department was entrusted not only with the responsibility of acquiring Western reserves but also with the task of streamlining the entire process of reserve management within these coal companies. Large reserves had generally been collected in the past as appendages to the acquired coal mines. Supplemental reserves had been acquired on an ad hoc basis to suit operating needs. The reserve-acquisition department was expected to change all that. Long-term planning for reserve acquisition and exploitation became an important new activity for coal companies. Consol centralized its reserve-management function under a vice-president in 1973 and called it the exploration function. NACCO created an exploration department in 1973 under a vice-president. Reserve acquisition, exploration, reserve or resource management were various synonyms that described a brand-new activity in coal companies—the centralized planning of reserve exploration, acquisition, and exploitation.

The spate of proposed and actual regulations that followed the Clean Air Act led many coal companies to set up other new functional departments. The Surface Mining Control and Reclamation Act of 1977 was one such regulation. Fought for years by the industry, the law was enacted in early 1977 in part to prevent the rape-and-run syndrome that had devasted so much of Appalachia. For the first time, strict federal control of strip-mine reclamation was established in those states that had lower standards than those decreed by Congress. The direct cost of the new act was estimated at $1 per ton in the West, where the rules were already strict, to $8 per ton in states where small mines had had less scrutiny.[5]

Coal companies became aware of two new realities: (1) The new regulations implied new administrative responsibilities at the divisional and corporate management levels—a regulatory-affairs function, also called the environmental-affairs function, was formalized to deal with this challenge; and (2) if further regulation had to be minimized, coal companies had to place their case strongly before the Congress and the general public—the public-affairs function was created for this purpose.

Coal companies which were predominantly surface miners faced several constraints on environment protection. Large Western coal companies like Amax and Utah International found it advantageous, therefore, to have a separate department to deal with environmental matters.

In Amax, as of November 1973, an environmental-engineering department was created under the Vice-President (Engineering) with three areas of responsibility: environmental studies, environmental planning, and environmental services (see Figure 3–3). The department was staffed with individuals possessing skills and backgrounds previously unheard of in the coal industry. For example, Amax had four wildlife biologists, a physicist, a hydrologist, a geographer, and an environmental engineer among its environmental-engineering staff. In a similar vein, Utah International set up an environmental quality department in 1971. The department was headed by a director, who reported to the president of the company. The department had three roles: (1) environmental conscience of the company—always keeping a finger on the pulse of the environmental movements, as reflected by pressure groups within the society as well as the legislative process; (2) advisor/consultant—in this role the department assessed the problems of the operating projects in light of legislative requirements and Utah's environmental policy; and (3) direct service—field surveys, program designs, and data analyses were done for projects which had neither staff nor expertise for such work.[6]

Table 3–8. An Economic Analysis of Alternate FGD Technologies

System	Capital investments† for emission-control alternatives		Cost of electrical power via alternate emission-control systems (mill/kw hr.)		
	Total fixed investment ($ million)	($/kw)	Coal	Emission control system	Total
Base case*			8.4	2.7	36.1
FGD					
Limestone	105	210	8.8	12.1	45.9
Wellman-Lord	115	230	8.8	12.9	46.7
ACP	120	240	8.7	10.9	44.6

*3.5 percent sulfur coal was used for comparison.

†All amounts are in 1980 dollars, assuming no interest during construction, no escalation beyond 1980. Capital costs were escalated to 1980 at a rate of 9 percent per year from 1977 costs.

Source: Lawrence H. Weiss, "Clean Fuel and Scrubbing Compared," 1977 Keystone Coal Industry Manual.

Table 3–9. Statistics on Petroleum Companies Active in Coal, 1976

Company	Nature of Entry	Reserves (billion tons)	Production (million tons)	Percent of U.S. Production
Continental Oil	Acquisition (Consol)	13.7	55.9	8.4
Exxon	De novo	8.4	2.8	—
Occidental Petroleum	Acquisition (Island Creek)	3.6	17.6	2.6
Gulf Oil	Acquisition (Pittsburg & Midway)	2.8	7.9	1.2
Mobil Oil	De novo	2.5	—	—

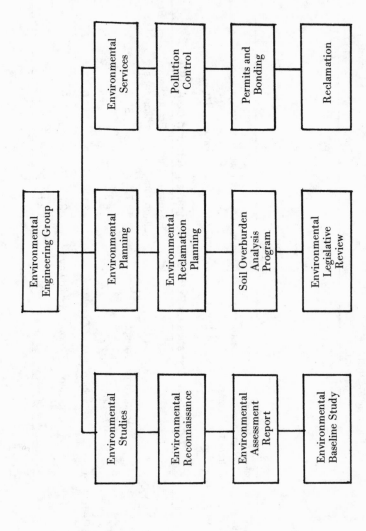

Source: John Cassady, "Obstacle Course for Permits and Approval," *Mining Congress Journal*, September 1975.

Figure 3-3. Environmental Engineering Functions at Amax

Coal companies that were predominantly deep miners did not see the need to set up elaborate environmental-affairs departments as Amax or Utah International had done. Nevertheless, a formal function called environmental affairs was recognized and a corporate director or vice-president was designated to head the new function.

Coal companies also became increasingly public-relations conscious. Reflecting the new trend, *Coal Age* in its editorial of 1976 titled "Come Blow Your Horn" stated:

> Although modesty is often an admirable trait, it's a luxury that coal cannot afford to indulge in. Coal simply can't play the shy maiden whose superb qualities will certainly and ultimately be discovered. Those are chances that coal and U. S. can't afford to take.

While industry associations like the National Coal Association, The Bituminous Coal Operators' Association, and the American Mining Congress (AMC) were all active in projecting coal's case before the legislators, individual companies were also initiating aggressive publicity campaigns for coal in general and for their projects in particular, and they began battling the legislators for a more pragmatic approach to coal.

THE ENTRY OF PETROLEUM COMPANIES

During the last two decades, almost every major petroleum company has entered the coal industry. There were broadly two types of entries: acquisition of or merger with operating coal companies, and de novo investment in coal operations. Of the oil and gas affiliates that entered the coal industry, the top five reserve holders are listed in Table 3–9.

Coal companies that were acquisition targets were large and profitable. Managers of these companies welcomed the acquisition by rich oil parents. Given the history of scarce financial resources experienced by the coal industry, access to the stronger capital base of an oil parent offered the acquired coal companies prospects of steady growth and expansion. However, complementarily, the oil parents also expected their coal subsidiaries to contribute consistently to corporate profits and to help enhance the value of the parent's shares. Both Island Creek and Consol have contributed more than their share to corporate profits since their acquisition. By the same token, management of both companies acknowledge the financial support of their parents, Oxy and Conoco, respectively, in the execution of their expansion plans.

The oil parent typically did not interfere with management of the acquired coal subsidiary, since those companies that had been acquired were some of the better-managed ones in the industry. However, formal long-term planning systems and financial controls were invariably introduced to the coal subsidiary by its oil parent. Transfer of managerial personnel was restricted to the planning and finance areas. In the 1970s, as coal-company managers struggled to cope with the Safety Act and Clean Air Act, they increasingly sought the help of their oil parents in the areas of personnel management, environmental, regulatory, and public affairs.

In contrast, oil companies that entered the industry de novo seem to have built their coal subsidiaries around a strong oil-company culture. They found it prudent to recruit coal-industry personnel only for mine operations. Other functions were staffed with personnel from the parent, especially at the supervisory and managerial levels. The orientation of the oil companies to their coal subsidiaries was long-term, with a willingness to absorb short-term losses. The coal operation was not expected to provide any significant profit contribution for nearly a decade.[7] In fact, the coal operation was originally aimed at providing raw material for the synthetics projects that the oil companies hoped to have in the 1980s. It was the Arab oil embargo of 1973 and the worsening energy crisis since, that have made the de novo entrants take a hard look at conventional steam-coal markets. Many of them now have grand plans to compete in that segment.

The entry of petroleum companies to the coal industry has raised concerns in some quarters about the increasing concentration of economic power in a vital industry such as energy. Other studies[8] point out that the competitiveness of the coal industry would not diminish with the entry of oil giants, and that in fact the oil companies are needed to provide the large amounts of capital necessary for future expansion in the coal industry. The entry of oil companies, however, did bring about an important restructuring of the industry. The industry now has three distinct types of coal companies: old independents, coal companies acquired by oil parents, and new coal companies owned by oil parents. The strategic orientations of these three types of companies may be expected to be different because of the differences in the nature and extent of managerial and financial resources that they command. A coal-company manager must, therefore, now contend with a diverse spectrum of competing strategies in setting a course for his own company.

THE DAWNING OF THE SECOND COAL AGE

The United States is called the Saudi Arabia of coal, with a reserve holding estimated at over one-fifth of the world's coal reserves. And yet it is ironically the Arab oil embargo of 1973 that led to the rediscovery of coal as an important energy fuel. Coal has since formed a major component of federal energy policy.

President Carter's energy program, first announced in 1977, hoped to encourage coal in a number of ways. Proposals to prohibit industry or utilities from burning natural gas or oil in new boilers have been discussed. A tax penalty on industrial users and utilities that fail to convert from oil and gas to coal within set time boundaries has also been considered. Industry projections reflecting such a strong coal orientation show near-doubling of coal demand in the industrial and utility segments for the decade following the announcement (see Table 3-10).

In interpreting these projections, certain factors that dampen demand need consideration.

Table 3-10. Projection of Market Segments for Coal in 1985 (million tons)

Major market Segments	1976 Actual	1985 Projected
Domestic		
Electric utilities	446	820-850
Coking coal	84	80-110
Industry	60	130-160
Export and others	67	90-130
	657	1120-1250

Source: National Coal Association, "The Outlook for Coal Demand and Supply," October 12, 1977.

Electric Utilities

Utilities are torn between the low-sulfur and lower-cost-per-BTU advantage of Western coals, and the plentiful and proximate location of high-sulfur Eastern coals. The reclamation regulations affecting strip mining did raise the cost of Western coal, and clearly transportation is a major cost disadvantage for these coals.

Despite these cost disadvantages, Western coal has the potential to be a low-cost competitor to Eastern coal. In fact, in the long run its competitiveness is estimated to improve.[9] However, two recent measures of the federal government: (1) mandating stack-gas scrubbers on all stacks irrespective of the sulfur content of the fuel burnt, and (2) the granting of permission to state governors to order utilities to burn coal produced in their states, have shored up the declining competitiveness of Eastern coal. The relative cost advantage of Western coal has consequently been neutralized in some of the coal-consuming states. Some analysts have made the accusation that the slant in the federal regulation in favor of Eastern coal is political. An article in the *National Journal* stated:

> Driven by three neatly converging factors—employment, environ-
> ment and election returns—the Carter Administration clearly has sided
> with the easterners . . . Carter, who failed to carry 10 of the 11 West-
> ern coal-producing states last year [1976], has been more attentive to
> the problems of unemployment and economic lag in the coal states east
> of the Mississippi, where he fared much better at the polls.[10]

Regardless of the validity of the accusation, it is clear that regulation in the coal industry will be influenced by political feuding in the Senate "over which region of the country will cash in the fastest on President Carter's ambitious plans to double U. S. coal consumption by 1985."[11] In the mean-while, managers of utilities confused by the changing economics of Western and Eastern coals have become cautious in their expansion plans. There seems to be increasing reluctance on the part of utility companies to make commitments to long-term supply contracts for coal, till the East vs. West debate is finally settled by the new Reagan administration.

Industrial Markets

The coal industry's sale to industrial customers dropped steadily from 130.6 million tons in 1940 to 60 million tons in 1976; despite the fact that the industrial market segment grew at a yearly rate of 5 percent or more in the same period. The coal industry's contacts with this segment have at-rophied with time. The industry does not have the marketing skills to recap-ture these markets from oil and gas with their clean-burning properties.

The industry will, therefore, face a tremendous marketing challenge in doubling the demand for steam coal in industrial markets; a task made more difficult by the fact that coal does not offer significant economies, and at any rate not enough to offset the convenience of oil and gas.

Besides the marketing and regulatory problems that cloud the prospects for an early coal boom, transportation is another major bottleneck.

Transportation

As of 1977, rail movement accounted for 49 percent of coal shipments, while river movements (18 percent), trucks (12 percent), conveyors (8 per-cent), Great Lakes shipments (7 percent), and tidewater shipments (1 per-cent) accounted for the rest. The U. S. Bureau of Mines expects the rail-road's share to increase marginally through 1985.

Coal has been historically important to the U. S. railroads. Ever since the railroads were built, coal has provided the very backbone of their operations. The cause for the misfortunes of many a railroad company in the East has been the loss of coal tonnage since the mid−1960s. Conversely, the Western railroads have benefited financially from the boom in Western coal transportation.[12] The controversy over low-sulfur Western coal vs high-sulfur Eastern coal is, therefore, of utmost concern to railroad companies.

Railroad companies have blocked every new form of competition to their business. They have joined hands with the environmentalists in blocking the construction of the $500 million lock-and-dam complex near Alton, Illinois, on the Mississippi. The same duo is also fighting a battle with barge operators over construction of a waterway that would connect the Tennessee and Tombigbee Rivers, a $1.6 billion project.[13] Railroads have denied privately owned slurry-pipeline developers the legal right of eminent domain. And yet, railroads have set themselves an almost impossible task of transporting all coal exports from the West (see Table 3−11).

Table 3−11. Unit-Train Taffic. Projected unit-train departures from important Western coal fields with and without slurry pipelines.* (Departures per day)

Capacity, tons per train Indicated capacity (166 mty exported)	Number of slurry pipelines			
	None	One	Two	Three
at 8,000	57	48	40	31
at 10,000	45	39	32	25
at 12,000	38	32	26	21
Indicated and possible capacity (200 mty exported)				
at 8,000	68	60	51	43
at 10,000	55	48	41	34
at 12,000	46	40	34	29

*Assumes 25 million tons per year per slurry pipeline.
Source: "Coal Development and Government Regulation in the Northern Great Plains: A Preliminary Report," Rand Corporation, as reported in "Coal Transporters Face Challenge," *Coal Age*, January 1977.

With 68 departures per day, a unit train will have to leave or arrive every 18 minutes. The interval between trains will be 15 minutes. That high a frequency of train movements will certainly cause upheavals in the farming communities located near the railroad route. Not only is the scenario unacceptable from a societal-impact standpoint, but the investment required to be made by the Western railroads to deliver that kind of a service seems so high as to be doubtful. Participating railroads expect to increase their Western-originating coal traffic by 323 percent, from 66 million tons in 1977 to about 279 million tons in 1980. Their expansion calls for 29,000 new 100-ton-equivalent cars, 1,500 locomotives rated at 3,000 hp, and over $1 billion in fixed-plant facilities.[14] Railroad companies are hesitant to make this multibillion-dollar investment with the future of Western coal hanging in thin balance.

In the short run, should the coal boom be a reality, coal companies may have a severe transportation bottleneck. The Eastern railroads are financially incapable of expanding capacity and the Western railroads are adopting a "wait and watch" policy. The bitter opposition of the railroads to the improvement of barge transportation or the laying of slurry pipelines only limits the transportation options available to coal companies.

The coal industry has been traditionally separated from its customers by an established railroad industry. There are consequently very few forward-integrated firms in the coal industry. Utility companies, like American Electric Power, that have backward integrated into coal have begun using their own rolling stock. Mine-mouth power generation is another development. In this system of power generation, power plants are located close to coal mines, eliminating the need for rail transportation of coal and using conveyors instead. Mine-mouth power generation may find increasing popularity, if losses in power transmission can be minimized. High-voltage power-transmission technology is being perfected to this end.

Synthetics from Coal

Coal companies have been encouraged recently to commercialize coal-liquefaction and coal-gasification technologies. With the exception of Consolidation Coal Company, other coal companies have had virtually no exposure to research and development in synthetics from coal. Whereas the federal government is eager to promote the use of synthetic fuels, it is only the oil and gas companies that are currently active in this field.

As of mid−1976, the U. S. Bureau of Mines identified 36 proposed U. S. synthetic-fuel projects from coal. Of these, 15 were managed by gas companies and 7 by oil firms.[15] Given the ability of these firms to manage complex R&D projects, they have assumed leadership in the attempts to establish a synthetics business in the coal industry. Traditional coal companies have neither the finances nor the manpower required to manage the complex synthetics plants. Their role in synthetics appears to be limited to that of potential suppliers of feedstock coal.

Even the giant oil and gas companies have found it wise in the recent past to collaborate on their synthetics R&D. For example, the two originally separate gasification projects proposed by Peoples Gas and American Natural Resources in North Dakota were merged into a single project in 1977. In mid—1978, three other natural-gas firms, Transco, Tenneco, and Columbia Gas System, joined in sponsoring a joint project. Even a firm of Exxon's resources has found it prudent to collaborate with the Electric Power Research Institute, ERDA, and the Phillips Petroleum Company on the $240 million coal-liquefaction project at Baytown, Texas. Exxon will, however, manage that project. The rationale for these collaborative efforts is based on several uncertainties.

For gasifying coal, there are several technologies available. Some of the technically proven first-generation technologies (pre—World War II) are Lurgi, Koppers-Totzek (KT), and Winkler. The post—World War II second-generation technologies that are being developed include HIGAS, BI-GAS, COGAS, CO_2 Acceptor, Synthane, Atgas, Kellogg Process, and the Exxon High BTU nitrogen-thwarting process. Liquefaction technologies under consideration include the Synthoil process, FMC's COED process, and Exxon's "put-and-take technique."[16] The technical and commercial superiority of these competing processes has not yet been established. Federal R&D funding supports both the development of new technologies and the commercialization of old ones. Given the technological uncertainty in these projects, even large firms expect the federal government to share part of the financial risk in their research efforts.

A related uncertainty is the eventual economics of producing synthetics. The federal government is expected by some oil and gas companies to help in the financing of their synthetics plants and also to provide some form of price protection for the sale of synthetics. For the successful commercialization of the synthetics technologies, both federal R&D support and a strong market pull are required (Abernathy & Chakravarthy, 1979). It is this combination of federal actions together with the initiative of oil and gas companies that will determine the pace of introduction of the synthetics business.

In summary, it seems on the one hand that there is a great future for coal, both in the conventional utility and industrial markets, as well as in the emerging synthetics business. However, the future is clouded by several uncertainties: regulatory uncertainty caused by the swaying political balance, uncertainty over modes and cost of transportation, and technological uncertainty. The challenge faced by coal-company managers is not only to cope with these uncertainties but also to help their customers and transporters share their faith in the future for coal.

THE CHALLENGE IN HUMAN-RESOURCES MANAGEMENT

Assuming that the projection of a 1.2-billion-ton coal consumption in 1985 becomes a reality, the industry's manpower will have to expand at an annual rate between 3 and 5 percent (see Table 3−12).

In an industry already beset with labor-management problems, the challenge of managing an expanded work force is truly of major concern to many coal-company managers.

Labor Management

The coal industry has long been known for its labor−management strife. In the last ten years, the industry has been characterized by wildcat strikes, excessive absenteeism, and high labor turnover. Productivity has fallen steadily from a peak in the late 1960s (see Table 3−13).

Table 3−12. Manpower Forecasts

	Actual 1974	Projected 1985*	Annual growth rate (%)
Manpower			
Management, professional, and technical	9,000	15,000	5
Supervisory nonprofessional	14,000	21,000	3
Wage and nonexempt	144,000†	219,000	3
Total	167,000	255,000	
Ratio of wage to salaried employees	6.3	4.5	

*At 1.2 billion tons production.
†Half of this work force is expected to retire by 1985.
Source: The Carter Oil Company.

The reasons for such turmoil are many. It is attributed in part to the heritage of the miner. Despite the fact that today's miner is "very much in the American mainstream,"[17] enjoying an affluence equal to if not better than that of his blue-collar colleagues in American industry, he is troubled by his heritage of exploitative wages, unsafe working conditions, and disease. He feels an obligation to redress the past and yet finds few tangible provocations in his current work environment. This dissonance, it is claimed, explains his

Table 3-13. Productivity Trends in U.S. Coal Mines. Output per man per day (net tons of 2,000 pounds).

Year	Underground mines	Surface mines
1920	4.50	9.91
1930	4.80	15.00
1940	4.86	15.63
1950	5.75	15.66
1960	10.64	22.93
1965	14.00	31.98
1970	13.76	35.96
1975	8.50	26.00

Source: U.S. Bureau of Mines.

militancy. Wildcat strikes are perhaps symbolic of miners' efforts to get back at management for past grievances.

An aggravating factor has been the changing composition of the work force in the mines. The median age of a coal miner in 1957 was 42 years, in comparison with 37 years for all U. S. workers.[18] The massive recruitment in the 1970s to compensate for productivity losses and retirement of older miners changed the work-force mix drastically. A number of untrained young men and women were recruited. The average age of coal miners dropped from 49 years in 1968 to around 31 years in 1978. That average represented two distinct groups, one substantially older than 31 and the other substantially younger. The young miner was independent, outspoken, and not really "addicted" to regular work. Many took three-day weekends, especially during hunting and fishing seasons.

The UMW, which has fought for miners' rights all through this century, enjoys strong allegiance. In the past, a strong UMW leadership, such as under John L. Lewis, had been a stabilizing influence on the miners. The UMW leadership has been in disarray ever since Lewis's retirement in 1960. The scandal-ridden term of Tony Boyle, and the weak leadership of Arnold Miller have eroded the respect of the miners for their leaders. This has definitely been a contributory factor in the worsening of discipline in the coal mines. While these and other extraneous reasons are often cited by coal-company managers to rationalize their incapacity to cope with their labor-management problems, part of the blame must also rest squarely with the management.

The industry's tradition of three yearly labor contracts between the UMW on one hand and the BCOA on the other in a sense casts labor management as an interinstitutional problem. Since both the institutions represent heterogeneous interest groups, a contract is often a compromise from the standpoint of local labor–management relationships. Moreover, the time, energy, and egos invested in the contract tend to make the contract inclusive—i.e., a boundary within which labor relations have to be practiced, rather than just a definition of one aspect of labor–management interaction. Until recently labor relations in most coal companies were oriented exclusively toward contract administration. This narrow legalistic focus certainly did not help calm the labor turmoil in the coal mines.

In coping with this labor-management challenge, coal-company managers may find comfort in some recent trends. The new UMW leadership under Sam Church, Jr., is gaining wide acceptance and will hopefully be a stabilizing factor. Moreover, the young militant miners of the early 1970s are maturing and beginning to settle down in life. Both these factors have brought a new harmony in the UMW[19] and relative peace in the nation's coal fields. Further, the growing importance of the Western coal fields has diluted the monopolistic power of the UMW. UMW-controlled mines produced only about 50 percent of the nation's coal in 1979, compared with nearly 70 percent five years ago. Managers, especially in the West, have the option of remaining nonunion. Where managers do have to cope with the UMW, the labor situation is rapidly improving to a point where managers will have a much bigger say in labor management. The challenge is in the efficient use of this newfound influence.

Supervisory and Managerial Personnel

Three to four decades ago, a foreman in a coal company was the man who ran the show. He had broad responsibilities and wielded corresponding authority over his men and their work. The foreman of today, however, is being held responsible for functions over which he no longer has any real authority or control. He cannot hire, fire, or set production standards. He cannot transfer employees, adjust the wage inequities of his people, promote deserving people, improve methods of production, or freely plan the work of his department. Most of these have become matters of company policy, union agreement, or subjects for staff experts. He is subjected to standards, budgets, laws, procedures; most of which were formulated without his participation.[20] And yet the foreman is the link between management and miners. As one mine superintendent remarked, "If there's no production we are down his throat. And he's got to keep you out of Dutch with state and federal safety inspectors."[21]

Today's increasingly sophisticated equipment requires that the foreman be more technically expert. Given the current labor militancy, he also has to be an industrial-relations expert. More often than not, he has received no special training for his job. And to top it all a section foreman's salary is not more than $700−$1,000 higher than the top annual wage of his most skilled crew members. "Management has been willing neither to recognize the seriousness of this condition nor to accept it."[22]

Through intensive training programs and careful recruitment of professionals, the coal industry is trying to strengthen its supervisory and managerial cadre. But as Table 3−12 projects, the annual growth rate for this cadre is higher than that for the direct workers. Despite the recent influx of managers and supervisors from other industries such as oil or mining (other than coal), management of underground mines, in particular, requires prior background in the coal industry. Coal companies will face the simultaneous challenge of retaining their good supervisors and managers, and recruiting and training new personnel.

SUMMARY

The concept of adaptation is most useful in an industry environment that is rapidly becoming complex. It is only in a taxing environment that the internal working of affected firms will be both revealed and distinguished (Simon, 1969). The coal industry seems an especially suited environment from such a standpoint. The industry has suffered a long history of decline, posing coal companies a major challenge for mere survival. More recently, since the mid-1960s, the industry has been subject to a wide variety of federal interventions that have adversely impacted on productivity and operating costs, and have distorted the markets for steam coal.

The coal industry at its zenith, in the 1920s, provided the primary fuel for the United States. Since then, it has steadily lost its markets to oil and gas. The more successful coal companies introduced mechanization to the mines in order to improve efficiency, and they also resorted to mergers and acquisitions to strengthen their financial base.

The industry enjoyed a revival in the 1950s with the rapid growth of the utility markets. Coal seemed to have finally found an expanding niche. Long-term contracts with utilities became common industry practice by the 1960s.

But just when the growth in utility demand and rise in labor productivity seemed to have restored the health of the coal industry, a spate of regulations hit the industry. The Federal Coal Mine Health and Safety Act of 1969 and the Clean Air Act of 1970 had severe impact on the operations of coal companies. The former, while improving the safety in mines, contributed in part to the drop in productivity, forcing companies to recruit at short notice in order to maintain production levels committed to under long-term contracts. The Clean Air Act has placed the traditional coal producers in the Eastern coal fields at a severe disadvantage by imposing stiff stack-gas emission standards not normally achievable given the high-sulfur content of Eastern coal.

The post—John L. Lewis era of chaos in the UMW has made labor management another critical stumbling block for the coal companies. The Eastern Coal companies married to the UMW through contractual arrangements suffered a traumatic era of increased wildcat strikes and declining productivity all through the 1970s. Western coal companies, being largely non-UMW, suffered much less. Coal companies have sought Western coal because of its lower sulfur content and the relatively peaceful labor conditions in the Western coal fields.

The Federal Energy Policy which was announced in 1977, supposedly formulated to encourage the expanded use of coal, was perceived by many in the industry to be proenvironmental and naive in its goal of forcing conversion to coal through fiscal measures. The proposed mandatory use of scrubbers on all boilers, announced in 1977, clouded the future for Western low-sulfur coal (a favorite under the Clean Air Act of 1970). These in turn have led to a "wait and watch" attitude among utilities that consume coal and railroads that transport it. The coal industry's euphoria in the early 1970s over an anticipated revival has been considerably dampened. And yet coal companies have to be ready to anticipate new demands and predict new markets so as to be ahead of the competition.

Competition in the coal industry has always been keen. The advent of the big oil companies has made it keener. Major oil companies entered the coal industry either through acquisition of operating coal companies (mostly in the East), or as de novo entrants (mostly in the West). The Arab oil embargo of 1973 made these companies pay serious attention to the conventional markets for steam coal, even where their original motive for entering the coal industry was to secure a feedstock source for their future synthetics-from-coal operations.

Faltermeyer[23] likens the challenge in the coal industry to that faced by "a somewhat frumpy middle-aged ballerina rushed out of semi-retirement to fill an unanticipated gap in a show that must go on." He should have added that the show is a crazy one with a constantly changing choreography.

Finally, the coal industry has the opportunity of sponsoring the synthetics business in the near future. Gasification, projected for commercialization in

1985, and the more distant possibility of liquefaction offer the coal industry, for the first time, options to forward integrate.

The managerial responses of coal companies to such a challenging environment present interesting cases of adaptation.

Part III
A Spectrum of Adaptation:
Four Case Studies

4. The North American Coal Corporation

The North American Coal Corporation (NACCO) is one of the large independent coal companies in the United States. It ranked sixth in the industry in 1976 in terms of reserves (5.1 billion tons) and tenth in terms of production (10.9 million tons). The company is headquartered in Cleveland, Ohio. It is a closely held corporation, with the founding Taplin family owning nearly 40 percent of the company's equity.

This case study describes the growth of NACCO into a major producer in the industry. The decision of the principal shareholders of NACCO to retain close control of the company has limited its financing options. But the aspirations of growth nourished by NACCO's management have led the company to some innovative business arrangements. The subsidiary arrangement, with the customer arranging and guaranteeing the financing of project expenditures, is one such. The growth in production and earnings which resulted as a consequence of the arrangement has made NACCO an important coal company.

EARLY HISTORY

The forerunner of NACCO was a coal-trading company founded by Frank E. Taplin in 1913 in Cleveland, Ohio. In 1925 his company was named the North American Coal Corporation. By the time Taplin died in 1936, NACCO was selling over 4 million tons of coal, of which slightly less than

NOTE: The original case study has been abridged and re-edited for this book.

50 percent was produced by the company's own mines. The rest was either purchased by the company to provide tonnage for its docks on the Great Lakes or sold on behalf of other producers for an agency fee.

Encouraged by the spurt in coal demand during World War II, NACCO acquired four subsidiaries, three of which were coal companies, while the fourth was a dock operation. As of 1946 the company owned coal mines in Ohio, West Virginia, and western Pennsylvania. Except for some low-volatile metallurgical coal produced by the Mead mines in West Virginia, NACCO was predominantly a steam-coal producer for the railroad and home-heating markets. The company had three dock operations then, located in Minneapolis, Minnesota; Milwaukee, Wisconsin; and Cheboygan, Michigan. All of NACCO's docks were located at various ports on the Great Lakes, and were substantial forwarders of Lake coal, principally to one another. NACCO's docks not only sold coal produced in the company's own mines but also coal procured from others. They acted to some extent as warehouses that balanced irregular production at NACCO's mines.

The war years provided NACCO growth in both sales and profitability (see Table 4−1). But as the war drew to an end, the company's sales started dropping. Companies like NACCO that were organized by the UMW suffered the additional burden of industrywide coal strikes, sponsored by that union. Schmidt, the then Chairman of NACCO explained the consequences of these strikes:

> One result has been to increase the price of coal and put it at a competitive disadvantage in relation to gas and oil.
>
> An even more serious consequence has been the weakening of the confidence of large consumers of fuel in the dependability of coal as a source of supply.[1]

For NACCO, this meant losing its railroad markets to diesel and its industrial markets to oil and gas. By 1950 its production had dropped to 2.7 million tons.

Table 4−1. Profitability Trends, NACCO, 1942−1946

Year	Tonnage produced (million tons)	Purchased & agency coal (million tons)	Total Coal sold (million tons)	Sales ($ mil)	Net-income/ sales (%)
1942	2.4	2.7	5.1	13.1	1.1
1944	3.4	2.7	6.1	18.5	5.7
1946	3.1	2.7	5.8	18.2	3.3

Source: Annual Reports.

PRODUCT—MARKET POSTURE

Efforts at Diversification

The drop in consumption of NACCO's coal in the early 1950s had prompted its management to consider diversification. In 1956, the company appointed Dr. Robert L. Savage from the Case Institute of Technology as Vice-President (Research). The research department had two objectives: (1) to find more profitable uses for conventional products, and (2) to provide diversification into new products, particularly chemicals. Being a chemical engineer, Dr. Savage was expected to guide especially the latter activity.

Commencing in 1958, a research program for converting mine wastes to useful commercial products such as alumina and aluminum sulfate was conducted in cooperation with Strategic Materials Corporation of Buffalo, New York. A $500,000 pilot plant was planned as of 1959. The pilot plant confirmed the technical feasibility of converting mine wastes to aluminum sulfate and decomposing the latter to alumina, a raw material for aluminum production. As a first stage, $1.3 million was approved in 1960 by NACCO's board to set up a commercial plant for processing mine wastes to aluminum sulfate (alum). An additional $450,000 was spent that year for assessing the economic feasibility of the decomposition of alum to alumina. As of 1962, the company had not ascertained the commerical feasibility of the alumina-decomposition process, and its alum-production plant at Powhattan Point, Ohio ran into unforeseen mechanical problems. In 1963, NACCO's board abandoned the project and exchanged its shares in Strategic Materials Corporation for complete patent rights, privileges, and know-how inherent in the alum—alumina venture. The loss on the venture to NACCO was $1.25 million.

The company was also unsuccessful at a few other efforts at diversification. In 1963 the company's research department was dissolved and Dr. Savage resigned from NACCO's board.

Shift to Utility Markets

R&D efforts were not the only attempts by NACCO to respond to the environmental changes. NACCO's top management looked to new markets for shoring up the company's shrinking sales. In 1951, Schmidt announced NACCO's major shift toward utilities for its future business:

> We believe that we'll lose almost the entire tonnage previously purchased by the railroads and perhaps will lose to a large extent, the tonnage of coal consumed by home owners. However, for our company there is a bright future for the sale of coal to the electric utilities and

their consumption of coal is increasing yearly. . . . Fortunately, for our company, our three large Powhattan mines are on the Ohio River. We can, therefore, transport and ship a large part if not all our coal by river. Important electric utilities and industrials are building and expanding in this vicinity.[2]

In the decade that followed, the company turned increasingly toward utility markets. The rapid growth in electric-power output since World War II and the emergence of NACCO as a major producer of coal were highly correlated:

> In 1946, NACCO was the twenty-second largest commercial coal producer with about 10 percent of its output going to the electric power industry. Today (1964), with about 76 percent of its tonnage used for the generation of electricity, the company is the ninth largest commercial producer.[3]

In keeping with its thrust toward utility markets, the top management of NACCO acquired the Dakota Collieries Company, North Dakota, in 1957. The company was a small supplier of steam coal to home-fuel markets. NACCO's management saw potential for entering Western utility markets through the North Dakota property.

NACCO also merged several of its subsidiaries in 1952 to streamline its organization. After the merger the company had only three active wholly owned subsidiaries: The Powhattan Mining Company with mines in Ohio; The North American Coal and Dock Company with mines in West Virginia and two dock divisions on the Great Lakes; and a Canadian dock company, Canada Coal Limited at Toronto.

The shift toward utility markets coincided with the phasing out of NACCO's metallurgical coal operations in West Virginia. These mines, being old, were not cost-efficient. Moreover, given the uncertainty of metallurgical-coal markets in the late 1950s, NACCO's management decided in 1960 to dispose of these mines. The company also sold all its dock properties in the United States in 1960, the Canadian dock having been sold in 1959. That decision was influenced by a number of factors. The dock operations became less profitable, due to the increasing supply of oil and gas to the north central United States. NACCO's preference for long-term utility contracts minimized the need for these coal-distribution outlets.

NACCO's management signed in 1953 one of the first long-term contracts in the coal industry for supply of coal to utilities when it agreed to supply part of the requirements of the Ohio Valley Electric Corporation (OVEC).

The contract was for the supply of 1.5 million tons of coal annually to the Kyger Creek plant of OVEC at Gallipolis, Ohio.

Encouraged by its favorable experience with the OVEC long-term contracts, NACCO's management decided to adopt long-term contracting as a standard business procedure. The certainty of demand that these contracts provided allowed NACCO to invest in mining equipment for improving efficiency and expanding capacity with much less apprehension than before.

With the restructuring moves complete, NACCO became essentially a steam-coal producer for utility markets. Its growing reliance on utility markets is shown in Figure 4−1.

Long-Term Plans

NACCO has essentially remained a steam-coal producer. It has no metallurgical-coal reserves and has no plans for acquiring any in the future. Over 80 percent of NACCO's reserves are located in North Dakota. Given its vast Western reserves, it is not surprising that nearly half of the company's proposed production of 25 million tons by 1984 is projected to come from its Western division.[4] Further, out of the 25-million-ton proposed production, nearly 75 percent of the coal is projected to be produced through the subsidiary arrangement referred to earlier.

Should the subsidiary arrangement be threatened, NACCO's expansion plans will naturally be subject to revisions. While most of the old contracts with subsidiaries do not expire until the late 1980s, the bulk of NACCO's new production may face difficulties on account of the changing political scene, which has neutralized the low-sulfur advantage of Western coal for consumption in Eastern utility markets. The other option of supplying coal to gasification projects, such as that of American Natural Gas, is also shrouded in the uncertain financial future for gasification and the difficulty in obtaining government help for raising the large capital resources required for the project.

These uncertainties must dampen NACCO's expansion plans for the future. However, given the fact that most available private coal reserves in the United States have been acquired, and the leasing/acquisition of the remaining free reserves is becoming more difficult and expensive, companies like NACCO, which already have large coal reserves, are potential beneficiaries of new business opportunities that may arise in the coal industry.

MATERIAL RESOURCES

NACCO's expansion in the past has been through joint ventures wherein the company provides coal reserves, management, and engineering exper-

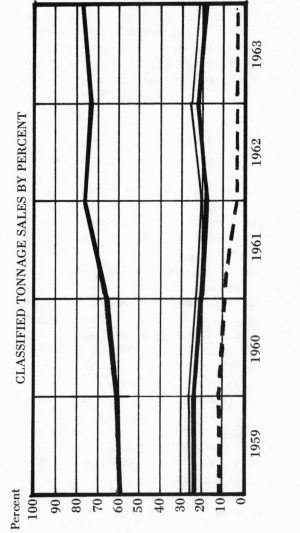

CLASSIFIED TONNAGE SALES BY PERCENT

ELECTRIC
UTILITIES

GENERAL
INDUSTRIES

OTHER

Source: Annual Report 1963.

Figure 4–1. Emergence of NACCO in Utility Coal Markets

tise, and the customer utility arranges the necessary financing either directly or through financial guarantees for bank loans. NACCO created subsidiaries to handle each such joint venture. The first two subsidiaries set up under the new arrangement were the Helen Mining Company and the Florence Mining Company. Describing the financing arrangement for the Helen Mining Company, the 1966 Annual Report stated:

> Financing will be arranged entirely by the subsidiary, with no guarantee on the part of the parent company. Basically the loan to Helen Mining will be underwritten by the utilities through the terms and conditions of the sales contract which is for thirty years. Under certain conditions and after five years from full operations the power companies may purchase the subsidiary for its net worth, but NACCO will continue to lease the coal to the mining company at a reasonable royalty rate irrespective of who operates the mines. It is not expected that the utilities will exercise their right to take over the property at any time so we fully expect to be the operator and manager of this property for the indefinite future and as long as the power plant is in operation.

The financing arrangement for the Florence Mining Company was similar. In 1969 the company formed two new subsidiaries, similar in arrangement to the Helen Mining Company. The two subsidiaries, the Quarto Mining Company and the NACCO Mining Company, were both located in Ohio. A fifth subsidiary company, the Oneida Mining Company, was formed in Pennsylvania in 1970.

The forming of these subsidiary companies helped finance NACCO's expansion (see Table 4−2). The growth in NACCO's production from 1966 to 1970 was 2.2 million tons, of which 1.8 million tons came from the new tonnage of the subsidiaries. The growth in fixed assets was all largely in the subsidiary operations, financed through long-term loans either provided by or guaranteed by, the customer utilities. As a consequence, NACCO's debt-to-equity ratio was a conservative 1:4 in 1970.

Given the preference of NACCO's principal shareholders not to dilute their holdings, raising additional equity is out of the question. The continued acceptance by utilities of the subsidiary arrangement is, therefore, crucial to the financing of NACCO's proposed expansion.

Coal Reserves

NACCO's reserves had grown very modestly up to 1967 (see Table 4−3). They were largely added through acquisitions of mining companies. Since those reserves were more than adequate to ensure nearly one hundred years

Table 4-2. Impact of Subsidiaries on NACCO's Expansion

Year	Addition to gross assets ($ Million)	Long-term debt		Net worth ($ million)	Production (million tons)
		All subsidiaries ($ Million)	Parent ($ Million)		
1966	10.4	2	9	24	7.4
1968	14.9	14	10	27	8.8
1970	21.4	47	7	28	9.6

Source: Annual Reports.

of production at NACCO's then output level, NACCO's management felt no pressing need to aggressively seek reserves. Moreover, NACCO did not have the financial strength required to acquire and carry idle reserves on its books. However, in the span of a decade since 1967, NACCO has built its coal reserves to 5.1 billion tons (see Table 4−3). The bulk of these additions have been in the West. The rationale for this addition is described in the following paragraphs.

Table 4-3. Growth in Reserves, NACCO, 1955-1976

Year	Reserves (billion tons)
1955	0.40
1965	0.70
1967	0.95
1970	1.2
1973	3.9
1976	5.1

NACCO went West with the acquisition of the Dakota Collieries Company, North Dakota. The Dakota Collieries became the lignite division of NACCO in 1957, soon after its acquisition. Its only mine, the Dakota star mine, was renamed the Indian Head mine. The mine produced 250,000 tons of surface-mined lignite annually, and served exclusively the home-fuel market in adjoining communities. The production at Indian Head remained constant until 1966.

In 1966, as part of its general strategy to acquire long-term contracts for its coals, NACCO negotiated a million-ton-per-year contract with a North

Table 4—4. Divisions and Their Operational Jurisdiction

Division	Subsidiary companies under divisional jurisdiction	Parent company mines
Eastern (Pennsylvania)	1. The Florence Mining Company 2. The Helen Mining Company 3. The Oneida Mining Company	Other NACCO mines in the state of Pennsylvania
Central (Ohio)	1. The NACCO Mining Company 2. The Quarto Mining Company	Other NACCO mines in the state of Ohio
Western (North Dakota)	1. The Falkirk Mining Company 2. The Coteau Properties Company	Indian Head mine, North Dakota

Dakota utility. The new contract forced NACCO to look for additional lignite reserves around its Indian Head mine.

In 1967, a coal geologist from a railroad company, Virgil Carmichael, joined NACCO. He had surveyed the coal reserves in North Dakota and Wyoming as part of his earlier job and was eager to put that knowledge to use by working for an operating coal company.

Carmichael's initial efforts at reserve acquisition were unsuccessful. His first project was exploring in Montana a large block of reserves which was under the control of an association of farmers. Since the farmers were opposed to coal mining, the proposal had to be dropped. In 1968, he identified another large block of reserves in Wyoming but could not persuade NACCO's top management to acquire it.

Meanwhile, Carmichael's efforts at locating reserves close to the Indian Head mine were more successful. In 1969, over 20 million tons of lignite reserves were identified and eventually acquired. These reserves offered adequate coverage for the utility contract signed in 1966 for the Indian Head mine.

As already mentioned, by the late 1960s, labor productivity in the Eastern mines of NACCO had dropped. The proposed Clean Air Act placed Eastern high-sulfur coals at a disadvantage in comparison with the Western low-sulfur coals. Otes Bennett, who became President of NACCO in 1966, was worried about the long-term competitiveness of NACCO's Eastern mines. Moreover, since the mid-1960s, giant oil companies and mining companies had started acquiring large coal reserves in the West. Bennett realized that further delay in the decision to expand in the West could deny NACCO good-quality coal reserves. Furthermore, the company's liquidity position had improved tremendously with the sale of its dock operations. As of the end of 1969, NACCO had a cash balance of $7.8 million. Given the low cost of leasing Western reserves ($1-per-acre per year), Bennett recognized that NACCO had an excellent opportunity to expand its reserve base substantially.

Bennett became Chief Executive Officer of NACCO in 1970, and soon thereafter launched an aggressive reserve-acquisition campaign in the West. In the meanwhile, the bulk of the low-overburden-medium-BTU coal in Wyoming had already been acquired by other large coal companies, mining companies, and oil companies entering the coal industry. NACCO, therefore, concentrated its search in North Dakota, an area which Carmichael had surveyed extensively.

In the first five years of their intensive Western efforts, Carmichael and his team assembled 3.5 billion tons of reserves, which was thrice the reserve holding that NACCO had in 1970. NACCO's Western reserves had a stripping ratio[5] of 6−11:1 and a heat value of 6,000−7,000 BTU. The sulfur content of the coal was between 0.6 and 1.2 percent.

An exploration department was formally created in late 1973. Bennett sanctioned the recruitment of additional geologists and geological engineers to bring the exploration department to its full staff strength of fourteen professionals. The final staff strength consisted of a chief geologist, a senior geologist, three geologists, a geological engineer, a senior land agent, two land agents, and a geological/land drafts person. Carmichael was elected Vice-President (Explorations).

Although NACCO had established two joint ventures, the Coteau Properties Company (in 1972) and the Falkirk Mining Company (in 1974), to develop its Western coal reserves, its management believed that the southwestern United States was the area with the best potential for coal. That area was running out of natural gas and coal was a feasible substitute. NACCO acquired nearly 400 million tons of coal in Texas and entered into a joint-venture agreement with the Getty Oil Company for development of the Texan reserves.

FORMALIZING NACCO'S ORGANIZATION

Despite impressive growth in the utility markets, NACCO encountered two problem areas in 1969 and 1970. The first was on account of the Mine

Health and Safety Act, which forced the company to spend millions of dollars for equipment and supplies to comply with the new standards. Besides, there was a sharp drop in industrywide productivity subsequent to the Act, especially in underground mines. NACCO suffered all the more, since a major share of its production came from underground mines. The increasing militancy of the UMW led to a further deterioration in productivity. While NACCO produced 8.9 million tons of coal in 1969 with 2,300 employees, its work force nearly doubled by 1972 for a 35 percent increase in production. The productivity drop meant an increase in production costs, which NACCO was fortunately able to recover from customers because of provisions in the long-term contracts. Drop in productivity also meant massive recruitment of workers and, consequently, supervisors to ensure that production was maintained. Since it was an industrywide phenomenon, the labor market became very tight. Bennett identified recruitment as the biggest problem area for NACCO in the early 1970s. The company established training programs not only to meet the mandatory requirements of the Mine Health and Safety Act but also to train unskilled recruits in mining jobs.

The second difficulty for NACCO was the Clean Air Act of 1970, which placed the high-sulfur Eastern coals at a disadvantage. Though NACCO was protected by its long-term contracts from any immediate repercussions from the Act, its top management decided to aggressively acquire lower-sulfur Western lignite as reserves for the future. Reserve acquisition gathered momentum in 1971, and as mentioned earlier, an exploration department was formally created in late 1973.

NACCO organized itself into three divisions as of 1974. The divisions and their operational jurisdiction are outlined in Table 4−4.

The operational arrangement in the divisions has had no major changes since 1974, except for the opening of additional mines and the sale in 1975 of the Oneida Mining Company to its utility customer. The sale was the consequence of an alleged contract-default claim by the utility and of NACCO's management's agreeing to sell the property rather than to continue the relationship with a dissatisfied customer. The company's production in 1976 was distributed among its various divisions as per Table 4−5.

NACCO also realigned its organization structure in 1974. Figure 4−2 shows NACCO's organization structure in 1977.

ORGANIZATIONAL STRUCTURE

NACCO's organization can be broadly conceptualized as having three levels:

1. The policy level consisting of the President and the executives reporting directly to him, i.e., the Senior Vice-President, Vice-President (Sales),

Table 4–5. Production Statistics, NACCO, 1976

Division	Parent company production 1976		Subsidiaries' production 1976	
	No. mines	Millions of tons production	No. mines	Millions of tons production
Eastern	3	.8	6	2.6
Central	4	3.5	4	2.9
Western	1	1.1	2	-0-
Total		5.4		5.5

Source: "NACCO Aims for Doubling of Output," *Coal Age*, October 1977.

Legal Counsel, and the Vice-President and Treasurer. The latter is responsible for both the controllership and the finance functions.

2. The operations-planning level consisting of the Senior Vice-President and the executives reporting directly to him, i.e., Vice-President (Explorations), Vice-President (Engineering), and the divisional presidents.

3. The plan-implementation level representing the divisional presidents, who are responsible for the implementation of the plans worked out at Level 2.

The Policy Level

The key staff functions at this level are sales, finance, and accounting. The latter two functions have been placed under the supervision of Robert Hawekotte, Vice-President and Treasurer of the company.

The finance and accounting functions are completely centralized at NACCO. Though Hawekotte has field staff at the divisions to collect data for financial and cost-accounting purposes, these field accountants are not responsible to the divisional presidents on any accounting matter. Division-performance reports are prepared centrally and sent monthly to the divisional presidents from the Cleveland office.

Sales is another centralized function at NACCO. The Vice-President (Sales), Herschell Cashion, Jr., has major responsibility for bringing NACCO's vast coal reserves to the market. Given the company's preference for long-term utility contracts, he has to constantly look for new projects. As Table 4–6 indicates, NACCO has relied heavily on subsidiaries to contribute to its sales revenue and profits. However, the subsidiary arrangement is favored only by certain types of utilities. The sales department has to locate such utilities that can provide the kinds of financial guarantees that NACCO desires of its subsidiaries. In an increasingly competitive market this is a

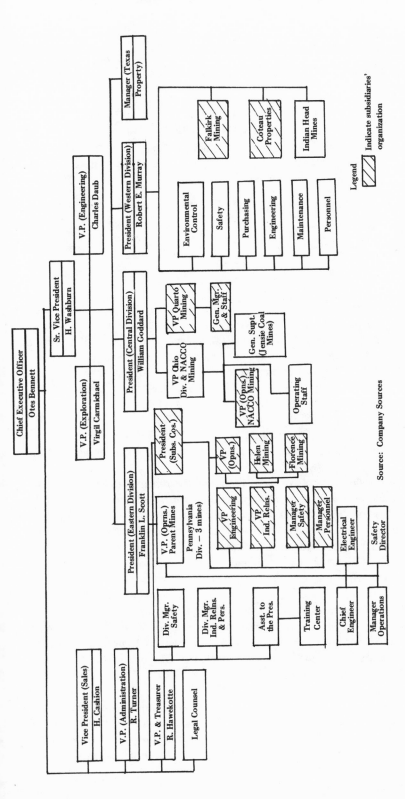

Figure 4–2. The North American Coal Corporation Organization Chart, 1977

Chief Executive Officer
Otes Bennett

Sr. Vice President
H. Washburn

V.P. (Engineering)
Charles Daub

V.P. (Exploration)
Virgil Carmichael

Manager (Texas Property)

Vice President (Sales)
H. Cashion

V.P. (Administration)
R. Turner

V.P. & Treasurer
R. Hawekotte

Legal Counsel

President (Eastern Division)
Franklin L. Scott

President (Central Division)
William Goddard

President (Western Division)
Robert E. Murray

President (Subs. Cos.)

V.P. (Oprns.) Parent Mines

Pennsylvania Div. – 3 mines

Div. Mgr. Safety

Div. Mgr. Ind. Relns. & Pers.

Asst. to the Pres.

Training Center

Chief Engineer

Manager Operations

Electrical Engineer

Safety Director

VP Engineering

VP Ind. Relns.

Manager Safety

Manager Personnel

VP (Oprns.)

Helen Mining

Florence Mining

VP (Oprns.) NACCO Mining

VP Ohio Div. & NACCO Mining

VP Quarto Mining

Gen. Mgr. & Staff

Gen. Supt. (Tensie Coal Mines)

Operating Staff

Falkirk Mining

Coteau Properties

Indian Head Mines

Environmental Control

Safety

Purchasing

Engineering

Maintenance

Personnel

Legend

⧄ Indicate subsidiaries' organization

Source: Company Sources

Table 4-6. Contribution of Subsidiaries to Sales Revenue and
Profits, NACCO, 1976

1976 Statistics	NACCO-owned mines	Subsidiary operations
Production (mill tons)	5.4	5.5
Average selling price per ton ($)	16.1	27.2
Average profit per ton ($)	.8	.5
Percent contribution to sales	35.0	65.0
Percent contribution to profits	57.0	43.0

Source: Annual Reports.

difficult assignment. NACCO's sales department has recently turned its attention to markets for coal in the emerging synthetics industry. Since not all oil and gas companies interested in synthetics are well endowed with coal reserves, NACCO has the potential for negotiating cooperative ventures with such companies. The joint venture with Getty in Texas and American Natural Gas in North Dakota are examples.

The Operations Planning Level

The two important departments at this level are Explorations and Engineering.

Exploration: The role of the exploration department was outlined earlier. Besides acquiring reserves the exploration department has also to analyze reserve holdings for potential development from a mining-cost or coal-quality standpoint. Though sequentially stated, the two tasks of exploration and development have become a composite and complex geological task at NACCO. Articulating the changing nature of his job, the Vice-President (Explorations), Virgil Carmichael, stated:

My job is to sell proposals for reserve acquisition/development prepared by my staff to my boss—the Senior Vice President. If I don't succeed, my men feel disappointed. Infrequently, a proposal rejected earlier finds favor with the top management later on. We are trying to avoid such situations.

Another matter of grave concern to the Vice-President (Explorations) is the very limited direct contact that exists between his department and the mining division of NACCO. He recalls how he, as a geologist, had helped identify a "washout" problem in one of the mines in the Eastern Division,

thereby saving it a lot of operating expense. However, the operating divisions have not fully overcome the traditional reluctance to consult geologists
on mine-engineering problems. The Western Division has set a new trend in
this area by hiring a geologist to its engineering staff.

Engineering: Though engineering is also a centralized function at
NACCO, the divisions have considerable autonomy on engineering decisions. The small corporate engineering group comprises a Vice-President
(Engineering), two mining engineers, a preparation engineer, a geotechnical
engineer, and a draftsman. The group has a prominent role in the preparation
of initial project proposals and in the scrutiny of detailed project reports prepared by the divisional engineering staff.

The engineering function at NACCO is computerized at both corporate
and divisional levels. Standard software packages are used through local
terminals connected to a central time-share computer belonging to Compu-
Serv. The central engineering group is responsible for identifying new engineering software packages.

Divisional Operations

As can be seen from the organization chart, NACCO does not have a
central personnel, industrial-relations, public-affairs, or regulatory-affairs
function. The divisional president has authority over all the above functions
as pertaining to his division. He has authority to tailor the recruitment and
training systems of his division to its special needs, he obtains all licenses
and permits from the government, and he is free to establish his own
community-relations program. In turn, he is totally responsible for the production and productivity of his division and has to meet the capital and
operating budgets set for him.

OTHER ADMINISTRATIVE SYSTEMS

Corporate planning at NACCO is the clear prerogative of the corporate
officers, located in Cleveland.

As described earlier, NACCO sells most of its coal to utility customers on
long-term contracts. Each of NACCO's mines is generally committed to a
single contract. Thus a new customer often means a new project. These
projects are centrally conceived and planned. When a market opportunity is
seen, the sales department notifies Bennett. Bennett also receives customer
enquiries directly. He selects the enquiries that seem useful to investigate
further and passes them on to Washburn. Washburn in turn works out a preliminary physical plan for servicing that enquiry, using the assistance of
Carmichael and Daub. At this, the proposal stage, divisional presidents are

asked to participate only on a limited basis. The physical plan is then costed out by Hawekotte's staff, who also evaluate its financial merit. Based on their recommendations, Bennett selects the proposals to pursue further. The central finance department also suggests financing options for the project. With the help of the above information, Bennett and his Vice-President (Sales) begin preliminary negotiations with the targeted customer.

At the second stage of planning, the physical plans are worked out in greater detail by the divisional president in whose jurisdiction the project is likely to be executed. The detailed physical plans are costed out once again by the controller's department at Cleveland. A project report is prepared by the concerned divisional president, incorporating all the physical and financial details of the project. If NACCO's proposal is for wholly owning the operation, a conventional bid is made in response to the customer's enquiry. In cases where the creation of a subsidiary company is conceived, the project report acts as NACCO's proposal for the subsidiary arrangement. The potential customer often has NACCO's report evaluated by an outside consultant. The negotiations that follow determine the project parameters.

The approved project report, whether it is for a company-owned mine or a subsidiary-owned mine, is then handed over to the selected division president for implementation. He is responsible for both implementing and then managing the project when it goes into operation. He has total authority in both activities, within the guidelines set by the project report. The planning system described above is summarized in Figure 4−3.

In the implementation phase the project report is first translated into a five-year master plan, which is updated yearly. The annual capital budget is prepared on the basis of the master plan and updated every three months. The project is assigned to a project manager, whose role it is to complete the project on time and adhere to the capital budget given to him. While ordering of capital equipment is approved centrally by the Senior Vice-President (Operations), the equipment-selection decision is that of the project manager. Specific limits are set for the amount of capital-expenditure appropriations that can be sanctioned at the level of divisional president. Larger appropriations require the sanction of corporate headquarters, and often the customer utility (in the case of subsidiaries).

Typically, the project manager stays on to head the operations of the new mine. The project report once again serves as a guideline for his operating budget. The control exercised on an operating manager is also shown in Figure 4−3. The divisional organization has no accounting function formally attached to it. But the corporate controller has some field staff located at the divisional headquarters. The formal financial-performance reports are prepared at the corporate headquarters for all divisions. However, the account-

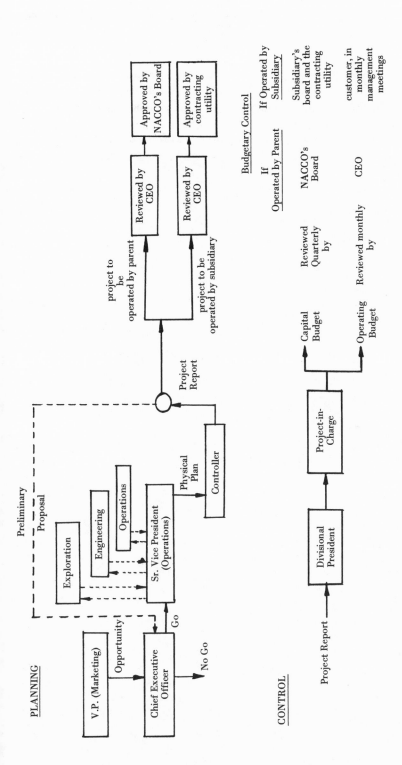

Figure 4-3. Planning and Control Systems at NACCO

ing field staff in the divisions provide informal performance data to the divisional president on a daily basis to help him control his division's performance. The daily performance report includes information on production, productivity, and cost per ton of coal produced. The daily reports have a lag time of about a week to enable the accounting staff to collect and process the relevant data.

5. Island Creek Coal Company

In 1904 Island Creek Coal Company sold its first ton of coal. Since then it has steadily grown to become the fourth largest coal producer in the United States, with an annual production of 16.6 million tons in 1976. Island Creek serves both the steam-coal and metallurgical-coal markets, and has sizable reserves of both types of coals.

The company has a history of constantly exploring new avenues of profitability. It has relied on acquisitions and product diversification, as well as internal administrative devices, to sustain its profitability over the years. Consequently, Island Creek has operated at a profit since 1907. The company was acquired by Occidental Petroleum in 1968. The added financial backing that the acquisition provided has made Island Creek a favorite among financial analysts.

EARLY HISTORY

Island Creek actually started as part of a petroleum company, the United States Oil Company. In 1901, Albert Holden, an employee of the oil company, was sent to West Virginia to look for some coal property. In 1902, the company acquired 30,000 acres of bituminous-coal lands in that state. Holden, who had been assigned the job of setting up the coal mine, had a host of problems to tackle: no rail or road access, a scarcity of skilled local labor, and a lack of community infrastructure such as houses, schools, and stores. Coal production started in 1904, and the town of Holden was established in 1906. Describing the accomplishment, the journal *Coal* reported in its issue of January 6, 1906:

NOTE: The original case study has been abridged and re-edited for this book.

85

A purely mining proposition of this magnitude, taking into consideration the excellent buildings and modern equipment throughout has rarely, if ever before, been attemped in the state. The appointments, in general, are such as should insure the best class of workmen, and from these, efficient service.

Island Creek Coal Company was formally organized in 1910. In 1915 it took over the actual ownership and management of the U. S. Coal and Oil Company properties. From a production peak of 2.2 million tons in 1916, production began to drop steadily due to a shortage of men and railroad cars during the war years as well as government controls on wage scales, distribution policies, and selling prices. However, by 1921, the mines were back to full production and during that year produced about 3 million tons of coal. Island Creek continued to open new mines throughout the 1920s, and it had twenty operating mines by 1929.

During the 1930s Island Creek experienced the economic problems of the Depression. In addition, Island Creek was unionized in 1933 by the United Mine Workers of America (UMW). At a time when sales of coal were dropping off, James D. Francis, the then President of Island Creek, helped create and then headed the Appalachian Coals, Inc., which acted as a selling agent for 127 different coal operations including Island Creek. In addition to the special sales effort, Island Creek's management invested $2 million in mechanizing its mines and improving the company's coal-processing techniques. Shuttle cars, mechanical coal-cleaning equipment, and cutting machines were introduced to Island Creek operations. The mechanization move was in keeping with the company's tradition of adopting innovative ideas to improve its efficiency. *Fortune*[1] described this tradition as follows:

> Once the possibilities of a new technique have been demonstrated, Island Creek will give heed as rapidly as anyone. It was one of the first to become completely electrified underground. Probably there is no more efficient miner in the U. S.

Its simultaneous attention to sales and efficiency, as reflected in its responses in the 1930s, made Island Creek "that rarity—a prosperous coal company. It is probably the bituminous industry's one enduring success story."[2]

During the World War II era, there was a spurt in demand for coal. Island Creek acquired the United Thacker Coal Company in 1941 and also organized the Marianna Smokeless Coal Company in that year. From 1944 to 1949 Island Creek's management invested nearly $14 million in plant, equipment, stores, docks, and yards. The acquisition phase continued through the 1950s. The important acquisition in that period was the Red Jacket Coal Corporation, which owned a large tract of Pocahontas Number 3 Seam, a coal which is one of the highest quality low-volatile coking coals in the world. That acquisition, together with the merger of Pond Creek Pocahontas Company, which had operated under Island Creek's management since 1923, gave Island Creek ownership of some of the highest-premium coals in the country.

PRODUCT—MARKET POSTURE

In the 1950s Island Creek's management established joint ventures with steel companies to exploit the company's rich reserves of metallurgical coals. The use of joint ventures grew, and by 1976 1.6 million tons of coal were being produced through four joint ventures.

Until the early 1960s, Island Creek's coal was primarily sold to the profitable metallurgical and industrial steam-coal markets, both of which required high-quality premium coals. The company's excellent reserves of these premium coals and its marketing abilities, built up internally as well as through Appalachian Coals, Inc., helped Island Creek establish a strong position in the two markets.

In the early 1960s, Island Creek's management decided to enter the utility-coal market. This move was prompted by the rapid rise in consumption of coal by electric-power utilities in the 1950s. In contrast, the metallurgical and industrial steam-coal markets shrank during that period. To help its entry in the utility market Island Creek acquired the West Kentucky Coal Company in 1964.

Island Creek was acquired by Occidental Petroleum in 1968 as part of Oxy's diversification strategy as a natural-resource and energy company. A year and a half after the merger with Oxy, the Maust Coal and Coke Corporation, with operating properties in northern and central West Virginia and Pennsylvania, was acquired to provide growth in the utility markets. Utilities became the major market segment for Island Creek by 1976 (see Table 5–1).

The acquisition of the Maust properties coincided with the Federal Coal Mine Health and Safety Act of 1969. Island Creek had been a "safe" operator even before the Act. Nevertheless, implementation of the Act meant a drop in productivity for Island Creek as for others in the industry. The productivity at Island Creek subsequent to the Act is shown in Table 5–2.

The drop in productivity was more pronounced in the underground mines. Surface-mining productivity suffered much less. Island Creek had

Table 5-1. Coal Production in 1976, Island Creek

		Coal production (million tons)
Steam		10.6
Utility	8.9	
Industrial	1.7	
Metallurgical		6.0
Own production	5.4	
Share of joint ventures	0.6	
Total		16.6

surface-minable reserves primarily in southern West Virginia. The company opened the Pevler mine in that region in the early 1970s. Pevler accounted for over 2 million tons of surface-mined coal by 1975.

The Pevler mine also helped Island Creek in another area. The Clean Air Act of 1970 induced utilities to look for low-sulfur coals in order to comply with the government standards on pollution from stack gases. Under the new circumstances the Pevler reserves assumed unique importance. Stonie Barker, Jr., now President and Chief Executive Officer of Island Creek, described their uniqueness:

In the late 1960s, when we acquired the Pevler reserves, they were uneconomical to mine and were referred to as low BTU quality coals. Those reserves only came into being in the early 1970s, and they turned out to be one of the few low-sulfur compliance coals in the Appalachian area. They are in great demand today by the utility companies in this country.[3]

In the West, Island Creek's affiliate—Sheridan Enterprises—is adding to its reserve base and has plans for the construction of a 3-million-ton-per-year surface mine in Wyoming. This mine will produce low-sulfur steam coal.

Table 5-2. Productivity in Tons per Mine Man per Day, Island Creek, 1969-1975

Year	Average for Island Creek
1969	24.9
1971	14.7
1973	14.5
1975	11.1

Source: Company records.

Long-Term Plans

Any projection of Island Creek's future role has to be prefaced by the fact that the company has been opportunistic in the past. Projections become somewhat meaningless in that context. However, as per the company's expansion programs in January 1978 nearly 90 percent of the new production will be in metallurgical coal (Table 5–3).

Table 5–3. Production Program, Island Creek, 1978

Metallurgical coal		(Million tons)
Deep	4.1	
Surface	1.0	5.1
Steam coal		
Deep	0.2	
Surface	0.4	0.6
		5.7

Since that time, the prospects for growth in steam-coal demand have substantially improved despite continuing uncertainties over the choice between Eastern vs. Western and high-sulfur vs. low-sulfur coals. Island Creek has been responding to these steam-coal opportunities in a number of ways. Low-sulfur steam-coal production at its present Eastern mines has been stepped up, and new production from other Eastern low-sulfur reserve areas is scheduled to begin shortly. Some of its present metallurgical-coal production, even portions of the new mine output currently coming on stream, are being switched into the faster-growing utility and industrial steam-coal markets. Given its good-quality reserves the company has unique strengths to exploit the domestic growth in utility and industrial steam-coal markets, as and when that growth occurs.

Island Creek will continue to be a dominant domestic metallurgical-coal producer. The company has a strong export business and is also trying to locate metallurgical-coal reserves overseas. In both steam- and metallurgical-coal expansions, it is surmised that Island Creek will continue to stress profitability, as opposed to mere volume, and maintain a broad product range of coals, a strategy that has been beneficial in the past.

As for synthetics (oil, gas, or chemicals from coal), Island Creek will not be directly involved for it does not have the large resources required to finance the synthetics business. All the technical know-how on synthetics is concentrated at its parent's research facility, the Occidental Research Center. Oxy is seeking to commercialize its synthetics technology, primarily through joint ventures involving governmental and private partnerships that share the financial burdens but allow Oxy to retain an economic interest in its proprietary and patented technology. If this technology is commercialized, Island Creek will possibly get new markets for its coal.

RESPONDING TO OTHER STRATEGIC CHANGES

Island Creek's top management recognizes that labor management would be one of the most critical functions of the 1980s. J. E. Katlic, an executive with vast and varied experience in the coal industry, was hired as Executive Vice-President (Administration) in 1975 to coordinate various efforts at improving labor productivity and reducing absenteeism and wildcat strikes. Some of Katlic's perceptions of the mine worker were:

1. The miner has this macho image of himself, yet we keep telling him how much safer it is and how nice he has it. We are eroding away at his image of himself.
2. His contractual gains *are* good and his heritage *does* lie in strife. But *he* has not paid his "dues." He has the gains but did not really contribute to getting them.[4]

The implications of the above were:

The union tells him how "bad" it is. Nothing has changed. We're ready to sacrifice him for a ton of coal. We're out to break the union. He loves it! Not because it's true, but *because it fits his image of himself* and his heritage. Realistically, he doesn't have a whole lot else going for him. Why does he strike for an insignificant reason? Dues. Peer image. Tradition. He's a miner. He is going to *contribute* to the gains. He is going to *earn* the right to be comfortable with them.[5]

Katlic realized that the broad problem of "cognitive dissonance," a negative-drive state which exists when a person has two contrasting beliefs or ideas simultaneously, was not easy to resolve. Katlic reasoned:

The higher the credibility of the source, the greater the dissonance—because the less sense it makes to be in disagreement. . . . Moreover, the more expert management becomes, the more dissonance the miners have to go through. Time may eventually see him coming to terms with his "new look," but it could be a *long* time with continued dissonance. We cannot expect rapid response, for some of our managers have dissonance of their own. Their image of mine managers is not what they've known or believed. We have a job to do on the management side, also.[6]

It was Katlic's hope that by sensitizing the foreman to the problem of dissonance described above, he could be made to empathize with his crew. That could be the first step in a long process of neutralizing the historical antagonism between miner and manager. The operations management at the top level has discussed the possibilities and potential of using this "dissonance theory." The next step is to communicate with the 1,500 foremen of the company through a training program.

In the meanwhile, Katlic believes that it is important that all company communications to the miner "quit telling him how good he has it and how safe it is," even though work continues toward his welfare and safety.

"Black and White Hat" Functions

A coal miner historically has had to bargain through his union for all concessions that he has got from management. His day-to-day interaction with the industrial-relations department has been either to redress a grievance or to be disciplined for a misconduct. Island Creek's management reasons that the impersonality inherent in the former and the adversary relationship generated by the latter have caused the miner to perceive industrial relations as a "Black Hat" function. While Island Creek has sought to complement the important contract-administration activity with more employee-centered activities, its management believes that the perceived stigma of industrial relations as a "Black Hat" function cannot be effectively erased by merely enlarging the scope of the industrial-relations department. Contract administration is often impersonal and very quickly gets rigidified in "win-lose" settings. Island Creek's management, therefore, seeks to establish employee relations, training, and human-resources development as "White Hat" functions autonomous in *operation* from the "Black Hat" function of industrial relations. "Black Hat" and "White Hat" are merely labels used by the company to describe miners' perceptions of these functions and are not descriptions of actual management styles at Island Creek. As Table 5−4 illustrates, the two functions together represent the full range of labor-management activities.

Pete Dulaney, Executive Vice-President, Operations, pointed out that "Black Hat" and "White Hat" were conceptual labels that helped the divisional management in organizing their labor-management program. However, the special settings and the nature of rapport existing between labor and management in a division decides the exact administrative arrangement

Table 5–4. Organization for Labor Management

Department Function	Industrial Relations (IR)	Employee Relations (ER)	Human Resources Development (HR)
"Black Hat"	Contract Administration		
"White Hat"	Personnel Administration (including recruitment)	Community Services Employee Welfare	Training Public Relations

in that division. At present, not only are the administrative arrangements different in the four divisions, but there are also divergent preferences among the divisional presidents for the way these departments should be regrouped.

When the "White Hat" function gets established at Island Creek, the management hopes that the resulting improvement in communication will provide advance warning of brewing labor crises. It further aspires to nip grievances in the bud before they assume major porportions, and before union and management egos are placed at stake.

Grievance Handling

Island Creek tries to follow the advice "keep grievances in the pit." Its management has been successful in settling close to 70 percent of all grievances in 1977 at Step 1, i.e., the section foreman's level. Of the remaining 30 percent, nearly 21 percent were settled at Step 2, i.e., the mine superintendent-mine committee level. An additional 8 percent were settled at Step 3, i.e., the divisional industrial-relations and district field-representative's level. In short, only 1 in every 100 grievances went up for arbitration. The latest contract with the UMW provides more encouragement to the section foreman in the settlement of grievances by protecting his decision from being used as a precedent in the settlement of other grievances.[7] The increasing responsibility of the foreman for settling grievances once again calls for more training. There are plans to intensify Island Creek's training for its foremen.

Training and Motivating the Miner

Island Creek's training extends beyond its contractual obligations, especially in the case of new recruits. The company tries to use the mandatory orientation-and-training period for new recruits to familiarize them not only with the mining job, but also to brief them on the company and its policies.

This is related to a much broader effort on the part of the administration department to try to build a sense of loyalty to the company.

Katlic sees a close similarity between the mining crew and a platoon in combat. He wonders whether the same pride that a platoon has for its regiment cannot be inculcated in a crew for its division. His staff is currently working on proposals for a distinctive logo and color for each division. There already exists a sense of camaraderie among the miners in a crew. If only that can be given anchor in a broader sense of divisional loyalty, a major attitude change would have been achieved among the miners at Island Creek.

Incentives

Industrial engineering at Island Creek is a well-established function, having started more than four decades ago. The Manager (Industrial Engineering) is currently working on an incentive scheme for the miners. Island Creek's work force is young and nearly half of it has been recruited in the 1970s. The top management of Island Creek is, therefore, hopeful that a good incentive scheme, attractive to the young miners, will help the overall labor-management effort.

MATERIAL RESOURCES

Despite its long record of profitability, Island Creek was not rich enough in financial resources to undertake on its own the many expansion plans it had in the 1960s. Its acquisition in 1968 by Occidental Petroleum provided Island Creek the much-needed financial support. As Stonie Barker summarized:

> In fact, Island Creek would have had difficulty providing the money for expansion on its own, and probably would have been precluded from doing many of the things we are doing today. Without the capital money supplied by Oxy, Island Creek could not have built new mines.[8]

The acquisition of Maust Coal and Coke Corporation, the opening of the giant Pevler mine, and the establishment of a Western coal operation were all subsequent to the Oxy acquisition. Island Creek's access to large financial resources through its Oxy connection, when coupled with its excellent coal reserve holdings, offer the company a variety of strategic options.

Coal Reserves

As mentioned earlier, Island Creek has an outstanding mix of coal reserves (see Table 5–5), consisting of prize metallurgical coal and substantial tonnage of low-sulfur steam-grade coal in the East.

The preference for low-sulfur coal subsequent to the Clean Air Act has

Table 5-5. Coal Reserves, Island Creek, 1976

	Coal reserves* (billion tons at 12/31/76)
Steam	
Sulfur content 1% and under	0.52**
Sulfur content over 1%	1.83
Metallurgical	
Premium (under 1% sulfur and 8% ash)	1.04
Other (over 1% sulfur and 8% ash)	0.19
Total	3.58

*Based on company reported data and August 1977 analysis by Dean Witter & Co.
**Includes 0.25 of Sheridan Enterprises.

encouraged Island Creek's management to consider acquisition of reserves in the West. Island Creek went West in 1976 through its parent. Oxy established a separate subsidiary, Sheridan Enterprises, responsible for acquiring and developing Western coal reserves. By the end of 1976 Sheridan owned or leased coal lands in Wyoming estimated by its geologists to contain approximately 250 million tons of recoverable reserves of steam coal. Approximately 90 percent of this reserve is minable by surface-mining methods. The coal is generally of compliance quality. Sheridan's management plans to set up a surface mine of 3-million-tons annual capacity at an estimated cost of approximately $30 million. It has also recently acquired some federal coal leases in Colorado. The property is estimated to contain approximately 100 million tons of low-sulfur steam coal recoverable by current underground-mining technology.

Whereas Island Creek is certain to seek and exploit opportunities for growth in both the steam- and metallurgical-coal markets, its reserves have not grown substantially in the 1970s with the exception of Western reserves acquired by Sheridan. Part of the reason may be the fact that it already has an excellent mix of reserves.

In terms of profitability the ranking of coals is premium metallurgical, low-sulfur compliance or marginal metallurgical, and high-sulfur steam, in that order. Island Creek has excellent reserve tonnage of the more profitable coals, metallurgical and low-sulfur steam. These reserves are difficult to add to. High-sulfur steam coals are more readily available, but management has not made any significant reserve additions of these coals. Given the lower profitability of these coals and their consequent unattractiveness to Island Creek's high-profitability aspirations, it is conceivable that the management may decide that its present holding of 1.8 billion tons is adequate for its foreseeable expansions in that market segment.

Reorganization

Soon after the acquisition of the Maust Coal and Coke Corporation in 1969, Island Creek was reorganized into four operating divisions. These were the Island Creek Division, located in southern West Virginia; the Northern Division, located in central and northern West Virginia and southwestern Pennsylvania; the Virginia Pocahontas Division, located in southwestern Virginia; and the West Kentucky Division, located in western Kentucky. The sales function at Island Creek continued to be a separate company, the Island Creek Coal Sales Company. A new organization structure was introduced to administer the expanded operations. That structure has remained largely unchanged through the 1970s.

Island Creek's organization structure in 1978 is shown in Figure 5–1. Under the present organization structure, Island Creek depends on Oxy and trade associations like the National Coal Association, Bituminous Coal Operators Association, and American Mineral Corporation for all major interface with the government. Other governmental liaison work of a procedural nature such as expediting a permit or seeking clarifications on a new law is done by the operations function. Dulaney, with his staff or the help of other corporate staff, helps the divisional presidents interface with the relevant government agencies. Similarly, while the divisions continue to seek development in mining methods with the help of their industrial-engineering staff, they undertake no research and development on new uses for coal. The Occidental Research Corporation (ORC) is responsible for all research on coal gasification and liquefaction. The President of ORC reports directly to the President of Oxy.

Organizational Structure

Island Creek's current organization can be highlighted under two broad headings: central services and operations management.

Central Services

The present organization provides Island Creek with three strong central services: finance, planning, and engineering.

The *finance* function was combined from the former controller and treasurer functions. A vice-president's position was created to head the new function. The reorganization reflects the corporate setup of the finance function at Oxy's headquarters in Los Angeles.

The *planning* function needed streamlining so as to mesh Island Creek's planning process with Oxy's corporate-planning activities. B. V. Postell, who helped establish and later headed Oxy's corporate-planning activity,

CHAIRMAN OF THE BOARD — Albert Gore
> Secretary — Linda Slone

PRESIDENT AND CHIEF EXECUTIVE OFFICER — Stonie Barker, Jr.
> Deputy to the President — J. E. Katlic
>
> Secretary — Frances McLaine

SENIOR VICE-PRESIDENT — J. J. Dorgan

VICE-PRESIDENT and SECRETARY — P. C. Hebner
> Ass't Secretary — W. G. Allen
>
> Ass't Secretary — R. B. Metcalf
>
> Ass't Secretary — Marguerite Glueck

VICE-PRESIDENT, FINANCE — C. M. Cooper
> Treasurer — R. B. Casriel
> > Director of Treasury Operations — A. V. Regan, Jr.
> >
> > Ass't Treasurer — R. B. Metcalf
> >
> > Ass't Treasurer — Fred W. Gruberth
> >
> > Manager, Texas — R. B. Metcalf
> > > Ass't Manager, Texas —J. W. Warden
> >
> > Manager, Credit Sales — Fred Painter, Jr.
>
> Controller — D. G. Kelsay
> > Ass't Controller — Gary Kendrick
> >
> > Ass't Controller — L. L. Williams
> > > Consolidation Accountant — E. E. Ranson
> >
> > Manager, Data Processing — G. R. Clifton

EXECUTIVE VICE-PRESIDENT, OPERATIONS — R. L. Dulaney
> Ass't Exec. Vice Pres., Operations — G. S. Matthis
>
> Safety Coordinator — E. E. McBurney
>
> Manager, Industrial Engineering — C. W. Rountree

Figure 5–1. Island Creek Coal Company Organization Chart, 1978

Manager, Preparation — E. F. Burch

Corporate Director, Environmental Affairs — J. L. Lombardo

President, Island Creek Division — Kenzie Jones

President, Northern Division — T. A. Salvati

President, Virginia Pocahontas Division — John Turyn, Jr.

President, West Kentucky Division — A. W. Petzold

EXECUTIVE VICE-PRESIDENT, ADMINISTRATION — J. E. Katlic

Vice-President, Employee Relations — J. J. Yorke

Manager, Labor Relations — J. P. Rouse

General Manager, Purchases — G. A. Williams

Security Director — B. L. Watson

Manager, Human Resources Development — Mike Musulin

VICE-PRESIDENT, PLANNING AND PROJECTS — B. V. Postell

Manager, Economic Serices — Lloyd Kelly

VICE-PRESIDENT, ENGINEERING — W. F. Diamond

Ass't to VP–Engineering — Donald Hunter

General Manager, Projects — Earl Boggs

Manager of Ventilation — J. D. Kalasky

Corp. Mgr., Explorat'n/Mineral Acquis. — C. L. Glover

VICE-PRESIDENT, SALES — W. W. Mason

President, Island Creek Coal Sales Company — W. W. Mason

PRESIDENT, ISLAND CREEK STORES COMPANY — L. A. Ware

GENERAL COUNSEL — W. G. Allen

Ass't General Counsel — R. P. Reineke

Ass't Corporate Counsel — W. K. Bodell

Ass't Corporate Counsel — M. S. Peace

Sup'r, Corporate Records — Marguerite Glueck

Source: Company records.

Figure 5–1. Island Creek Coal Company Organization Chart, 1978 (Cont.)

was brought in to establish the planning function at Island Creek in 1974. The positions of Vice-President (Planning and Development) and Vice-President (Production Planning) were eliminated. Postell was designated Vice-President (Planning and Special Projects).

Central engineering was strengthened in the early 1970s. The Vice-President (Engineering) was responsible for engineering and construction of all new mines and major facilities and for monitoring the capital expenditures on all projects. A portion of his responsibility in the area of project development has been delegated to his assistant, General Manager (Projects). The central-engineering staff also provides specialized engineering consultation to supplement the engineering skills already available in the divisions. The Manager (Exploration and Minerals Acquisition) also reports to the Vice-President (Engineering). This manager evaluates all reserve-acquisition proposals. He has, however, more of an advisory function, in that the final purchase and price decisions are made by the President of Island Creek.

In the *sales-management* area, Island Creek has one of the largest sales organizations in the industry, with some unique strengths for exploiting future opportunities. The selling function at Island Creek is organized as a separate company—Island Creek Coal Sales Company. The sales company, however, functions as a division for all practical purposes. It sells coal for others besides Island Creek. The coal brokered by the sales company on behalf of other producers is said to yield a profit that supports its entire operation. The organization of the sales company is shown in Figure 5–2.

L. G. Evans, Executive Vice-President of the sales company, emphasized that coal was not a single product:

> It is a variety of products. For example, for steam coals, variety is determined by location of the reserves, and its size, BTU value of the coal, its sulfur and ash content. Its marketability is influenced by the type of combustion equipment that customers have and the reliability and cost of transportation to get the coal to these customers. Thus, for different markets, our coal assumes different product meanings.

Evans understands this variety as well as anyone else in the industry, since Island Creek has over 1,500 customers and sells nearly one-third of its coal in the spot markets. The company has six district sales offices to service its large base of customers, many of whom are small. Table 5–6 shows the percentage of large customers on long-term contract with Island Creek.

Island Creek's expertise in dealing with small customers and its knowledge of the industrial markets may provide the company some unique op-

CHAIRMAN AND CHIEF EXECUTIVE OFFICER — Stonie Barker, Jr.

PRESIDENT — W. W. Mason

  Secretary — Ellen Greer

Executive Vice-President — L. G. Evans

  Vice-President Utility Sales — E. R. Mook

    Utility Engineer — F. C. Belsak

    Manager — Utility Sales — (vacancy)

  District Sales Manager (Denver): J. H. Combes

    Industrial Engineer — L. J. Muskopf

  Manager — Western P/A — (vacancy)

  Manager — Welco & KOT P/A — (vacancy)

  Manager — P/A General — B. Christopher

Vice-President of Administration — R. H. Neilsen

  Manager Contract Administration — Larry Holt

  Manager Market Services — B. C. Daniel

  General Manager — Transportation — L. W. Kobitter

    Manager — Transportation — T. G. Slone

Vice-President Met Sales, U.S. — A. W. Simmons

Vice-President Met Sales, Export — M. A. Sofo

General Manager of Sales — J. H. Booher

  District Sales Manager (Cincinnati) — (vacancy)

  District Sales Manager (Chicago) — R. J. Blaising

  District Sales Manager (Greensboro) — J. C. Maynard

  District Sales Manager (Detroit) — R. G. Holloway

  District Sales Manager (New Jersey) — V. P. Kober

General Manager, Distribution — R. P. Wehle

  Senior Distribution Manager — R. E. Gee

Figure 5–2. Island Creek Coal Sales Company Organization Chart, 1978

Senior Distribution Agent — W. P. Hagy

Manager — Export Forwarding — A. Stapleton

Secretary — W. G. Allen

Assistant Secretary — R. B. Metcalf

Clerk — Hotham D. Pierce

Treasurer — A. V. Regan, Jr.

Controller — E. E. Clark

Figure 5–2. Island Creek Coal Sales Company Organization Chart, 1978 (Cont.)

Table 5–6. Long-Term Contracting, Island Creek, 1976

Market segment	Sales tonnage (1976)	Percentage of tonnage on long-term contracts
Steam		
Utilities	9.2	85–90
Industrial	2.2	35
Metallurgical		
Domestic	2.0	35
Foreign	4.5	75–80
Total	17.9	

portunities in the industrial markets, particularly if forced conversion or mandatory burning of coal becomes realities.

Operations Management

Island Creek also made changes in the operations management function. In the 1965 organization the mine manager had a number of staff functions reporting directly to him. In the present structure (see Figure 5–3 for the organization of a typical division), the mine manager is made responsible only for production. This is in keeping with the increasing demands placed on the mine manager's job by the Federal Health and Mine Safety Act and growing labor militancy. The staff functions have all been placed under the divisional presidents who are expected to take initiative in a number of areas other than production.

President and Chief Executive Officer — Stonie Barker, Jr.

Executive Vice-President, Mining Operations — R. L. Dulaney

President, Island Creek Division — Kenzie Jones

Secretary — Lucille Thomasson

Director of Purchasing — Curtis Testerman

Director Industrial Relations — R. L. Piercey

Director Human Resources Development — G. Johnson

Manager Engineering Services — M. A. Sharkey

Director Engineering — Hans Naumann

Division Controller — L. R. Wagner

Director Industrial Engineering — Ralph Herbert

Director Preparation — Joe Campoy

Director Safety — Tony Turyn

Manager of Mines — J. M. Hunter

Manager of Mines — T. Mosley

Supervisor Contract Coal — Roy C. Dotson

District Manager — D. Chaffins

Sup't — Pevler Mine

Sup'ts — Wheelwright & Spurlock Mines

District Manager — P. Cook

Sup'ts — Pond Fork, Nos. 9, 10, 12 Mines

District Superintendent — C. Evans

Sup'ts — Nos. 14, 25 Mines, Gund, Big Creek 1 & 2

District Superintendent — L. Derenge

Sup'ts — Guyan No. 1, Nos. 4 and 5 Mines

Figure 5-3. Island Creek Division Organization Chart, 1978

OTHER ADMINISTRATIVE SYSTEMS

Planning was a part-time activity at Island Creek until 1974. The annual operating budget was prepared by the controller, and the longer-range operating plans were coordinated by the sales division. The controller prepared capital-expenditure forecasts based on these longer-range plans. Since planning was considered an intrusion into executive time, it was no more than an annual ritual of numbers. When Postell, currently Vice-President (Planning and Projects), took charge of the function, he had two objectives: (1) streamlining of the planning process to make it consistent with Oxy's planning system, and (2) internalization of planning as an important management tool at all levels of management.

Postell introduced to Island Creek Oxy's three-tier planning system. The three tiers were (1) a five-year strategic plan, (2) a three-year capital plan, and (3) a yearly operating plan. Since Postell intentionally kept his staff small (only two professionals), a great deal of the basic planning effort was carried out under his direction and coordination by the production, marketing, and finance executives both at the corporate office and in the divisions. Thus planning has become a more pervasive activity.

Each divisional president participates in the company's long-term planning process. In the course of preparing capital budgets and annual operating budgets for his division, the president has to propose expansion programs, training programs, reserve-acquisition programs, and plans for contracting out mining of his division's reserves to small operators. All such proposals are discussed in detail with the Executive Vice-President (Operations) whose approval is a must before any action may be initiated. Thus, while the divisional presidents have plenty of encouragement to show their initiative in the planning process, commitment to a plan can only be made at Lexington, Kentucky (the company's headquarters since 1973).

The implementation of approved plans is again carefully controlled through formal review meetings. The divisional presidents meet the Executive Vice-President (Operations) in a monthly performance-review meeting which lasts two days. The four divisional presidents attend all sessions of the meeting so as to benefit from each others' experiences. The executives in charge of administration, sales, planning, finance, and engineering are scheduled to attend some sessions of the meeting. This helps in the sharing of mutual concerns and in solving problems of coordination with operations. The sales representative, for example, may help modify dispatch schedules in cases of anticipated excess or shortfall in production. Occasionally, one division's shortfall can be made up of the other's surplus, if acceptable to the sales division. The President attends these meetings frequently as a way of keeping in touch with the operations. The top management of Island

Creek is convinced that its style of delegation with careful control represents the appropriate management style for running an efficient operation.

Table 5–7. The Executive Incentive Program

Factors	Basis for incentive
1. Safety	Performance against budgets for frequency and severity of lost-time accidents.
2. Production	Tonnage produced in excess of budget.
3. Productivity	Performance against budgeted ratio of clean coal produced to attended man days.
4. Capacity utilization	Targeted ratio of depreciation and rental dollars to ton of clean coal produced.
5. Cost	Evidence of an improving trend in the cost per ton of coal produced.

Table 5–8. The Supervisory Incentive Program

Factors	Basis for incentives
1. Production	Standard performance has been set at 80% of normal performance. Performance in excess of standard is rewarded on a straight-line bonus formula.
2. Cost budgets	If the supervisor stays within 15% of the cost budget, he is entitled to a bonus.
3. Safety-compliance bonus	If there are no safety violations in any two random inspections of his area of jurisdiction, or there is not more than one violation in three inspections, a supervisor is eligible for a safety bonus. The bonus is ranked as follows: Inspections Violations Bonus rank 3 — 1 2 — 2 1 —⎫ 3 1⎭ 3
4. Control of overtime	Performance against budget.

Note: The above incentives are arranged in the descending order of their monetary attraction. The supervisor loses all his incentive earnings if there is any fatal accident or mine closure in his area of supervision. The incentive is paid once a month.

Incentive System

In order to reward executives whose performance exceeds budgeted levels, Island Creek also has incentive programs. It has two types of incentive schemes.

The first incentive scheme is for mine managers and divisional presidents; it has been in existence for over a decade. The factors on which this incentive is based are outlined in Table 5—7.

Incentives payable under the above scheme are all subject to one condition, i.e., a fatal accident or a mine closure would wipe out the benefits. The incentive is paid quarterly. A special bonus at the discretion of the Executive Vice-President (Operations) is payable over and above these incentives for excellence in management.

The second incentive scheme, introduced in 1972, is for supervisors up to the rank of divisional superintendent. Their scheme is outlined in Table 5—8.

6. Consolidation Coal Company

Consolidation Coal Company (Consol) is one of the leading coal companies in the United States. It has the largest coal reserves and is the second largest coal producer in the country. Consol possesses an interesting blend of strengths. Firstly, it derives all the traditional wisdom about the coal business from its long association with the industry; an association marked by professionalism in management and leadership in technological innovation. Added to that strength is the financial and managerial backing of its parent, the Continental Oil Company (Conoco).

This case study describes the growth of Consol and the efforts of its management in the last decade to consolidate its strengths. Consol's management aspires to retain the company's dominance in the conventional coal markets, while attempting to find new markets for its vast coal reserves. Its ambitious expansion plans make it an important energy company.

EARLY HISTORY

Several small coal operators in Maryland combined their interests to form the Consolidation Coal Company in 1864. Coal mining was then done with pickaxes and shovels. At first coal was transported to the surface using mule carts and shipped to the market by wagons or flat-bottomed river boats, but soon it was moved in massive amounts by railroad. The Spanish–American war gave an impetus to Consol's coal production. It produced 1.7 million tons of coal in 1899.

In the early years of the twentieth century, Consol's management decided to expand geographically. Between 1902 and 1904, Consol acquired rich

---

NOTE: The original case study has been abridged and re-edited for this book.

coal fields in northern West Virginia and controlling interests in two operating coal companies in Pennsylvania and northern West Virginia. The acquisitions contributed 5 million tons of coal production each year. They also provided Consol a large dock for river transportation and a successful coal-distributing facility. In 1909 Consol entered Kentucky.

There was a brief lull in geographic expansion during the World War I years. Consol played a prominent part in supporting the war effort. Consol's then President helped organize the bituminous-coal industry into a national body for more effective cooperation with the Federal Fuel Administration. After the war, Consol acquired two operating mines in West Virginia, and by 1926 the company became the leading commercial producer of bituminous coal in the country. Its production had reached 12 million tons.

The company reorganized several departments in 1927 in the interest of increased efficiency. More than $3 million was spent on additional plants and equipment, enlargement of certain units, greater safety, better preparation of coal, and improvement in the working and living conditions of employees. Although fewer mines were operated in 1927 than in the previous year, the tonnage exceeded the 12 million tons that was reached in 1926. The company also pioneered in 1929 a group life-insurance plan providing sick and death benefits to further improve the financial security of its employees and their families.

With the onslaught of the Depression, however, Consol was in serious financial trouble and in 1930 went into receivership in the midst of severe worldwide recession. The company regrouped its operations after the Depression into five divisions: Maryland Division, Pennsylvania Division, West Virginia Division, and two divisions in the Millers Creek Division and the Elkhorn Division. The company's work force was organized by the UMW during the 1930s.

During the World War II years demand for coal grew and consequently Consol attained financial stability. But as the war drew to an end, Consol's management feared that the demand would start declining. Traditionally there had been short periods of extreme demand followed by longer periods of oversupply. Properties of the Christopher Coal Company, which had high-quality coal reserves in West Virginia, were acquired during the war and just after. In 1945, Consol merged with another large coal company, the Pittsburgh Coal Company. The merger was conceived by the top management of both companies who dreamed of a unified large coal company, financially strong enough to afford the best mechanization and to undertake research. The merger was also in anticipation of increased competition from oil and natural gas after the war. In 1946, Pittsburgh-Consolidation, the merged company, acquired Hanna Coal Company's bituminous-coal-producing properties in Ohio.

In keeping with its policy of concentrating its efforts on the primary functions of mining and distributing coal, Consol disposed of certain properties no longer considered necessary and acquired others that lent themselves to greater diversification in mining methods and in the types of coal produced. It also sold in 1946 the Montour Railroad, the Youngstown and Southern Railway, and other private rail properties that it owned through past acquisitions to major railroad companies.

George M. Humphrey, who had been President of the Hanna Coal Company since 1929, was elected Chairman of Pittsburgh-Consolidation. George H. Love of the Consolidation Coal Company became President of the new Pittsburgh-Consolidation Company.

In a reorganization move that was made soon after the merger, the company's mines were organized into the following separate and distinct operating units: Consolidation Coal Company (Kentucky); Hanna Coal Company (Ohio); Pittsburgh Coal Company (Pennsylvania); and Consolidation Coal Company (West Virginia). Steps were taken to delegate responsibility for decisions to the points of operation, by assigning capable executives to head the four operating units.

Finance and sales continued to be central functions, handled directly from Pittsburgh. In explaining the rationale for their centralization, a Consol vice-president suggested:

> We have historically had a central sales organization, that has allowed us to sell our coals without duplicate effort to markets geographically diverse from those available in the proximity of our mining operations.
>
> Likewise, a central finance function was not only necessary to integrate the operations of various divisions into a common company balance sheet, but also to coordinate the cross transfer of financial resources between divisions to suit the larger interests of the corporation.

The reorganization in 1946 had two other important features. A Vice-President (Engineering) was elected and made responsible for coordinating the modernization and mechanization of the company's forty mines in four states. Another position, that of Vice-President (Research and Development), was offered to a Consol executive who had spent several months of 1946 in South Africa investigating the possibility of complete gasification of coal. The two positions respectively symbolized Consol's concern for improving the efficiency of its mining operations and its efforts at generating new markets for coal. Consol's emphasis on research was rather unique at that time in the coal industry.

Consol began mechanization of a number of its mines. New cutting equipment, modern shuttle cars, and new haulage locomotives were purchased. In the period 1946–1948, the company spent more than $48 million in modernization and mechanization of existing mines, and acquisition of new mines and additional coal reserves. Net coal production in 1948 jumped to 26 million tons.

The period 1947–1949 also saw rapid progress in the company's research on coal gasification. Work involved the evolution of a process design in cooperation with Standard Oil of Ohio (Sohio), based on data sources in the United States and abroad. Sohio terminated its research interest in gasification soon after, and Consol hired a number of research engineers from the oil company's defunct gasification project. Eric Reichl, the current President of the Conoco Coal Development Company, was one of the several engineers who joined Consol. The then President of Consol, George Love, gave strong support for the R&D activities. He approved the construction of a pilot coal-gasification plant in Library, Pennsylvania, which was completed in late 1948. In addition, a pilot plant involving an important step in the refining of tar from a carbonization process developed by Consol was built during that year. The assembly of technical staff and facilities required for a basic exploratory-research program was completed in 1949.

PRODUCT–MARKET POSTURE

Consol together with three major metallurgical-coal-consuming steel companies formed in 1951 a joint venture—Mathies Coal Company. Consol acquired its equity in the company by relinquishing its ownership of coal reserves to the subsidiary. Mathies Coal was the forerunner of four other Consol joint ventures with steel companies. The affiliated and/or supervised companies produced nearly 9 million tons of low- and high-volatile metallurgical coal by 1965. Consol owned approximately 25 percent of this tonnage as its share, based on its equity holding in the joint ventures. The joint-venture mines were operated by Consol, and it received a management fee on each ton of coal produced. Since the mines were largely captive to steel producers, their production remained fairly stable even during downturns in the steel industry. The arrangement thus offered Consol a steady income from the metallurgical-coal reserves that it had assigned to these joint ventures.

In the early 1950s, the R&D department of Consol had begun to look at problems beyond coal conversion. The department successfully experimented with a coal-slurry pipeline for transporting coal. In 1957, a 108-mile pipeline was operational, supplying coal to a Cleveland utility from one of Consol's mines in Ohio. The major impact of the slurry pipeline, according to a company document, was to spur "the railroads to hold down costs and to develop the unit train, another innovative way of transporting coal from mine to market."[1] Eric Reichl, presently the head of synthetics research, emphasized the importance of the slurry-pipeline innovation in the following words:

> Small as the project may now seem, the enormity of the savings in railroad freight rates that it induced have perhaps paid for all R&D expenses incurred by the company in the three decades since 1946.

During the same era, Consol entered the chemical business, by purchasing a coal-tar-refining and chemical plant in New Jersey. The new plant produced cresylic acids for plastics and general industrial use. In 1956 Consol acquired the large Pocahontas Fuel Company, which was a major producer of low-volatile coking coals for steel making. The A. L. Lee Company of Ohio was also acquired in the 1950s and became the Lee Engineering Division of Consol. The division pioneered the development of radically new types of drills, electric safeguard systems, and underground-to-surface communications. In the next few years three other coal companies were acquired by Consol.

In 1963, Consol was awarded a contract by the Office of Coal Research of the United States Department of the Interior to continue research on the conversion of coal to gasoline, and, upon successful completion of the laboratory work, to design, construct, and operate a pilot conversion plant in West Virginia. In addition, the R&D department of Consol got another contract from the Office of Coal Research in 1964 to convert coal to synthetic pipeline gas.

Consol acquired a rich parent, Continental Oil Company, in 1966 to strengthen its resources. In the aftermath of the Arab oil embargo of 1973, Consol, like other coal companies, had an overnight turnover in its financial situation (see Table 6−1).

As evidenced by Consol's doubling of capital investment on coal, surface lands, and equipment, its management foresaw good opportunities for expansion of coal production. In view of the restrictions imposed on burning of high-sulfur Eastern coal, Consol's management planned for development of its Western coal reserves.

Reflective of the corporate thrust toward development of low-sulfur coal reserves was the following Consol long-term plan (Table 6−2) announced in 1975. Over 50 percent of Consol's planned production was in low-sulfur Western coal.

Table 6-1. Financial Statistics, Consol, 1973-1974

	1973	1974
Production tonnage (million tons)	54	47
Revenue (million $)	474	747
Net income (million $)	(13)	44
Capital investment (million $)		
Plant and equipment	32	66
Coal and surface lands	7	11

Source: Annual Reports.

Table 6-2. Proposed Long-Term Expansion (in million of tons)

	End use foreseen			
Region	Steam coal	Gasification	Metallurgical	Total
West	13	4	—	17
East	4	2	1.5	7.5
	17	6	1.5	24.5

Source: Keystone Coal Industry Directory, 1976.

The 6 million tons of coal proposed for gasification included both Eastern high-sulfur coal and Western coals. Gasification was one possible marketing outlet for high-sulfur Eastern coal. Conoco's subsidiary, the Conoco Coal Development Company, had planned a major demonstration project in Noble County, Ohio, for converting coal into synthetic natural gas. The Federal Energy Research and Development Administration and six pipeline companies together with Conoco have shared the cost of the project. In highlighting the importance of the project, a company report stated:

> The plant must use the high-sulfur, high-ash coal characteristic of Appalachia. If this coal can be converted into methane without releasing ash and sulfur dioxide into the atmosphere, one of the region's major environmental problems will be solved. The plant is expected to do this.[2]

The low-BTU Dakota lignites of Consol are good feedstock coals for gasification. A gasification project in the Dakotas could provide interstate markets for the otherwise difficult-to-transport lignite. Consol also has a demonstration project in Rapid City, South Dakota. If the project succeeds,

Consol's vast Western reserves, especially the noncompliance variety, could find new markets.

Currently Consol is predominantly a steam-coal producer. It is a major supplier to both the utilities and industrial segments (see Table 6−3).

Table 6−3. Production and Distribution Statistics, Consol, 1976

	Production/distribution (millions of tons)	
Produced by Consol		55.8
Consol's share of production		50.6
Sale by market segments		
Utility	42.8	
Industrial	2.2	
Metallurgical	5.6	50.6

Source: Company sources.

Long-Term Plans

Consol has ambitious plans for expansion in the conventional steam-coal markets. Consol announced in 1977 plans to increase its steam-coal production by 19 million tons in the East and 14 million tons in the West before 1985. Consol's projected production of steam coal for then is about 78 million tons (total production about 90 million tons).

The oscillating competitive advantage between Western and Eastern coals, caused by changing environmental legislation, has paralyzed decision-making in utility companies and consequently may slow down the growth in demand for steam coals. Nevertheless, the recently proposed mandatory use of scrubbers on all new coal-burning plants could eventually favor Consol. As Ralph Bailey[3] pointed out:

> Although we question the merits of the inflexible approach to the sulfur emission problem from a cost standpoint, the fact remains that Consol would be in a stronger competitive position because a significant portion of our reserves and production is located in the east and midwest.

The bulk of Consol's additional production is, therefore, likely to be in the East and Midwest for utility markets.

While Consol's marketing department does forecast some growth in demand for steam coals in industrial markets, it does not expect that market to grow strongly. Industrial users are less price-sensitive to fuel costs and are more concerned with the convenience and cleanliness of burning a fuel. Forced conversion to coal through the proposed system of taxes and rebates may, therefore, not result in the expected growth in demand for coal in the industrial markets.[4] Moreover, active penetration of this market would require technical expertise in areas related to conversion from oil- and gas-fired furnaces to coal-fired furnaces and the ability to service a large number of small orders, often less than a unit train in size. In view of these factors, Consol's sales department does not seem to have any special plans to expand its share of the industrial steam-coal market. Consol sells 2 million tons of industrial steam coal and will continue to grow modestly in that market segment.

In financing the proposed expansion, Consol will experience two problems. The first is the rapidly inflating "price" of capital for every new ton of coal produced. There are three factors that influence this inflation: inflation in the prices of capital equipment, the falling labor productivity, and capital intensity in operations. An underground mine of 2-million-ton capacity is estimated to cost over $50 million, and a surface mine of similar capacity would cost over $20 million.[5] A growth of nearly 40 million tons in total production capacity as envisaged by Consol would cost the company nearly a billion dollars, even without considering the additional inflation in the prices of capital equipment during the period of expansion. This investment would need an upward revision, if labor productivity were to drop any further in the future. Consol estimates that the additional dollar investment required solely on account of productivity loss to maintain the same level of production in 1976 as in 1969 is 33 percent of the 1969 investment.[6] In trying to offset productivity losses, Consol has relied in part on technology. New technology implies higher capital intensity because of the automation involved. When all the three factors are combined, the problem of "price" inflation in capital is a serious one for Consol.

The second problem in the financing of Consol's capital expenditures is the slow buildup in self-generated funds because of the poor profitability of some of the old sales contracts. Contracts negotiated prior to 1974 accounted for 46 percent of Consol's 1976 shipments sold under base-price-plus-escalation contracts. Consol has successfully renegotiated many of the unprofitable contracts from among the pre−1974 ones. It has ensured that the new contracts (post−1974) not only provide improved base prices but also incorporate more realistic escalation provisions which protect Consol against potential impairments due to productivity declines, new legislation, or other unanticipated factors.[7] But it is only with time that all of the older, less profitable contracts can be phased out.

Securing Options for the Future

As was described earlier, the R&D activity at Consol was initiated soon after World War II to generate new markets for coal. In the early years of its existence, the activity got ample funding, since under the tax laws then in vogue, each R&D dollar spent by Consol in effect cost the company only 10 cents.

By 1962, the Office of Coal Research (OCR) was established by the federal government. Eric Reichl, the then Vice-President (Research), successfully sought funding for his R&D projects from the OCR. While Consol continued to provide the seed money for R&D on the basis of which Reichl could draw on federal support, the increasing managerial diversion and financial squeeze imposed by the Safety Act of 1969 and subsequent events temporarily slackened the research activity at Consol.

However, the Arab oil embargo provided the impetus to accelerate R&D on coal synthetics. In April 1974, Conoco disbanded the R&D department of Consol and announced the formation of a new subsidiary, Conoco Coal Development Company (CCDC). Reichl was named President of that company. CCDC was expected to coordinate research, long-range planning, and facilities for production of synthetic fuels from coal and for removal of sulfur dioxide from coal-fired power plant stack gases. The administrative implications of the forming of CCDC are shown in Figure 6−1. The creation of CCDC was not merely a legal change, for it also represented management's thinking, at both Consol and Conoco, that research on gasification and liquefaction was best carried out under Conoco's auspices. Further, since CCDC was meant to launch businesses of the future, it was placed under the charge of the Executive Vice-President for corporate planning at Conoco, Samual Schwartz. Commenting on the thrust of his organization in the field of synthetics, Reichl stated:

> The status of technology in this field is sufficiently undetermined, still subject to development. It is still being treated within CCDC as R&D, though its specific assignment is to go commercial.

Of the two kinds of synthetic fuels, synthetic gas is nearer to commercialization than liquid coal. However, even a pilot plant such as the one in Ohio, where CCDC plans to produce 60 million standard cubic feet of high-BTU gas per day, is expected to cost between $250 million and $300 million. Consequently, CCDC has only a small portion of the equity. The rest is financed by a consortium of partners. The problem with many gasification projects, Reichl points out, is that:

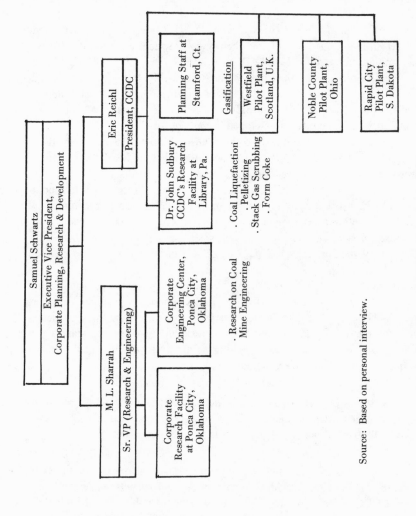

Figure 6–1. Organization of Research and Development

Source: Based on personal interview.

The projects are too big and the companies sponsoring them are relatively small. The projects have to get smaller and they have to be jointly sponsored by a consortium of companies. That is the only way gasification projects will get on stream.

Reichl maintains that the opportunities for synthetics will come not through industry action in technology development, but through political action by the government. The federal government could, for example, mandate the mixing of a certain percentage of nonpetroleum-based fuels with gasoline. Such a regulation would in effect ask the consumers to subsidize the higher production cost associated with the synthetics technologies. But by juggling the mix percentage carefully, the government can keep the price increase to the consumer within politically prudent limits. Companies that are able to lower the cost of producing synthetics can offer lower prices on their "mixture" gasoline. The proposed regulation would, therefore, make the development of synthetics technologies a competitive dimension and thus would lead to the quicker commercialization of these technologies. However, the government would have to brave the political risks of slightly higher fuel prices to the consumer in the short run.

In summary, while CCDC certainly has the technical expertise, the massive capital investments required for a synthetics project exceed the amount Conoco currently wishes to expose. Moreover, until the return on these vast investments looks more favorable, CCDC cannot be expected to launch commercial ventures for manufacturing synthetics from coal. Reichl summarized CCDC's position as follows: "If the nation eventually decides that it needs a synthetics industry, our company will have the coal and the expertise to lead in the development."

Responding to Other Strategic Changes

Consol suffered a steady drop in productivity since 1969 as did the rest of the coal industry. Ralph Bailey pointed out in this report to a group of security analysts:

Since 1969, machine productivity at our underground and surface operations has declined about 40% and 25%, respectively. In addition to lower productivity, production also has suffered from increased work stoppages. For those mines that were in operation in both 1969 and 1976, we estimate that these factors have caused a loss of about 17 million tons per year. Obviously, the loss would have been greater if we were able to estimate the impact of these factors on our new mines;

however, we have no basis of comparison. Had we been able to achieve the same level of productivity and operating time in 1976 as we did in 1969, we would have produced about 68 million tons as compared with the 51 million tons actually produced.[8]

Over the past few years, Consol has actively sought to improve productivity through capital expenditures, industrial engineering, and industrial and employee relations.

Consol's capital budgets in the recent past have earmarked nearly 30 percent of the funds for efficiency improvement and maintenance of production. A good example of the types of projects that are undertaken in this area is the hydraulic transportation system being erected at a cost of $10 million in West Virginia. The system not only minimizes many health and safety hazards, but eliminates massive underground transportation vehicles. The Lee Engineering Division of the company has been involved in the development and testing of new mining equipment and has pioneered a wide variety of mining equipment. Gene Shockey, Assistant to the President, added:

> We do consider technology to be a part answer to the productivity problem. We have 13 longwalls[9] in operation now. We hope to get them to 45 by 1985. They are expensive, $5 million a piece, but are also at least 3—5 times more productive than the continuous miners.

An industrial-engineering function was organized a year ago under Gene Shockey to identify the causes of lost productive capacity at individual mines. The new engineers who currently staff this function are gaining experience by gathering data on mine conditions, mining methods, and production, hoping to eventually build standards.

Industrial and employee relations at Consol are focused around improving the understanding between management and labor, and increasing the scope of training programs. As B. R. Brown, the then Executive Vice-President of Consol, remarked in 1977:

> Understanding does not mean agreeing. Labor and management may disagree with one another, but they must understand each other. Understanding comes from predictability. A person cannot work for another unless the supervisor is predictable. Consistency of action and predictability of behavior are key supervisory traits—if grievances are to be minimized.

Brown believed that Consol's labor problems can be loosened through a planned approach of taking fair, equitable, consistent, and affirmative action. Such actions can become routine through a comprehensive management-development program that is directed specifically to the needs of the participant and carried through from the section-foreman level to that of the superintendent. Recently, a Management Development Institute (MDI) has been proposed to provide such training.

The core and optional curriculums of the MDI are shown in Figure 6–2. In highlighting the MDI concept, a company report asserted:

> To make our MDI work at all levels, each level must be familiar with the same material. Programs for the section foreman are introduced at the superintendent level, but the emphasis is different. He views it as doing the right thing, whereas the section foreman will receive the point of view of doing the thing right.[10]

The MDI is designed to be the vehicle through which senior management's directions on critical issues are translated at each level of supervision. The Institute plans to draw on in-house personnel as trainers.

An advisory committee to guide the institute's operations, chaired by B. R. Brown and comprising all the regional operating heads, has been proposed.

Consol's training program for lower levels of employees was formalized in 1972 as part of an intense safety effort. The current training program covers all new hires, annual retraining for all new miners and supervisors in new work assignments (see Figure 6–3).

Consol places special emphasis on training and communication at its Western Division, where it has a local contract with the UMW. Consol's management wants to use that opportunity to inculcate a sense of loyalty for the company among its Western Division miners. Effective communication is considered crucial to that process.

MATERIAL RESOURCES

Conoco acquired Consol in 1966 as part of its diversification strategy. Conoco in 1965 was the eighth largest in crude-oil production, and among the top fifteen in refinery runs and refined-product sales, when compared with the 1965 worldwide operations of other American-based integrated petroleum companies. Its acquisition of Consol made Conoco a major supplier of fuel to the rapidly growing electric-ulitity industry. The demand for electric power was expected to grow at an annual rate of 6–6.5 percent, and coal was expected to supply a growing share of the domestic-energy needs of electric utilities.

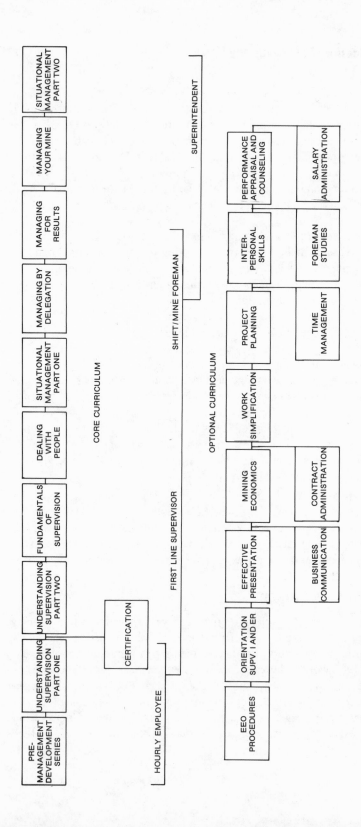

Source: Company Records.

Figure 6–2. The Management Development Institute's Curriculum

MANAGING FOR
RESULTS
New Shift Foreman
Annual Retraining   (one week)

First Aid   FOREMAN
Self-Rescuer   TRAINEE
Roof & Rib Control   New Foreman (six weeks)
Mine Rescue & Fire
   Fighting
                       CONSOL TECH
                   Pre-supervisory (14 four-hour sessions)
             MAINTENANCE PROGRAM
               New Mechanic (18 months)
          SAFETY ACTION
          New Machine Operator
ORIENTATION
New Miner

Source: Company Records.

Figure 6–3. Consol's Training Program

Conoco's annual report of 1966 described the benefits of the Consol acquisition as follows:

> The outcome [of the acquisition] was to give Conoco one of the strongest positions in either the coal or the oil industry in terms of a basic energy raw material position. Furthermore, the company could now broaden its energy base and capitalize on new markets. The coal industry, after many successes and failures over the years, had gained a position of prominence, with attractive growth prospects.

Consol's management saw two advantages in being acquired by Conoco. The acquisition was expected to provide a strong financial base for Consol's expansion, and to strengthen Consol's research on gasification and liquefaction of coal.

Utilities were the biggest market segment for Consol at the time of its acquisition. Nearly all of the sales to electric utilities of steam coal produced by Consol were made under contracts having terms of one year or more. Approximately 80 percent of such sales were made under contracts ranging from two to thirty years. The acquisition by Conoco provided Consol the necessary financial base to be more discriminating in its contracts. As described earlier, Conoco also formed the Conoco Coal Development Company in 1974 in order to give special attention to the synthetics business. The added financial and technical strengths accruing to Consol through its connections with Conoco, together with its impressive coal reserves, offer Consol a rich set of strategic options.

Coal Reserves

Consol has the largest coal reserves in the industry, covering a wide variety of coals (see Table 6–4). The company's reserve acquisition was decentralized up until 1973, the reserves being built through acquisition of and mergers with other coal companies. The bulk of Consol's reserves through the 1960s were in the East (see Table 6–5).

The Clean Air Act of 1970 made it unattractive for utilities to burn high-sulfur coal beyond 1975. This put pressure on coal companies to plan for the supply of low-sulfur compliance-quality[11] coal. Compliance coal was available mainly in the West. Consol's reserve acquisition in the West had been slow and came under the jurisdiction of its Western Division.

The slow acquisition of Western reserves was rudely interrupted when the federal government, which owns approximately 80 percent of the coal in the West, placed a moratorium on federal coal leases as of 1971. Even though Consol's reserves in the West have grown substantially since (see Table 6–6),its late response has meant that 34 percent of its reserves have 0.7 percent or less sulfur, when nearly 70 percent of the Western lignites and sub-bituminous coals have that low a sulfur content.[12]

The resource-management function was centralized in 1973. One of the motivations for the centralization was the realization that, as the nation's largest reserve holder,[13] managing the reserves of the company was a full-time activity. Divisional management was likely to pay only scanty attention to resource management, in view of its increasing operational headaches arising from new regulations and labor militancy. After the centralization, specific targets and budgets were set for reserve acquisition. Evaluation of existing reserves became a systematic activity. Today, the central-resource-management function under Dell Adams, Vice-President (Exploration), is consolidating Consol's vast reserve base and is buying, selling, and leasing reserves. Dell Adams reports to William Poundstone, Executive Vice-President (Engineering).

ORGANIZATIONAL CONSOLIDATION

Consol had grown to be a giant by 1968, producing 51.9 million tons of coal in that year. Nineteen-sixty-nine was the first year of a decade of radical changes. New regulations forced Consol to centralize some functions.

The Federal Coal Mine Health and Safety Act of 1969 imposed new requirements on working conditions in Consol's mines. The Act, together with

Table 6-4. Reserve Position, Consol, 1976

	Recoverable reserves (billion tons)	
	Compliance quality	Total
Steam coal		
Eastern United States	0.3	5.6
Western United States	2.3	6.8
Metallurgical coal		
United States		1.3
Canada		0.6
Total	2.6	14.3

Source: Company sources.

Table 6-5. Consol's Recoverable Reserves: 1967-1971 (in billions of tons)

Year	Western steam coal	Eastern steam coal	Total steam coal
1967	0.9	4.0	4.9
1969	1.3	4.4	5.7
1971	2.0	4.8	6.8

Source: *Annual Reports*.

Table 6-6. Recoverable Reserves: 1971-77 (in billions of tons)

Steam coal	1977	1974	1972	1971
Eastern	5.6 (0.3)	5.5	4.9	4.8
Western	6.8 (2.3)	6.9	4.5	2.0

Note: Figures in parentheses indicate coals having a sulfur content of less than or equal to 0.7 percent. These sulfur levels do not meet EPA short-term criteria for compliance in the case of all coals. The figures have to be revised downwards to arrive at compliance-quality reserve tonnage.
Source: Company reports.

the increasing militancy of the UMW miners at Consol, led to a sharp drop in productivity.

The drop in productivity experienced by Consol in the late 1960s meant that additional employees had to be recruited to maintain production levels. This recruitment need was over and above the massive recruitment program that Consol had launched in 1966 as part of its first major internal expansion program. Whereas Consol had grown in the past through acquisition of operating companies and their employees, its $130 million investment from 1967–1969 in expanding the capacity at several existing mines required large-scale recruitment of various skilled employees. The service of Roger Haynes from Conoco's personnel department was requested in 1966 to help set up the recruitment function centrally at Consol's headquarters. The growing recruitment activity and the intricacies of administering the new safety law led to the centralization of the personnel function. The rising militancy of the company's workers (all represented by the UMW) reinforced the need for a central personnel policy making body.

The central-engineering coordination function, set up in 1946, had atrophied partly on account of the impressive pre-1969 industry-wide rise in labor productivity, both in underground and surface mines. Another reason for its lack of success was the distinctive engineering culture that each division of the company had inherited, which made it difficult to exchange ideas or to standardize mining practices. However, the events of 1969 once again made productivity and efficiency key issues. As one executive recollected:

> Divisions were reinventing the same engineering solutions that other divisions of the company had successfully implemented. There was duplication of effort and inefficient use of critical engineering resources.

The central-engineering department was rejuvenated in 1972 and placed under William Poundstone, Vice-President (Engineering). Whereas the operating divisions retained their engineering staff, they could not implement major engineering projects without the approval of Poundstone. Furthermore, as the central-engineering function got adequate staffing, the planning of all new mines became a corporate activity. Only projects less than $1 million in size fell under divisional jurisdiction. Even on such projects, engineering advice was offered from the headquarters.

Reorganization in 1975

Ralph Bailey became President of Consol in 1973. The changes in the previous five years in the operating environment of Consol had strained its efficiency. Bailey believed that the time had come for some major reorganization. Divisions operated as separate companies and still had their old identities. There was no Consol image, and there were not many exchanges of new ideas between the divisions of Consol. Bailey queried: "Were we really Consolidation Coal Company—or the Unconsolidated Coal Company?"

In early 1975, Bailey became Chairman of Consol. As Roger Haynes [14] pointed out:

> It is but natural for every new Chairman to make realignments in the organization to suit his management style. In the case of Bailey, there was the added factor of mounting dissatisfaction with the then organization.

Bailey invited three of his executives to help him with the plans for reorganization, and also to remain as an informal and confidential advisory body. The executives chosen were Executive Vice-President Jarvis Cecil, Vice-President Roger Haynes, and Manager of Economics and Planning Thomas Norris, all of whom had joined Consol from Conoco. As Haynes speculated:

> I don't think we were selected because of our Conoco background. That was relevant only to the extent that we had not built our careers in Consol. So we had no empires to protect and consequently we could be more objective.
>
> Additionally, all three of us had either professional training or experience to work with organizational problems.

While narrating his perceptions of why the reorganization was important to Bailey, Haynes added:

> The lack of a Consol image was certainly a major concern of Bailey's But an important related issue was his perception of the organization's inability to cope with the strains of expansion under an increasingly tougher regulatory environment. When we played out our expansion plans creating paper divisions on the 1975 pattern, we needed 17 divisions to handle our operations by 1985. Bailey felt that it would be impossible for the President to handle 17 divisions with any effective control. Clearly we needed to reduce that number. He wanted a structure that could support at least the growth over the next decade.

Cecil stated:

> Bailey did not have an organization in mind that he wanted us to
> critique. He was open to alternative designs. However, he was clear on
> a few objectives that the reorganization should achieve. It should pro-
> mote a company image, and to the extent old divisional loyalties
> obstructed the achievement of that objective, these loyalties should be
> broken up. He had a preference for reducing the number of divisions.
> He also desired that they be approximately equal in size and preferably
> be grouped on the basis of geography. Geography in our business is
> often a good surrogate for type of coal, nature of mining and attitude of
> labor. Given our expansion plans and expected depletion, he desired
> that the new units should not grow or shrink at such a rate that a new
> organization would become necessary within a decade.

Bailey worked with alternate designs and had consultations with Conoco
from time to time. Haynes asserted:

> I don't think there was any pressure from Conoco to reorganize. But
> they were receptive to Bailey's initiative. Conoco's Chairman,
> Blauvelt, was planning his own reorganization at that time and there
> was opportunity for both Bailey and Blauvelt to use a common basis of
> organization to the extent that their diverse businesses allowed.

Months of careful planning and discussion finally led to a satisfactory organizational structure. But there were some key issues of implementation
that now worried Bailey.

On Bailey's promotion to the chairmanship of Consol, there was the vacancy of a President to be filled. After much deliberation, he had decided to
offer the job to R. E. Samples, who before he left Consol in 1973 had
helped in the reorganization of the central-engineering department. Another
important issue was the reshuffle of personnel that the reorganization would
cause. As Haynes recalled:

> Bailey worried about the implications of the reorganization for each
> member of the executive team. Can we minimize the adverse effects of
> our reorganization on executive personnel? How would those affected
> react? Can we face the consequences? Only when Bailey had thought
> through these questions for each executive did he feel comfortable that
> he had a viable plan.

Bailey invited all his executives to the company headquarters at Pittsburgh in October 1975 and announced simultaneously his reorganization plans and the appointment of Samples as President. He recognized that it was perhaps best to announce all changes at once, rather than create apprehensions of organizational instability that arise when changes are announced sequentially.

The main feature of the reorganization was the collapsing of nine divisions into five regions. The regions were: Eastern Region, Northern West Virginia Region, Southern Appalachia Region, Midwestern Region, and Western Region. The last two did not quite match the criteria of size and geographic proximity of mines that Bailey had stated as a guideline.

The basic organization structure is outlined in Figure 6−4. The regional organizations were similar to that of the Eastern Region, whose organization is shown in Figure 6−5.

ORGANIZATIONAL STRUCTURE

The key feature of the organization was highlighted by Bailey in his announcement of the reorganization to Consol executives:

I think any good organization has to be built on the basis of that magic triangle whereby the very tip of the triangle is delineated off as being strategic management. The next slice of the triangle, and the obviously larger one, is the tactical management; and the lower slice, and the largest of all, is operations management. If that triangle starts looking like a rectangle or a square−watch out− you are in trouble.

Strategic management was strengthened under the reorganization. A strategic-management team composed of Bailey and Samples plus Jarvis Cecil, Executive Vice-President (Corporate Affairs); Thomas Whyte, Executive Vice-President (Industrial, Employee and Public Relations); William Poundstone, Executive Vice-President (Engineering); and L. J. Huegel, Executive Vice-President (Sales) was identified.

With the exception of Huegel, the officers reporting to Samples formed the tactical-management team, and those reporting to the regional Senior Vice-Presidents formed the operations-management teams. The reorganization placed strong staff support under each regional Senior Vice-President. This simultaneously freed individual operations from maintaining staff, unlike in the earlier organization where each operation had to have its own staff expertise. The regional staff had functional (dotted-line) relationship with executives in the headquarters as per Table 6−7.

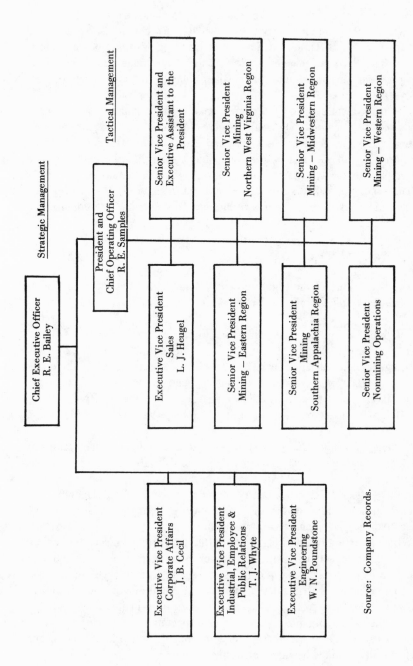

Figure 6—4. Strategic and Tactical Management Organization of Consol, 1975

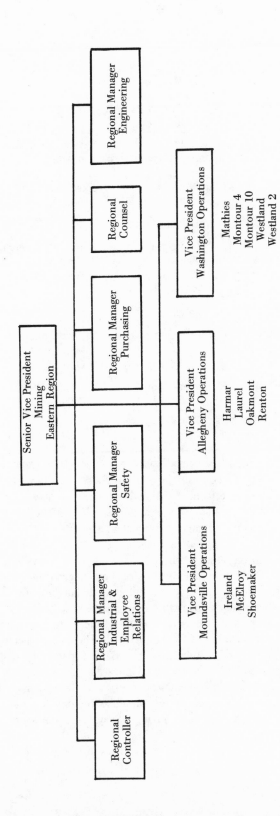

Source: Company Records.

Figure 6–5. Operations Management—Eastern Region of Consol, 1975

Table 6–7. Functional Relationships of Regional Staff with
Headquarters

Regional staff	Functional head at corporate headquarters	Senior executive in charge
Controller	VP and Controller	Executive VP (Corporate Affairs)
Counsel*	VP and Chief Counsel	—do—
Manager (Industrial and Employee Relations)	1. VP (Industrial Relations) 2. VP (Employee Relations)	Executive VP (Industrial, Employee & Public Relations)
Manager (Safety)	VP (Safety)	—do—
Manager (Purchasing)	VP (Purchasing)	VP and General Manager (Nonmining Operations)
Manager (Engineering)	VP (Engineering)	Executive VP (Engineering)

*This function has not been delegated to the regions.

The reorganization did cause major upheavals in job titles; some divisional presidents became vice-presidents of operations. Even those that became regional senior vice-presidents wondered whether their new titles were not perceived as a drop in status. The word 'division" was abolished, and instead the terms "operations" and "regions" came into vogue. "Divisional" groupings were reassigned in some cases into new "operations" groupings, to break up old associations. "Operations" were clustered into five new 'regions." Despite the massiveness of the change, it must be said to the credit of the prior planning that went into it that only four vice-presidents resigned from the company in the two years since 1975, and their reasons for leaving were not necessarily a result of the reorganization. Figure 6–6 shows the organization of Consol in 1977. The basic structure has remained unchanged. The only difference is that B. R. Brown, who replaced Thomas Whyte as Executive Vice-President (Industrial, Employee and Public Relations), was placed under Samples in order to bring about closer liaison between the functions under him and the regional operations.[15] Brown came to Consol from Conoco having headed the latter's personnel function for many years.

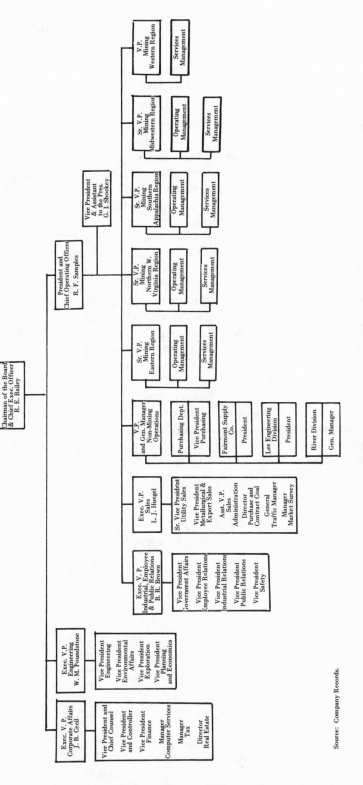

Figure 6–6. Management Organization of Consol, 1977

Source: Company Records.

OTHER ADMINISTRATIVE SYSTEMS

Conoco helped Consol establish a formal planning-and-control system, soon after Consol's acquisition. Consol's annual planning cycle was meshed with that of its parent. Regional managers now propose capital projects within guidelines established by Consol's strategic-management team. Consol's capital budget is in turn approved by Conoco's corporate management. Capital projects are evaluated on the basis of return on investment wherever feasible. Certain projects, such as for improving safety or for pollution control, may be approved on qualitative criteria.

The regions also have a good operational control system. All operating budgets are prepared on a per-ton basis, thus highlighting the major cost categories that need control. The operational-review system has helped identify several unprofitable sales contracts. These contracts have been renegotiated wherever possible. Performance against budgets is reviewed at the regions every quarter. These reviews are aimed more at helping regional managers identify problem areas, rather than at appraising their performance. However, Consol does have plans for installing, at all levels up to general superintendent, a merit-based reward system. The quarterly reviews would provide an important input to this reward system. Consol already has an incentive-reward system for its executives.

Each year, a corporate team of fifteen to twenty Consol and Conoco executives visits at least one mine in each of Consol's operations. These visits serve as an audit of that operation's performance. The quarterly-review and yearly-audit practices have helped Consol improve its operating efficiency.

7. The Carter Oil Company*

The Carter Oil Company, headquartered at Houston, was one of the several oil-company affiliates to enter the coal industry de novo in the 1960s. Carter Oil, a subsidiary of Exxon, has made impressive strides in its decade of association with the coal industry. Its coal reserves in 1977 ranked fifth in the industry, and its ambitious development plans will place it among the leading coal producers by 1985. Carter Oil's strong financial, technical, and organizational resources make it the leading contender for establishing a new business of producing synthethics from coal.

PRODUCT—MARKET POSTURE

Exxon had recognized even in the early 1960s that the projected domestic production of oil and gas would peak in the 1970s. Given the unabated domestic growth in consumption of petroleum products, the top management of Exxon reasoned that either the import of oil had to rise to meet the growing demand or else substitute fuels to replace oil and gas had to be found. A company report described Exxon's analysis of the then emerging scenario:

> We concluded at this early date that there would be substantial future needs for synthetic oil and gas. It also appeared that, since coal reserves are so plentiful in this country, a high percentage of the synthetic fuels would be made from coal. Since synthetic fuels from coal most probably would be direct raw material for our refineries and chemical plants, or directly substitutable in our marketing activities, they were deemed a logical extension of our business.[1]

---

*The Carter Oil Company has been renamed Exxon Coal, U.S.A.
NOTE: The original case study has been abridged and re-edited for this book.

In 1965, Exxon began to acquire coal reserves on private lands through the coal-and-oil-shale department of Exxon Company, U. S. A. Later, Exxon's domestic-coal, shale-oil, and synthetic-fuel interests were assigned to an affiliate, the Carter Oil Company. Carter Oil entered a stagnating coal industry. The average price of coal in 1965 at $4.44 per ton had not changed in two decades. Though Carter Oil had aspirations to sell steam coal, given the adverse industry condition in 1965 its management decided to focus on the synthetic business and keep its steam-coal-business aspirations in temporary abeyance.

In 1967, a small marketing department was set up to look for steam-coal customers in the Midwest. The marketing organization had no executive who had any experience in the coal industry. In an industry where personal contact had traditionally been an important aspect of selling coal, the lack of coal-sales experience[2] was a handicap for Carter Oil. Yet, its marketing executives believed that the company's name together with a professional approach to selling would launch them in the coal business. One executive described Carter Oil's marketing approach:

> We walked in with a slide projector and put on a half-hour presentation, demonstrating our ability to supply consistently good quality coal. We showed some of our plans to these potential customers and gave them every information they wanted, to convince them of our abilities. Of course, the Exxon name helped.

In 1969, the Monterey Coal Company, a wholly owned subsidiary of Carter Oil, was formed to mine coal in the Midwest and Eastern regions. The following excerpt from a company report outlines the rationale for the creation of the Monterey Coal Company (Monterey) at Carlinsville, Illinois:

> Since commercially viable coal synthetics operations were not projected to be developed for several years after initial purchase of coal reserves, a logical move was to start mining and selling coal as a boiler fuel. This would not only generate income on the coal investments, but would also provide the necessary operating experience in coal mining that would ultimately be needed to support the raw material production for coal synthetics operations.[3]

Monterey's first mine was planned for a yearly capacity of 3 million tons. Most mines in Illinois were organized by the UMW. Whereas the militancy of the UMW had been of concern to many coal-company managers in the past, the management of newcomers like Carter Oil felt confident of handling the problem. As one Carter Oil executive, with a vast coal-industry experience, remarked:

The oil industry is bringing a greater emphasis on technology to boost production and improve operating safety. It has also brought in more sophisticated management techniques. I think the coal industry has suffered from some of the worst labor relations in the history of American business, and we coal people have a lot to learn about improving this relationship. We need to bring our human relations into the 20th century with the rest of the world.[4]

Carter Oil's management believed that modern technology together with a professional approach to the management of coal companies could concurrently improve working conditions in the mines and raise productivity. Even in the older underground mines, partial conversion to continuous-mining methods had raised industry productivity from 10.1 tons per manshift in 1959 to 15.6 tons per manshift in 1969. Monterey No. 1 was built as a modern mine with emphasis on safety features and good working conditions. UMW organized all of Monterey Coal's miners soon thereafter.

Monterey's first ton of coal for direct-burning markets was mined in 1970. By then, the Federal Health and Mine Safety Act had been passed. Since Monterey was already planned for safe operations, the Act posed no major revisions in its construction plans. However, the 1970 Clean Air Act that followed made the 3–4 percent sulfur-bearing Illinois coal unacceptable for direct burning in new power plants and in many older plants unless additional capital investment was made by the utilities on scrubbers.

The increasing importance of low-sulfur coal made Carter Oil's Western reserves, which were predominantly low-sulfur, more valuable. Having been one of the early entrants in the West, Carter Oil had put together large blocks of coal reserves at relatively low costs. Moreover, its early start in the West was helpful from another perspective. Nearly all of Carter Oil's properties in the West were federal leases. In response to the growing opposition from environmentalists, the federal government placed a moratorium on federal leases in the West in 1971.

The Arab oil embargo provided the coal industry an unexpected shot in the arm. Spot prices of coal trebled in 1973. Carter Oil announced the formation of a Western subsidiary, The Carter Mining Company (Carter Mining), in 1974. The development plans for Western coal were, however, stymied by yet another phenomenon of the decade, environmentalism. The Sierra Club obtained a court order in 1975 restraining the Secretary of the Interior from issuing any mining permits in the West until a revised environmental-impact statement was filed by the U. S. Geological Survey. The stay order was eventually vacated by the Supreme Court in 1976. During the period of the litigation, Carter Mining developed its mining plans and began training its employees. It could, therefore, progress quickly on the opening of its first Western mine soon after the Supreme Court decision.

The marketing department at Carter Oil was able to secure long-term contracts for both the Eastern and Western coals. These contracts were won by emphasizing consistency in coal quality and reliability of supply. While price was also an important factor, Carter Oil's pricing strategy was guided by a computer program that took into account the desired return on investment and the anticipated capital cost to Carter Oil for fulfilling a contract. The marketing department tried hard not to compromise on this formula price.

Just when the first Western mine was nearing completion, the 1977 Amendment to the Clean Air Act was announced. Scrubbers were once again back in reckoning as they represented "best available technology." In fact, it was even proposed that they become mandatory by 1982. This neutralized the advantage of low-sulfur Western coal and placed the Eastern high-sulfur but high-BTU coal back in a more favorable competitive position. Whereas Monterey was already working on a second mine in Illinois and a new mine in West Virginia, given the severe competition in the Eastern markets from established coal companies, Carter Oil's management decided to also enter a third geographic region, the Southwest—an area which was fast running out of natural gas.

Long-Term Plans

The current production statistics and plans for future expansion are shown in Figure 7−1. If the market for steam coal grows according to Carter Oil's expectations, the company's projected production is expected to be in excess of 40 million tons per year by the mid-1980s. A predominant share (24 million tons by 1985) of the projected expansion is expected to be contributed by the Western coal fields of Carter Mining for utility markets. The mandatory imposition of scrubbers may alter the economics of Western coals, lowering that supply figure considerably. However, low-sulfur coals will certainly be demanded at least as a blend fuel. In anticipation, the company's resource-management group has been actively seeking low-sulfur coal reserves in the East.

Carter Oil's marketing department believes that the industrial coal market will be an important one. It sees a number of strengths in this market: (1) Exxon has experience selling industrial fuel oil, and its customers who are required to convert back to coal may provide useful entry points for Carter

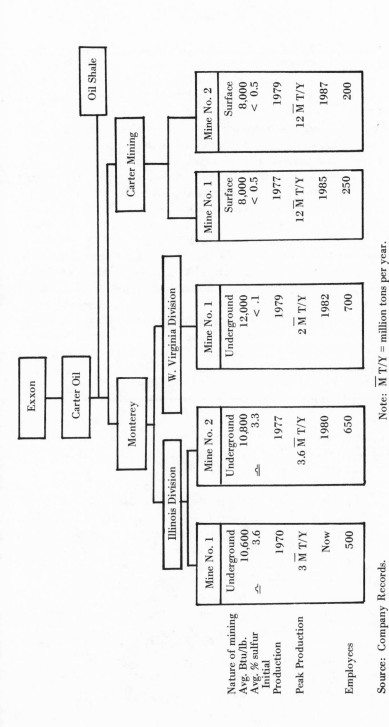

Figure 7-1. Current and Planned Production

Note: $\overline{\text{M}}$ T/Y = million tons per year.

Source: Company Records.

Oil; and (2) Moreover, Exxon's central-engineering department can provide two important expertises to Carter Oil—combustion analysis, enabling Carter Oil to suggest conversion options to its customers, and expertise in ash disposal, which is likely to be a major headache for medium-size industries converting to coal burning.

The marketing department is convinced that conversion to coal from oil will come not through legislation, but by coal companies suggesting an economical conversion option to industrial users currently burning oil.

The company does not have metallurgical-coal reserves and is actively looking for some. However, its marketing department is simultaneously initiating joint studies with steel companies to explore the possibility of substituting coke with "form coke" made from Carter Oil's low-sulfur coals, currently unsuitable for metallurgical applications.

A major role that is anticipated of Carter Oil is in the commercial conversion of coal to synthetic gas and liquids. Its gasification project is at an advanced stage of development, and Carter Oil's management has hopefully found that special niche it was seeking for entry into the synthetics business. Given the vast financial, technical, and human resources of Exxon that Carter Oil can draw upon, it is likely to be the pioneer in the commercial production of snythetic gas from coal. The endeavors of Carter Oil in this field will, therefore, be discussed at some length.

The Synthetics Business

R. C. Curtis, a Senior Vice-President at Carter Oil, summarized the decision-making process on the synthetics business as "equanimity in the midst of uncertainty." The synthetics project had uncertainties in three major areas: the suitability of Carter Oil's reserves of coals for conversion to synthetics, the economics of conversion, and the demand for synthetic fuels at the prices projected by Carter Oil for their supply. Carter Oil's synthetics project has consequently gone through a number of iterations and what seems like a viable business idea may yet go through more iterations before the synthetics business is established. In discussing synthetics it is useful to separate gasification, the likely commercialization option in the near future, from the more distant possibility of commercial liquefaction of coal.

Carter Oil's present plan for gasification is to set up a plant in Texas producing Intermediate BTU Gas to be supplied as fuel and chemical feedstock to industrial users in the state of Texas. The project is planned to be completed by the mid-1980s. In the area of coal liquefaction, Carter Oil is participating in a research-and-development project managed by Exxon Research and Engineering and funded in collaboration with the government, Phillips Petroleum Company, Atlantic Richfield, the Japan Coal Liquefaction Development Corporation, and the Electric Power Research Institute. The project will provide data to assess the commercial feasibility of coal liquefaction. It is also expected to be completed by the mid-1980s.

In the rest of this section, only Carter Oil's efforts in the commercial gasification of coal will be discussed.

Reviving the Synthetic-Gas Idea: Having entered the coal business with synthetics in mind, Carter Oil's sights broadened to other possibilities; and in fact in the period 1967–1973, the emphasis of the company was clearly on steam coal for utility markets. In the wake of the oil embargo, Carter Oil's management decided to have a fresh look at its synthetic-gas option. As Curtis recollected:

> It appeared as if the time had come for synthetics. The management committee of Carter Oil decided to search for good investment opportunities. As a policy, we wished to avoid a situation where we would be artificially subsidized. But we recognized that synthetics are high-cost fuels. We were not about to lose sight of the fact that it is always better to burn coal directly, whenever possible. But there are applications where gaseous fuels are indispensable because of special heat transfer needs. We were looking for opportunities to substitute natural gas in these markets.

In 1973, a commercial-gasification task force was created under Curtis. The other three members were loaned by Exxon, and included an operations manager who had refinery-construction and operations experience, and two analysts, one of whom had an international-oil-and-gas-marketing background and the other a chemical-marketing background. Curtis' own background had been in oil production.

The task force was assigned three tasks: (1) to evaluate the suitability of Illinois and Wyoming coals for synthetics production; (2) to study the market for synthetics; and (3) to evaluate the various process alternatives available to gasify coal.

Illinois coal was found more suitable for liquefaction and less suitable for gasification. However, Wyoming coals could be gasified using available technology. One obvious market was to provide synthetic gas to pipeline companies, who were running out of natural gas. Pipeline companies were, however, interested in large volumes, on the order of a billion cubic feet per day of synthetic gas. The task force looked at two gasification projects that were then being proposed. Investment on the order of $500 million was estimated for a planned production of 250 million cubic feet per day. A billion-cubic-feet-per-day synthetic-gas project was clearly a multibillion-dollar investment. Given the uncertainties in the steady offtake of gas by pipeline companies, and the then-existing price control on interstate gas supply, Carter Oil's management decided not to pursue the pipeline market.

The other option was to produce synthetic gas for use as chemical feedstock. Chemical companies used natural gas as a feedstock for several of their processes. The Carter Oil task force recognized that natural gas was in fact first processed to yield carbon monoxide and hydrogen, the two gases that were the real reactants in a chemical process. Synthetic Natural Gas (SNG),[5] on the other hand, was rich in carbon monoxide and hydrogen in its first stage of production. Highlighting the commercial significance of the above, a Carter Oil executive stated:

> In processing natural gas for use as a chemical feedstock, close to one-third of the gas has to be burned as fuel. In other words, if 3 cu. ft. of natural gas is taken in, only 2 cu. ft. is useful in the reaction. In contrast, the first stage SNG, before its final processing to methane, is an excellent choice as a chemical feedstock. The additional processing stage required for natural gas and the processing stages saved in the case of first stage SNG significantly tilt the economics in favor of synthetic gas over natural gas as a chemical feedstock.

The first-stage synthetic gas, or Intermediate BTU Gas (IBG), has a heating value of approximately 350−400 BTU per cubic foot. The task force concluded that IBG, produced through one of the three proven and available gasification technologies—Lurgi, Koppers-Totzek, and Winkler− would be a preferred way of entering the synthetics business.

The Focus on the Southwest: In pursuing the task force's suggestions, Carter Oil's management had concluded that the IBG idea was a good one. But there were a couple of issues to be resolved. While Wyoming coals would be good choices for gasification, using available technology, the gas would have to be piped interstate since there was no chemical market in Wyoming. Interstate transfer of gas was unappealing to Carter Oil's management because of the cost and the then-existing government price regulation on such gas sales. Carter Oil's management looked at regions that had a big intrastate market for gas and picked the southwestern United States for detailed study. The task force was assigned a revised set of objectives in 1975 that included a study of the possibility of gasifying Gulf Coast lignites and a determination of the Gulf Coast markets for synthetic gas. The task force selected Arkansas as the first site for study since the state had significant coal reserves, a construction-cost advantage, and a favorable economic climate.

The Carter Oil Company

139

The initial studies on Arkansas coal proved encouraging and the resource-management group started acquiring reserves in the state. Two large chemical companies were identified as potential customers for IBG. The task force reasoned that the companies had only one other option besides IBG when natural-gas supplies to them ran out, i.e., to partially oxidize petroleum residuum. While the cost of IBG was the lowest of the three options (see Table 7−1), the investment on an IBG plant was the highest. If the chemical companies could be persuaded to share the equity risk and also relocate their plants to Arkansas, IBG from Arkansas coal seemed a viable option.

Table 7−1. An Economic Comparison of the Options

	Approximate indices of comparison		
	Steam reformation of natural gas	Partial oxidation of residuum	Coal gasification
Investment for equivalent volume of CO & H_2	100	250	500
Feed-and-fuel cost for equivalent BTU	100	80	15
Cost of CO & H_2 for equivalent volume	100	120	85

Note: Investment and costs of steam reformation of natural gas are given an index of 100. The two other options are compared relative to this base option.

However, a number of factors killed the option. One of the chemical companies made a commitment to partial oxidation of residuum at an existing plant, thereby reducing the demand for Carter Oil's synthetic gas. Additionally, there were technical problems to be resolved if the Arkansas lignite was to be used. The Lurgi process was considered most economical because of its higher thermal efficiency, but could not be used because of the softness of Arkansas lignite. In the meanwhile, Texas lignite appeared to be better suited for gasification by the Lurgi process.

The task force, therefore, recommended to the management committee that the following combination be considered next: IBG for sale in Texas, converting Texas lignite by the Lurgi process.

The Current Status: The task force was disbanded until suitable reserves could be located in Texas. Acquisition of substantial reserves in Texas took a little more than a year.

Having identified the reserves, Carter Oil's management wanted to make quick progress. As Curtis observed:

There are some important natural gas contracts in the southwest that will come up for renewal in 1983–86. These contracts may be terminated then for want of natural gas. Chemical companies that use natural gas as a feedstock tend to be less concerned about the cost of the gas, as it is but a small fraction of their cost of production. They want surety of supply. They will be in the market for alternative sources of supply sometime in 1981–83. The present option for them is to partially oxidize heavy residual oil. If they commit capital expenditures on that process, synthetic gas will be out of the reckoning for a long while. It is, therefore, a one-time opportunity and we want to make sure that we are there to make a bid on synthetic gas. We have to prove our process to a point where we can guarantee regular supplies.

Instead of reassembling an ad hoc task force, four work groups were formed in 1977 (see Figure 7–2). The Planning work group and the Plant Design work group were headed by John Racz, Synthetics Operations Manager. Racz had just completed a refinery project for Exxon, and was transferred to Carter Oil to guide the implementation of Carter Oil's synthetics project. The Planning and Plant Design work groups had employees from both Carter Oil (Racz's assistants) and Exxon Research and Engineering (ER&E).

The Planning work group was responsible for developing a project recommendation, including process, size, and staging of implementation. It received input from the other work groups. The Plant Design work group was responsible for developing the design basis for the coal-conversion plant. It had to check the conversion suitability of Texas lignites, upgrade process by-products for commercial markets, plan for minimum pollution, etc.—in short, all aspects of plant design. This work group also had to estimate capital and operating expenses for the plant. The Marketing work group had to assess demand for synthetics, suggest a product specification most popular with potential customers, recommend selling price, and contrast the advantages of IBG at the suggested specification-price combination over other competing options for the customer. The Mining work group had to plan a coal mine to meet the needs of the conversion plant. A complete proposal including capital- and operating-cost estimates for the coal mine was expected of this work group. The work groups did not work to a fixed project outline, but in fact generated several project options. These options were synthesized by the Planning work group into alternate business proposals.

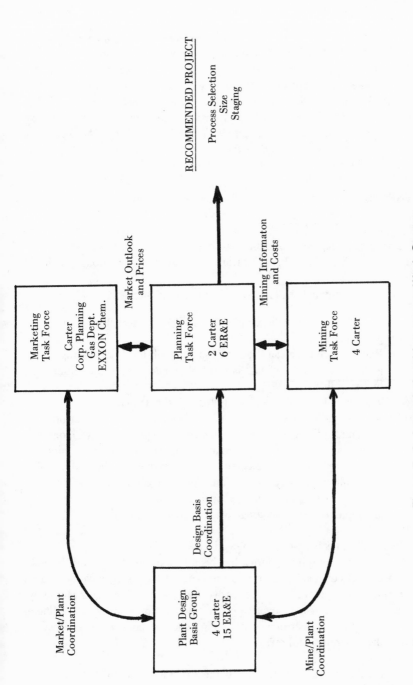

Figure 7-2. Interrelationships among Work Groups

All the work groups were staffed with expert personnel drawn from both Exxon and Carter Oil, loaned to the work groups on a full-time basis.

The alternatives that the work groups considered were: product—various chemical-feedstock options for IBG; process—choice between Lurgi, Koppers-Totzek, and Winkler. Beyond these, there were scale and scheduling options. The Planning work group has thus far come up with ten business scenarios, which are combinations of the above options. These alternate scenarios have been presented to the management committee of Carter Oil by Racz and representative members of the work groups.

RESPONDING TO OTHER STRATEGIC CHANGES

Human-Resources Management

Carter Oil's challenge in human-resources management is most clearly illustrated in Table 7–2. F. R. Curran, who heads this function, stated:

The key personnel challenges for us until 1985 are:

- Recruit and select the employees needed to meet the company's growth needs.
- Retain, encourage, and reward capable high-level performing employees in an industry that is short of people and has a tradition of high mobility.
- Train and develop employees to reach full potential.
- Manage the surface mining and synthetics labor relations effort so that employees will not feel the need to be represented by unions.
- Maintain good local labor relations at Monterey's coal mines, where employees have elected to be represented by the UMW and the resulting industry wide union contract negotiation.
- Develop and maintain a safe operating working environment for all employees and encourage off the job safety practices.

The action plans for the above objectives are as follows:

Recruitment: The primary thrust has been to look for new blood. In addition to normal company recruiting efforts, co-op programs[6] have been used to recruit mining engineers, supervisory staff, and technicians. Monterey, for example, has a very innovative co-op scholarship program with a liberal arts college, located near one of its mining sites. A company executive described the program as follows:

The college was turning out liberal arts graduates and not surprisingly had serious placement problems. We offered the students a co-op

Table 7−2. Manpower Forecasts

Manpower	Actual 1974	Projected 1985*	Annual growth rate (%)
Management, professional, and technical	9,000	15,000	5
Supervisory nonprofessional	14,000	21,000	3
Wage and non-exempt	144,000**	219,000	3
Total	167,000	255,000	
Ratio of wage to salaried employees	6.3	4.5	

*At 1.2 billion tons production.
**Half of this work force is expected to retire by 1985.
Source: Company Records.

program whereby through instruction and on-the-job training, these liberal arts students could qualify for mine operations. Those that joined us permanently from these programs were often good supervisory material. Their liberal arts training coupled with their experience made them suitable for supervisory positions within a year or two of their graduation.

Carter Mining has a much bigger co-op scholarship program with a local community college. Graduates from this program are awarded an Associate of Applied Science degree in Coal Field Technology and are hired as skilled technicians.

Retaining good employees: The anticipated rapid growth of the industry has brought great mobility among the supervisory and managerial cadres. A key element in retaining employees is providing career-progression opportunities. All salaried employees are offered a career plan. Salaries and benefits are also kept competitive.

Training: When Carter Oil started its training effort, the first thing its trainers recognized was the striking contrast between training in the oil and coal industries. One executive articulated these differences as follows:

- In the case of oil, training centers are generally located in densely populated cities. Coal training is centered more around small communities.
- Coal industry has to work against strong community biases. "Mothers want their sons to get away from coal." Oil industry work is more widely acceptable.

- Coal training is done in an environment of mandatory federal regulation and UMW inspection, unlike oil.
- It is difficult to provide job mobility in coal.
- Since coal mining requires special skills, employees have to be internally trained and are not available from a general pool of trained labor.
- In the oil industry, the API [American Petroleum Institute] provides training aids. The coal companies have to reinvent the wheel, and there is no industry-wide agency to provide training aids.

Carter Oil established a strong training program, since many of its miners and supervisors are recruited with little experience.

Training of miners: The primary emphases in training at this level are safety and productivity. Each task has been programmed into a training module. These modules are assembled to suit the differing training needs for various jobs. For example, training modules 10.54 M to 10.63 M (see Figure 7–3) can be assembled for orientation training. The same modules together with others (see Figure 7–4) can also be used for training for underground production jobs. The modules represent a method of working that will ensure safety, without compromising productivity. They are prepared by subject-matter experts drawn both from within the company and from other organizations. The programming of the training material is done by Carter's media experts. The training modules have been reviewed with the miners through the UMW or employee representatives,[7] and has the backing of supervisors. The modules, therefore, represent standard operating procedures. As one executive put it:

> The instructions in the modules are not just things that are nice to know and never used. They are things that an employee needs to know. In case of accident an employee can be pulled up for nonadherence to instructions given in these modules.

Besides the classroom instructions through video tapes, films, and slide shows, Carter Oil has also planned a full-fledged underground training section at Monterey No. 2 mine. The facility will be one of the first in the industry. All underground mines of Monterey Coal will have in the future their own underground training sections.

The National Coal Association and the Bituminous Coal Operators Association have agreed on a system, originally proposed by Carter Oil, for pooling industry's collective training knowledge. Carter Oil's management

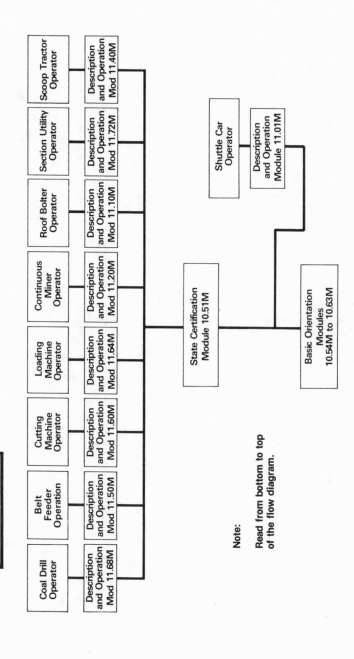

Figure 7-3. Training Modules for Underground Production

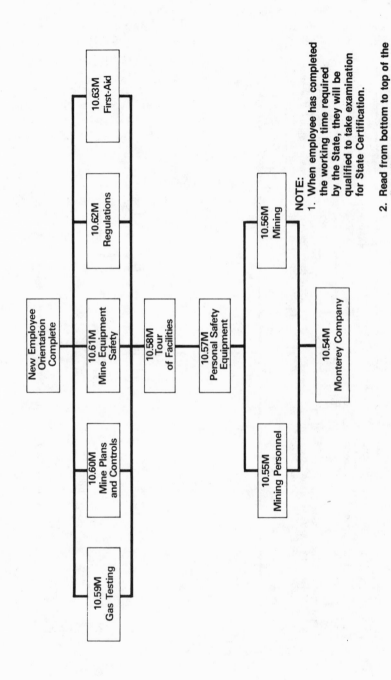

Figure 7-4. Orientation for New Employees

is making available to this system over 300 hours of training material that it has developed. The system (see Figure 7–5) aims at standardizing training methods, so as to make them available in canned modules at low costs to smaller coal companies with limited training facilities.

Training of supervisors: Carter Oil's training program for supervisors emphasizes labor-relations training. The company uses a "behavior-modeling" technique to highlight problems with supervisory styles. The technique centers around the filming on video tapes of what a "model" supervisor is supposed to do in a set of more frequently encountered supervisory situations. These films are shown to supervisors in training sessions and used as a basis for discussing problems of supervision and their possible resolution.

Professionals and managers: All professionals and managers have an induction program, introducing them to executives in the corporate headquarters. The orientation is considered especially necessary for personnel recruited from outside the Exxon organization. The induction serves as a means of orienting new employees to Carter Oil's distinctive style of management. Professionals and managers also have a variety of in-house and external training opportunities.

Nonunion operations: When Carter Mining was established in the West, its management desired to work directly with its employees so that they would not feel a need for a union.

The company's operations are currently nonunion. All miners of the Western subsidiary are called "technicians" and are salaried employees of the company. Carter Mining's salary-and-benefit package is one of the best in that region and its modern and safe operations make it attractive for miners to work for the company. C. E. Smith, Jr., the President of Carter Mining, worked hard at keeping his work force satisfied and settling employee complaints amicably. One member of the employee-relations department performs the job of a roving ambassador for his division, continuously assessing through informal channels the health of the supervisor–technician relationship. The management of Carter Mining and the corporate human-resources department constantly evaluate their employee-relations strategy in the West, and make appropriate changes in it.

Union operations: Monterey's experience with the UMW has been good. Monterey has lost less than seven days in wildcat strikes through the last three years, which is well under the average experienced by the industry. Good working conditions and training, constant efforts at improving supervisory abilities, and good engineering systems are some of the reasons for the satisfactory industrial relations and high productivity at Monterey.

Safe operations: One of the prime objectives of Carter Oil's training programs is safety. It is a part of every training module. The safety system and

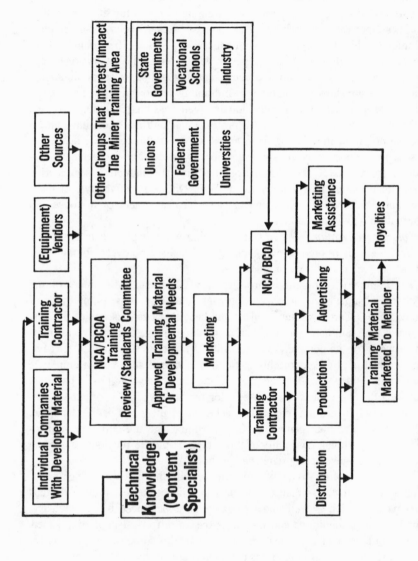

Figure 7—5. Proposed System for Developing Industrywide Standard Training Materials

safety equipment at its surface mine in the West are being imitated by several old, well-established companies. Carter Oil's midwestern underground-safety program is also among the leaders in the underground industry. The comparative worth of both safety operations was illustrated when they were both audited by MESA (now MSHA) in 1977. Both units received audit scores that MSHA considered excellent.

Public-Affairs Management

Carter Oil established a public-affairs department, in part to cope with the growing number of legislations on coal, and also to share information with communities involved with the company's operations. The main responsibilities of the public-affairs department may be classified under the headings:

(1) External: the department is responsible for presenting Carter Oil's case to the communities, political groups, government, and any other body which either affects or is affected by Carter Oil's operations; and
(2) internal: the department is responsible for informing the company's senior managers of legislation that affects the company's operations.

Figure 7–6 diagrams how the public-affairs department planned and implemented its campaign for public support for a new project in the southwest. The campaign was carried out in five stages: (1) recognition of the need for public support; (2) analysis of the positions of various interest groups; (3) planning a strategy of communication; (4) review and approval of the plan; and (5) implementation, using a combination of outlets. The five-stage process is replicated for all major public-affairs projects.

While Carter Oil used Exxon's resources in public affairs quite extensively, the initiative for and the coordination of all public-affairs programs pertaining to the coal business rests exclusively with the small public-affairs department of Carter Oil. Carter Oil's public-affairs department plans all media appearances for the presidents of the two subsidiaries and provides expert advice to the regulatory-affairs managers at Monterey and Carter Mining.

MATERIAL RESOURCES

When Exxon entered the coal industry, it clearly did not expect quick and big returns. In fact, even according to one optimistic estimate coal will provide only 3 percent of Exxon's profits by 1985. Exxon, however, seems willing to pump funds into its coal venture and wait for its returns.[8] Finan-

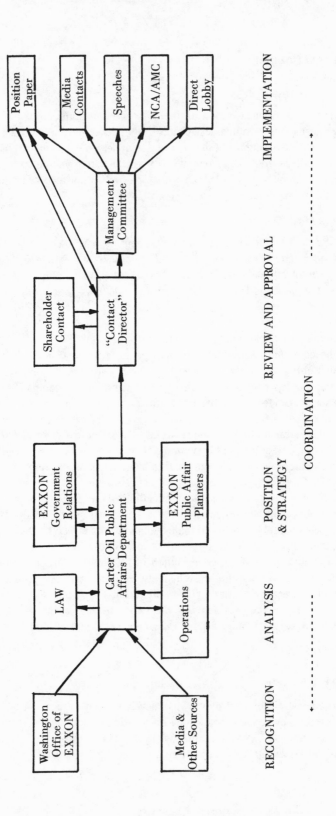

RECOGNITION ANALYSIS POSITION REVIEW AND APPROVAL IMPLEMENTATION
& STRATEGY

COORDINATION

Source: Adapted From Company Records.

Figure 7–6. Public Affairs Flow Chart

cial resources are consequently no real constraint for Carter Oil. In addition, Carter Oil enjoys access to the vast technological and human resources of Exxon. As the case study has already described, Carter Oil has benefited from these resources in the establishment of its coal-mining and synthetics-business ventures. The impressive coal reserves that Carter Oil has assembled in a short time provide the final complement to a rich array of material resources.

Coal Reserves

Rather than attempt to enter the coal-producing industry through the acquisition of an existing company with established reserves, Exxon decided to enter on a de novo basis and began a grass-roots program of acquiring reserves.

The services of a dozen geologists from Exxon were commissioned in 1965 to help acquire coal reserves. None of them had previously worked on coal. They were selected for their geological experience in the regions where coal deposits were known to exist.

Unlike oil, coal reserves were better documented and easier to establish. But by the same token, most of the better-quality reserves in the traditional coal fields of Appalachia and the midwestern United States had already been acquired. There were very few open leases available to Carter Oil. While persevering with their attempts in the East, Exxon geologists had also turned their attention by 1966 to the rich Western coal fields. Recollecting their efforts, a senior geologist said:

> Those were hectic days. We were working against tight time pressures. We had to make educated guesses. Nevertheless, backed by the faith that management had in us, we assembled approximately 7 billion tons of reserves in a record time of eight months, 4 in Illinois and 3 in the West.
>
> Moreover, in order to keep acquisition costs down, we went to "frontier areas," i.e., unexplored reserves, especially in the West. Over 75% of the reserves that we acquired were obtained without drilling a single core hole! We also selectively leased federal lands in the West.

However, the rapid acquisition of reserves meant acquiring reserves without careful evaluation of their coal characteristics. For example, the acquisition in Illinois was later found not entirely suitable for gasification, though amenable to the more distant liquefaction technology. Whereas Western coals were well suited for gasification, any viable-size plant would require the interstate transfer of gas, an option that Carter Oil did not favor because of the then governmental control of interstate gas sales. Reminiscing on those critical days, H. Pistole, the President of Carter Oil, told his management committee in 1974:

> We have a much better perception of some of the fine points in reserve acquisition and particularly the effect of such factors as sulfur content, heat value, reactivity, ash content and mining cost, and on coal usage. But if we had waited for all this knowledge plus assurance of how and where we would eventually use our coal, then our prime coal reserves would belong to somebody else. We, like other latecomers, would be paying premium prices for third or fourth class coal reserves.

Even as Carter Oil geologists recognized the poor reactivity[9] of the Illinois coal, a couple of factors led to a change in emphasis in Carter Oil's plans. Scientists and engineers at Exxon Research and Engineering Company realized that commercialization of coal gasification and liquefaction was further away than they had earlier expected. In the meanwhile, the staff at Carter Oil recognized the spurt in steam-coal consumption by utilities. The vast coal reserves found a ready outlet in the utility markets.

Having helped Carter Oil acquire large reserves, the resources group turned its attention to the consolidation of these reserves. Elaborate field work was initiated and the field data were carefully organized in computer files. At present, computer programs are available to evaluate quickly the desirability of new lease options. A formal monthly review of all leases and options has been instituted.

The formalization of the resource-management system was concurrent with the establishment of a resource-management department. The department was responsible for the exploration, evaluation, and acquisition of coal reserves in the United States. The organization of the department is outlined in Figure 7−7.

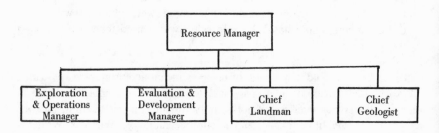

Figure 7−7. Resource Management Organization

Despite the growing expertise of the department's engineers, geologists, and landmen, they are always open to expert advice. The departmental staff seeks help from a number of external agencies. It gets direction for its search activities from the planning and marketing departments of the company; it consults mining engineers from the mines to assess difficulties in mining operations before acquiring new reserves; and it draws on the expertise of geologists and landmen at Exxon for technical help and supplemental help in its search and development efforts. Carter Oil's geologists maintain contact with universities in the vicinity of the company's operations for geological information and advice on site-specific reclamation procedures. Carter Oil uses professional land brokers to buy/lease coal reserves from private owners. This method has proven to be the most effective use of available manpower. The coal reserves held by Carter Oil in 1977 are summarized in Table 7−3; if the two railroad companies which hold vast coal reserves are excluded, Carter Oil's reserves rank third after the industry giants, Consol and Peabody.

Table 7−3. The Carter Oil Company. Approximate Distribution of Reserves by Region (1977)

Region	States	Reserves in billion tons
Appalachia	West Virginia	0.3
Midwest	Illinois	3.4
West	Wyoming, Montana, N. Dakota, Colorado	3.7
Southwest	Texas, Arkansas	1.0
		8.4

Source: Company Records.

The operating subsidiaries of Carter Oil have no responsibility for reserve acquisition. Based on approved long-term plans, certain reserves are assigned to them. In developing their mining plans the engineers at Monterey and Carter Mining consult the resource-management group for geological advice. The geologists at Carter Oil also periodically run a coal-quality workshop for engineers from the subsidiary companies to help the mining engineers understand coal-quality implications of various mining plans, given the geological specification of a given resource.

ORGANIZATIONAL STRUCTURE

Carter Oil's formal organization has two significant attributes: (1) The corporate–subsidiary relationship between Exxon and Carter Oil, and (2) the intraorganizational linkages within Carter Oil.

The Relationship between Exxon and Carter Oil

Carter Oil's position in Exxon's worldwide coal organization is described in Figure 7–8.

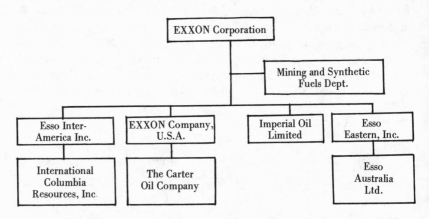

Source: "Coal, Energy Bridge to the Future," November 1977.

Figure 7–8. Organization of the Exxon Corporation

The President of Carter Oil reports to the management committee of Exxon Company, U.S.A., through a "contact executive."[10] Capital-investment plans are prepared for a four-year period and reviewed yearly with the management committee.

Carter Oil's management has drawn on a variety of staff support from Exxon Company, U. S. A., through a "contact executive."[10] Capital-quarters are located very close to the former's headquarters in Houston. Its management has sought and received from Exxon Company, U. S. A. support ranging from expert advice to direct assistance in the implementation of programs. Some of the important areas of support have been in public affairs, corporate planning, marketing, geological engineering, computer services, legal services, and training.

Exxon's worldwide pool of human resources has often provided Carter Oil with managers for some key appointments. In fact, except for jobs directly associated with coal mining, the bulk of Carter Oil's managerial manpower has come from the Exxon organization.

Exxon's research affiliate, Exxon Research and Engineering Company, has been active in coal-research programs for many years. Since 1966, these programs have had two principal goals: (1) to develop processes for manufacturing synthetic gas and oil from coal, and (2) to remove pollutants so that coal can be burned more cleanly. Exxon has spent through the end of 1976 more than $55 million for coal-synthetics research. ER&E has been a critical resource to Carter Oil in its aspiration of commercializing synthetics technologies. Exxon's research engineers have also been available as consultants to Carter Oil on problems of coal mining and coal conversion using technologies developed outside Exxon.

Intraorganizational Linkages at Carter Oil

The organization chart of Carter Oil as of 1977 is given in Figure 7—9. Carter Oil has its own management committee consisting of Pistole and his two senior vice-presidents. Pistole, at fifty-five, has years of experience in various executive positions with Exxon's domestic production operations. He became President of Carter Oil in 1973. The two senior vice-presidents also come from the Exxon organization.[11] The two senior vice-presidents act as contact officers for a set of functions, paralleling the role of "contact executives" in Exxon's management committee. Their major responsibility is to translate the company's goals in terms that are meaningful to the functional managers who work with these senior vice-presidents.

This practice helps in bringing a broad perspective to the management of various functional departments, since the senior vice-presidents do not work as functional specialists but as general managers.

Carter Oil provides several central services to its subsidiaries, Monterey and Carter Mining. There are two broad categories of central services: (1) functions performed centrally, such as management of coal resources, marketing, corporate planning, and public affairs, and (2) advisory services, such as those of the Administrative Coordinator, Mining Manager, and Controller and Treasurer. The subsidiaries have their own employee-relations, mine-engineering, and accounting staff, but draw on central expertise and advice fairly frequently. There is a dotted-line relationship in each of the above functions between the headquarters and subsidiary companies.

The subsidiary companies each have a president, who reports directly to the President of Carter Oil. The synthetics business of Carter Oil is looked after by a synthetics operations manager and his technical staff.

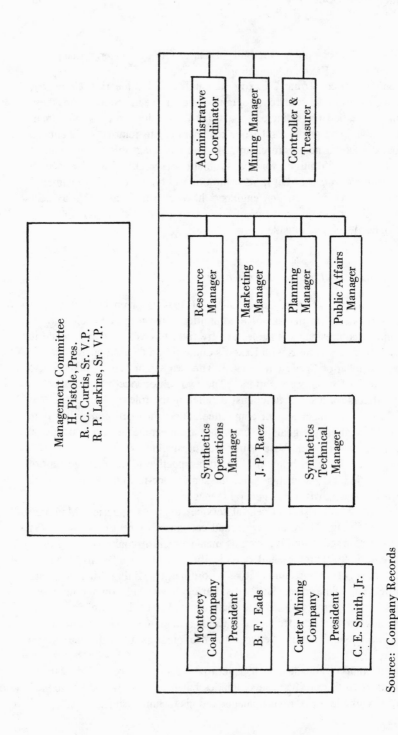

Management Committee
H. Pistole, Pres.
R. C. Curtis, Sr. V.P.
R. P. Larkins, Sr. V.P.

Administrative Coordinator

Mining Manager

Controller & Treasurer

Resource Manager

Marketing Manager

Planning Manager

Public Affairs Manager

Synthetics Operations Manager
J. P. Racz

Synthetics Technical Manager

Monterey Coal Company
President
B. F. Eads

Carter Mining Company
President
C. E. Smith, Jr.

Figure 7–9. Organization Chart for Carter Oil, 1977

Source: Company Records

The Carter Oil Organization

As may be seen from Figure 7−9, there are three main parts to Carter Oil's organization: operations, centralized staff functions, and advisory services.

Coal-Mining Operations: Carter Oil has two coal-mining subsidiaries that run its operations: Monterey (see Figure 7−10) and Carter Mining (see Figure 7−11). When Carter Mining's mines go into full production, its organization chart will be similar to that of Monterey's.

The current differences in structure not only reflect the differences in production maturation, but also the differences in the tasks assigned to C.E. Smith, Jr., the President of Carter Mining, and B. F. Eads, the President of Monterey.

Monterey was set up in an established coal-mining county, and the need was for quickly achieving efficiency in operations. Eads was recruited to set up the mines, because of his rich blend of operations and engineering experience in the coal industry. He later became President of Monterey. Given his personal background, the engineering and planning functions have been placed under his direct supervision.

In contrast, Smith came to Carter Mining from Exxon's commercial departments, having no experience in coal mining. He was Carter Oil's Vice-President in charge of coal sales before being asked to head Carter Mining. Smith's job was to establish cordial relations with a community that viewed coal mining with suspicion. The ranchers and farmers of Gillette were worried about the disquieting effects of the Western coal boom. They were concerned about the consequent pressure on town services, and damage to their land, water, and environment. Given the external orientation of his assignment and his own personal background, Smith decided to delegate all mining-related problems to his operations manager. Therefore, in Carter Mining the engineering manager does not report to the President, but instead to the operations manager.

Staff Functions and Services: Carter Oil has inherited Exxon's tradition of providing strong staff support to line management. Operations personnel are aided in their work by corporate services as well as direct staff assistance placed under them. They are taught the use of staff services through special problem-solving seminars. The central functions at Carter Oil are resource management, marketing, planning, and public affairs. The resource management function was described earlier. The marketing organization consists of a sales manager, three area managers—one each for the East, Midwest, and West—and one order-progress coordinator. The subsidiaries handle all day-to-day dispatching, and the corporate controller handles all billings to

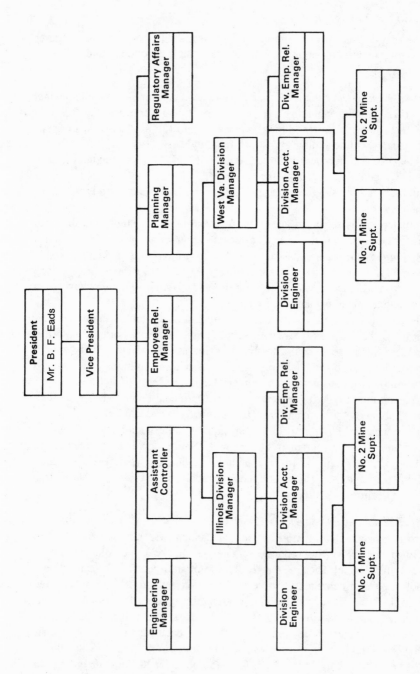

Figure 7–10. Organization of Monterey Coal Company, 1977

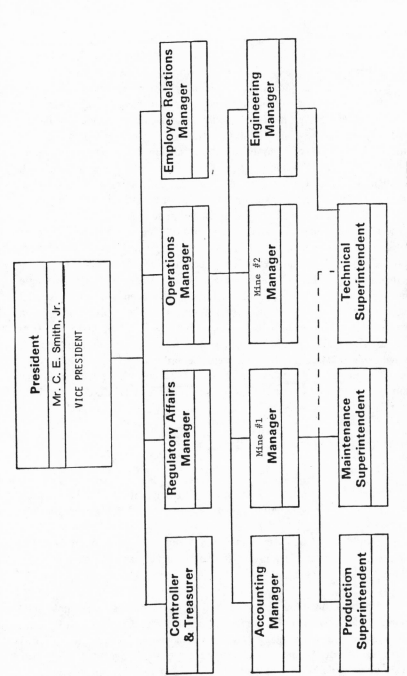

Figure 7–11. Organization of Carter Mining Company, 1977

the customer. The Planning department currently has a staff of five, including the manager. It has an MBA interested in the economic modeling of mining ventures. The rest are engineers who, with the exception of one, were assigned from either Exxon's planning or operating divisions. The exception now is a young mining engineer assigned to the planning department from Monterey Coal. In the long run, the planning manager hopes to have a regular system of personnel rotation between the planning department and Carter Oil's mining subsidiaries. Public affairs in Carter Oil means more than governmental lobbying or expediting papers through the governmental bureaucracy. Carter Oil is one of the few coal companies to have a formal and active public-affairs department. The company's system of public-affairs management was described in detail in an earlier section.

The three key areas in which Carter Oil provided advisory service to its subsidiaries were human-resources management, handled by the Administrative Coordinator, controllership, and engineering. At present, the mine-engineering expertise available to the company is restricted to that of a single mining engineer. A mine-engineering function has been conceived of at the headquarters, not only to help in the preparation of long-term plans and work on special projects, but eventually to help solve special problems of the subsidiaries. The central function needs to be staffed with experts, though currently limited to one person. The corporate controller provides advisory support to the controllers in the subsidiaries. The human-resources management is a very important function at Carter Oil; some of its practices were described earlier.

OTHER ADMINISTRATIVE SYSTEMS

Long-Term Planning

The current long-term plan for Carter Oil extends to 1990. The rationale for such a long-term orientation was explained by the planning manager:

> Utilities are our major customers today and will always be important to us. A utility typically takes 10 years to design and build its plant. That puts us on a planning horizon of 10−15 years.

The corporate-planning activity has four broad phases: (1) supply-and-demand survey on coal, (2) strategic scenarios for Carter Oil, (3) plans elaborating a selected strategy (both physical and financial), and (4) projections of production programs, capital, and profit budgets. The first two phases are essentially the responsibility of the planning department, though a lot of help is drawn from Exxon's corporate-planning department. The output from the planning department at the end of the two phases is a document "outlining assumptions about the long-term business environment and the suggested strategic scenarios that match the project environment." The document, after scrutiny by the top management, sets the guidelines for detailed planning. The subsidiary companies then help the planning department in preparing detailed physical and financial projections consistent with the guidelines. The formal planning process for synthetics is somewhat different and handled separately. Given the uncertainties associated with the project, there are three distinct planning stages, the accuracy of the capital-expenditure forecast improving progressively from $\pm$ 25% error in the I Stage to $\pm$ 10% error in the III Stage. The I Stage of the process is outside the scope of the formal long-term planning process described earlier. The next section describes in some detail the three stages in the planning for synthetics.

The Planning Process for Synthetics

The various tasks in the planning of the synthetics project are described in Table 7−4. There are three key decision stages in the process, as shown in the table. There is a year's gap between each stage. The project is funded in Stage I by a predevelopment budget authorization. The funding in Stage II comes from a development budget. In Stage III, the project expenditures are funded by a regular capital budget.

Though the synthetics-operations manager and his four work groups are primarily responsible for the project through all the three stages, other departments at Carter Oil are brought into the planning process at appropriate times. When Stage I decision was taken on the Texas lignite project, for example, other central services at Carter Oil began to make their contributions to the project. The marketing department began making initial customer contacts. The public-affairs department started planning its information-dissemination program for communities and power groups that may be concerned with the project. The human-resources department began its search for suitable manpower. As the project draws nearer implementation, the question of its organization will get increased attention within Carter Oil: Should the synthetics business be orgainzed as a separate company or should it be an operating subsidiary?

Philosophy of Planning and Control

Carter Oil's formal planning system has interesting distinctions when compared with those of other coal companies. Apart from these systemic differences, there seems to be another important difference. Carter Oil's planning is perhaps the most participative in the industry. As Carter Oil's President Pistole summarized:

Table 7-4. The Synthetics Planning Process

Decision stage	Process	Responsibility
I.	1. Preliminary planning. Class V investment estimates (±25% error)	The four work groups
	Abort project or provide funding for process-design detailed estimates.	
	Decision made by the management committee of Carter Oil, and appropriations for detailed estimates, approved by Exxon.	
	Broad product, process, and location decisions are approved.	
	2. Prepare detailed specs. for design, and offload engineering either to Exxon's engineering organization or outside consultants or both.	Plant Design work group and Planning work group.
	3. Prepare capital appropriation (±15–20% error).	Planning work group with the help of controller's organization.
II.	Project capital expenditure approved for inclusion in the long-term plan of the company.	
	4. Environmental-impact assessment, filing of statement and preparing for the hearings.	Synthetic Operations Manager.
	5. Offload detailed design.	Synthetics Operations Manager.
III.	Final capital budget approved (±10% error)	Synthetic Operations Manager.
	6. Prepare site.	Synthetic Operations Manager.
	7. Field construction.	Synthetic Operations Manager.
	8. Site operation.	

We believe in group decisions. I am not saying that an individual does not make decisions. He does; in fact, we seek his inputs into decisions all the time. But we aim at deliberately getting more than one input into a decision. We try to improve the quality of decision making of the team as opposed to improving an individual's decision-making abilities.

Carter Oil's style of management is also characterized by its rewarding of innovative, risk-taking behavior. As Curtis remarked:

I have experienced this. I have seen it experienced by others. There is reward for innovative behavior. You must remember, we have an oil company culture. You drill a five hundred million dollar dry hole and walk away from it. You don't lose sleep over it. Our decisions are risk weighted decisions. Their quality is evaluated by peers. Some of our projects are so long drawn, the decision maker has most probably moved on to another responsibility by the time the project is implemented. We can't judge on the basis of outcomes.

Finally, its decision-making style may be termed flexible, continuously open to questioning of the plan. As Curtis remarked:

You are doomed to failure if you have a rigid plan. Plans have to change in the light of new information. Quite often a project has to be dropped after a lot of effort. You do get frustrated. You go home and kick your cat. But you can't be emotional about the project. You go back the next morning and start all over again. As the project evolves, more areas get certain and the changes are hopefully few from one stage to another; but the project team has total authority to reject all decisions made in the previous go around.

Figure 7−12 summarizes the evolution of the synthetics-business idea:

The Control Dilemma

While Carter Oil's decision-making style certainly encourages innovations, the company faces a major challenge on the efficiency front. Like other de novo entrants in recent years, Carter Oil's cost of production tends to be high for three reasons: (1) inflated capital cost of a new mine makes its cost of production higher than that of the older mines; (2) Carter Oil's insistence on modern technology and safe and healthy work environments means capital spending well above the industry average; and (3) a built-in under-

	Strategic Parameters		Years			
Product	Process	Area	1974	1975	1976	1977
INTER/INTRA STATE						
Iteration						
1. SNG	Lurgi or KT	Wyoming or Illinois		▭		
2. IBG	Lurgi	Wyoming	▭			
INTRA STATE						
3. IBG	Lurgi	Arkansas		▭		
4. IBG	KT	Arkansas		▭		
5. IBG	Lurgi	Texas				▭

Figure 7–12. The Evolution of the Synthetics-Business Idea

utilization in the early phases of expansion. Carter Oil's management has to ride the twin horses of innovatioₙ and productivity, striking that delicate balance between short-term profitability and long-term growth. Its control system must likewise reflect a flexible approach, with managers being judged on differing criteria in keeping with their priorities.

A contrast between the efforts of Eads, President of Monterey, and Smith, President of Carter Mining, is illustrative of such a practice. Eads concentrated on the proper engineering of mines and establishment of engineering systems which would guarantee use of proper methods and minimize delays. Monterey had hired from a number of different coal companies. The rich variety of experiences that its employees brought with them was used by Monterey in the development of its engineering systems. Eads believes that the slow, painstaking process of building systems has finally started paying off. Systematic working has reduced the number of emergencies on the job, allowing the supervisor to concentrate on managing his crew instead of running from one crisis to another. The productivity of Monterey is said to be better than that of neighboring mines with similar seam conditions.

Smith's efforts at establishing good community relationships had various facets to it. Carter Mining was the first major coal company to be headquartered in Wyoming. A million-dollar office building was constructed, symbolic of the company's intent to stay permanently in Wyoming and experience at first hand the concerns of the people of Gillette. Carter Mining, together with a few other companies in the Gillette area, underwrote the construction by a private contractor of a residential complex in Gillette. The houses were of various types to cater to a broad cross-section of the Gillette community. The additional supply of houses also helped Carter Mining's own employees in securing proper residential accommodation.

Smith also encouraged his executives to assume leadership roles in the community. He reasoned that a healthy community would help Carter Mining retain and attract talented professionals to work at Gillette.

In deference to concerns about environmental damage, Carter Mining established programs in collaboration with the University of Wyoming to restore mined lands to equal or greater use.

The different orientations of the two subsidiaries reflect differing priorities, both encouraged by Carter Oil's control system.

Part IV
Managing Adaptation

8. Illustrating the Model

In Part II, the various changes taking place in the coal industry were described. Since the mid-1960s, new opportunities, tighter constraints, and richer resources have all contributed to the growing complexity of the industry. It is important to distinguish the adaptation in the industry prior to 1965 from that since. After a brief discussion of the early patterns of adaptation, this chapter examines in some detail the adaptive responses of four coal companies to the changes in their industry environment since 1965. The case studies on the four companies were presented in Part III. The case data will be analyzed with the help of the framework developed in Part I.

THE EARLY ADAPTATION

Three of the four companies in this study have had a long history of association with the coal industry. The North American Coal Corporation, Island Creek Coal Company, and Consolidation Coal Company have successfully survived the various challenges that the coal industry has had to offer. Table 8−1 summarizes the strategies of these companies from the time of their founding up until 1965. They have all resorted to acquisitions and mergers for growth and geographic diversification. Growth provided the coal companies with control over greater financial resources, allowing them to keep pace with the increased mechanization in the coal mines. Productivity improved as a consequence. Geographic diversification helped in the spreading of their marketing risks, this being additionally important to coal companies because of the significant transportation costs associated with coal. In the 1950s the coal companies tried to protect themselves from the fluctuating fortunes of the post−World War II coal markets through joint ventures, long-term contracting, and product diversification. The growing utility mar-

Table 8–1. A Comparison of the Evolution of Strategies of NACCO, Island Creek, and Consol until 1965

	NACCO	Island Creek	Consol
1. Year founded	1913	1902	1864
2. Year formally organized	1925	1910	1864
3. Nature of entry into the coal industry	Acquisition:	Building from the grass roots:	Merger:
	Franklin Taplin acquired operating coal companies and transportation lines, transforming a coal-trading company to a coal company.	Albert Holden acquired bituminous-coal lands in West Virginia, and built the coal mine from grass roots. The town of Holden was also established to provide supporting infrastructure for the mining operations.	Several small coal operators combined their interests to form Consol.
4. The pre-World War I era			
4.1 Product strategy	Steam coal	Metallurgical and steam coal	Steam coal
4.2 Market strategy	Railroads, home heating	Steel making and industrial	Railroads and industrial
4.3 Geographic diversity	Pennsylvania	West Virginia	Maryland West Virginia Pennsylvania Kentucky

5. 1920–1955

	NACCO	Island Creek	Consol
5.1 Overall strategy	Growth through acquisition	Internal growth and growth through acquisitions	Growth through mergers and diversification
5.2 Product strategy	Entered metallurgical-coal markets in a very limited fashion.	No change	Entered metallurgical-coal markets Established a strong R&D department in 1946 to explore new uses for coal especially in the synthetic-fuels market. Entered the chemical business, by purchasing a coal-tar-refining and chemical plant in New Jersey.
5.3 Market strategy	Utilities became an important market segment. In 1953, NACCO signed one of the first long-term contracts in the industry with a utility customer.	Established the Appalachian Coals Inc. in the 1930s to act as selling agent for 127 coal operators, including Island Creek, in order to shore up coal prices during the Depression. Established joint ventures in the 1950s with steel companies to exploit its rich reserves of metallurgical coal.	Utilities became an important market segment. Along with NACCO one of the first to sign a long-term contract in the industry with a utility customer. Established joint ventures in the 1950s with steel companies to exploit its metallurgical-coal reserves. Metallurgical-coal reserves were strengthened through the acquisition of Pocahontas Fuel Company in 1956.

Table 8-1. A Comparison of the Evolution of Strategies of NACCO, Island Creek, and Consol until 1965 (Cont.)

	NACCO	Island Creek	Consol
5.4 Geographic diversity	Expanded its operations to Ohio and West Virginia Became a strong coal company in Ohio and Pennsylvania	Essentially a West Virginia operator	Reorganized divisions in the 1930s by the four regions in which it operated, i.e., Maryland, Kentucky, West Virginia, and Pennsylvania. Entered Ohio through merger with Hanna Coal Company and strengthened Pennsylvania operations through merger with Pittsburgh Coal Company. Four regions in 1947: i.e., Kentucky, Ohio, Pennsylvania and West Virginia
6. 1956–1965			
6.1 Overall strategy	Increasing reliance on utility markets. Sold its dock operations and metallurgical coal interests in 1960. Abortive attempts at diversification. Long-term contracts became a predominant method of doing business.	Entered the utility coal markets in 1964 through acquisition.	Utility coal markets became a major outlet for Consol's coal. Increasing reliance on long-term contracts. Synthetics research did not provide new markets.

	NACCO		Island Creek		Consol	
	1956	1965	1956	1965	1956	1965
6.2 Product-market strategy						
Sales to various market segments (incl. agency coal) (in millions of tons)						
Steam coal utilities	2.8	4.7	1.5	9.0	13.6	24.6
Industrial & others	2.3	1.3	10.8	7.4	13.1	8.8
Metallurgical (domestic)	0.2	–	3.7	3.1	14.1	12.5
Export	0.3	–	2.5	1.5	6.2	2.7
	5.6	6.0	18.5	21.0	47.0	48.6
6.3 Geographic diversity	Entered the Western coal market for the first time, through acquisitions of the Dakota Collieries in North Dakota		Acquired steam coal property in West Kentucky		Acquired approximately 1 bt of Western Coal Reserves	
	Discontinued West Virginia operations with the sale of its metallurgical coal interests					

kets for steam coal provided the much-needed stabilizing force, contributing, as of 1965, over 40 percent to the sales tonnage of the three companies (see Table 8–1, item 6–2).

Through all these strategic moves the structures of the coal companies did not change significantly. The president of a coal company, not unlike his counterpart in other mining industries (Chandler, 1962) devoted little time to organizational matters. He often had an intimate understanding of all facets of his company's business, and influenced the company's profits directly by being involved in all major sales negotiations. His popularity in industry circles had beneficial effects on the company's business. An influential president could get good sales contracts, arrange financing for his company, and negotiate favorable acquisition and merger terms. Given the then nature of the coal business, a coal company president did not need many staff advisors. Most coal companies consequently had very thin staff at headquarters—mostly to handle sales, finance, and legal matters. Operations were totally delegated to divisions organized on the basis of geographic regions. With minor variations this arrangement continued through 1965 (see Figure 8–1).

The strategies and structures of the three coal companies showed a good deal of similarity as of 1965, though there were some distinctions in their product mix and in their corporate organizational arrangements. However, in the years that followed, varying responses to several environmental changes have positioned the three companies differently. The adaptive posture of Carter Oil, the most prominent of the new entrants to coal, offers yet another contrast. The spectrum of adaptations exhibited by the four coal companies will be explored in some detail, using the model developed in Part I.

THE NEW CHALLENGES

Part II identified at least three major challenges faced by coal-company managers since the mid-1960s: (1) adapting to rapidly changing market opportunities; (2) coping with mushrooming legislation; and (3) dealing with worsening problems in human-resource management.

Today for the first time since 1920, coal-company managers see hopes of a sustained growth in demand for coal. In fact, if the ambitious goals for coal do become a reality, coal companies should expect a near-doubling in demand for coal by 1985. However, these euphoric estimates cover three distinct markets, and the varying degrees of uncertainty one associates with them.

The utility market, the surest of the three, has slackened on account of the political tussle between Western and Eastern coals. Depending on what the

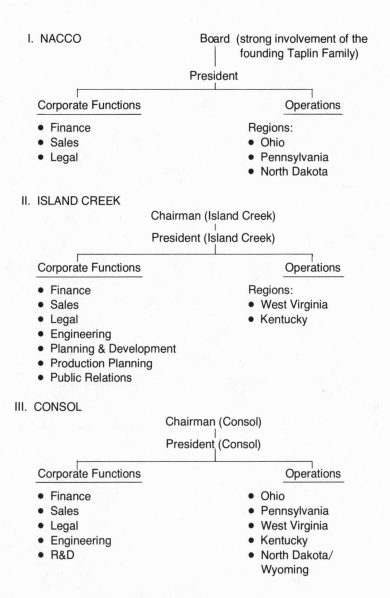

I. NACCO   Board (strong involvement of the founding Taplin Family)

President

Corporate Functions

- Finance
- Sales
- Legal

Operations

Regions:
- Ohio
- Pennsylvania
- North Dakota

II. ISLAND CREEK

Chairman (Island Creek)

President (Island Creek)

Corporate Functions

- Finance
- Sales
- Legal
- Engineering
- Planning & Development
- Production Planning
- Public Relations

Operations

Regions:
- West Virginia
- Kentucky

III. CONSOL

Chairman (Consol)

President (Consol)

Corporate Functions

- Finance
- Sales
- Legal
- Engineering
- R&D

Operations

- Ohio
- Pennsylvania
- West Virginia
- Kentucky
- North Dakota/ Wyoming

Figure 8–1. A Comparison of the Organizations of NACCO, Island Creek, and Consol in 1965

regulations favor, coal companies will find a growing demand for either their Eastern or Western coal reserves. A lead time of at least seven to ten years is, however, required for the development of coal reserves, depending on whether they are to be surface-mined or deep-mined. Committing capital resources ahead of time on the acquisition, development, and exploitation of coal reserves, without knowing which way the political wind will blow, is risky. Coal-company managers must make these risky choices if they wish to preempt competition.

The industrial markets for coal seem even more troublesome. Economics and convenience do not currently favor coal. However, future regulation and proposed penal taxation could make this market a reality.

As for synthetics, a commercially viable project is yet to be completed. The future for this market is still unclear. Technological development and governmental intervention are two major factors that can shape this market in several ways.

Thus each of the three product—market segments for coal seems to have some uncertainty associated with it. The range of product—market uncertainties faced by coal companies is summarized in Table 8−2.

Table 8−2. Range of Product−Market Uncertainties

Product-Market combination	Projected yearly demand in 1985 (million tons)	Product-market complexity
Steam coal for utility markets	820−850[1]	Moderate. (While markets have been identified, there is uncertainty over the preferences for Eastern or Western coal.)
Steam coal for industrial markets	130−160[1]	High. (Industrial markets are tough to penetrate, given current economies of coal-fired boilers, with attendant pollution problems.)
Synthetic fuels	188[2]	Very high. (Product and processing technology not finalized. Markets nonexistent at current costs of conversion.)

Regulation poses a different kind of challenge. The various laws enacted to ensure the safety of miners and to protect the environment can be treated at one level as laws, the letter of which has to be obeyed. At another, they can be seen as instruments seeking redress for a societal grievance. Coal-company managers could, therefore, choose to follow the spirit of these laws and undertake more changes than those mandated by law. And at yet another level, managers could even volunteer to formulate new laws, if necessary, and help others in the industry improve their safety performance and environmental-protection efforts.

The challenge in human-resources management is similar. Whereas the contractual obligations with the work force, whether unionized or otherwise, specify the bare minimum that a manager has to do, the challenge can be treated more broadly. Clearly, mere adherence to the letter of the contract has yielded neither productivity gains nor labor peace in the past. Perhaps a more enlightened approach is called for.

STATES OF ADAPTATION

In responding to the challenges mentioned in the previous pages, coal-company managers have used a wide range of strategies.

Product—Market Posture

The four coal companies in this study (Part III) have chosen to place varying emphases on the several product—market options open to them. NACCO has opted to concentrate on the utility markets. It has no major plans for penetrating the industrial markets, and as for the synthetics business it merely hopes to be a supplier of coal to others engaged in the synthetics activity.

Island Creek has also focused on utility markets in its long-term plans. Its strategy, however, seems more cautious. Given its excellent metallurgical-coal reserves, it has a unique opportunity in metallurgical-coal markets. The company has announced a major expansion in its metallurgical-coal production. It can wait until such time as the various uncertainties surrounding the steam-coal markets are resolved before making its moves in this segment. Whereas it has no current plans for exploiting opportunities for steam coal in the industrial segment, the company could change its stand depending on future developments. Some of its lower-grade metallurgical-coal reserves could be sold at a premium in industrial markets. The company has no definite plans for entering the synthetics business.

Consol has announced a major expansion program in its steam-coal production. The plan primarily focuses on expansion in utility markets. Industrial segments would be serviced, but at existing levels. Consol is very active in the commercialization of liquefaction and gasification technologies, and is readying itself to exploit opportunities in the synthetics field when and as they develop.

Carter Oil is the only company in this study that has definite plans to participate aggressively in all three of the market segments, utility markets, industrial markets, and the synthetics business. Its Intermediate BTU Gas (IBG) project should be on stream by the mid-1980s. Its experiments with form coke may also open up metallurgical-coal markets to Carter Oil in the late 1980s. Table 8−3 summarizes the orientation of the four companies.

Table 8−3. Comparing the Product-Market Orientations of the Four Coal Companies

	Expansion Plans		Complexity associated with response (see Table 8-2)
NACCO	Steam coal for utility markets		Moderate
	1976 (actual)	10.9 mt	
	1984 (projected)	25.0 mt	
Island Creek	Steam coal for utility and industrial markets		Moderate
	1976 (actual)	10.6 mt	
	1983 (projected)	11.2 mt	
	Metallurgical coal		
	1976 (actual)	7.0 mt	
	1983 (projected)	12.1 mt	
Consol	Steam coal for utility and industrial markets		High
	1976 (actual)	45.0 mt	
	1985 (projected)	78.0 mt	
	Metallurgical coal		
	1976 (actual)	9.9 mt	
	1985 (projected)	13.0 mt	
Carter Oil	Steam coal for utility and industrial markets		Very high
	1976 (actual)	3.0 mt	
	1987 (projected)	32.6 mt	
	Form coke in the 1980s		
	IBG in the 1980s		

Responding to Other Strategic Changes

The responses of the four coal companies in coping with regulation and managing human resources have also been distinct.

In the case of NACCO, responding to regulatory mandates on safety and environmental affairs is the responsibility of divisional managers. It is up to the personal initiative of divisional managers to go beyond the letter of the law. Since divisions are cost centers, there is a tendency on the part of divisions to control tightly the recruitment of personnel not directly useful for short-term performance. As Figure 4−2 shows, staff support in the areas of safety and environmental affairs varies widely within and across divisions. Likewise, NACCO's orientation to labor management also varies across divisions. It is a divisional prerogative. By and large, the contract with the work force establishes the norms for labor management. Given strict short-term performance goals, there is not much room for experimentation. While NACCO's response to the regulatory and human-resources-management challenge meets all legal and contractual obligations, it does not go far beyond them.

Island Creek, in contrast to NACCO, does have a corporate focus on safety, environmental affairs, and human-resources management. A Safety Coordinator and a Director of Environmental Affairs help shape the corporate response in the first two areas. The two executives report in turn to the Executive Vice-President of Operations (see Figure 5−1). Operating performance is closely linked to safety. Island Creek's incentive schemes require a minimum safety performance of an operations supervisor or manager before he can become eligible for a bonus (see Chapter 5). Likewise, Island Creek's top management also seeks to go beyond contractual mandates in the area of labor management. The Executive Vice-President for Administration is responsible for corporate response in this area. Chapter 5 described the elaborate efforts that are being planned at Island Creek to minimize miner alienation and to foster a sense of team spirit. A whole new program of motivation, loosely called the "white hat function," is slated for experimentation. The program represents the extracontractual efforts at Island Creek to better manage its human resources. Training is included as part of this program and is coordinated centrally by the manager for human-resources development.

Consol has an orientation very similar to that of Island Creek's. The company has a Corporate Vice-President for Environmental Affairs, who reports to the Executive Vice-President for Engineering (see Figure 6−4). The latter executive coordinates all of Consol's expansion projects. Environmental considerations can thus be routinely factored into all expansion projects. The company's labor-management policies are coordinated by the Executive

Vice-President for Industrial, Employee and Public Relations. Consol places much emphasis on training. It has an elaborate training program that covers all levels of employees up to shift foreman (see Figure 6−3). The training programs are designed to help safety and productivity in the mines. The company has also established recently a Management Development Institute (MDI) to help train its supervisors. A senior Consol executive[3] observed: "Consistency of action and predictability of behavior are key supervisory traits if grievances (of miners) are to be minimized." The MDI is expected to build these and other supervisory skills. Consol is clearly not constrained by mere legislative mandates or contractual obligations in its search to improve safety and productivity in its mines.

Carter Oil, being a recent entrant to the coal industry, has been able to build high standards of safety into its operations. Liberal capital expenditures have been a significant factor in this regard. However, the company is also distinguished by one of the most elaborate administrative arrangements, both at the division and corporate level, to cope with regulation and human-resources management (see Figures 7−5, 7−6, and 7−7). These reflect the company's commitment to safety and environmental affairs, beyond legal mandates. The company has, for example, set up a joint program with the University of Wyoming to restore mined lands to equal or greater use. It has also persuaded the National Coal Association and the Bituminous Coal Operators Association to consider an industrywide pooling of training skills for dissemination to coal companies, some being poorly endowed with training resources. Such a program is aimed at improving skill level and safety throughout the industry. Carter Oil has offered to share three hundred hours of its comprehensive audiovisual training modules in such an industrywide effort. Likewise, in other areas of human-resources management the company seeks to bring the coal industry "into the twentieth century."

The four coal companies must at the very minimum meet their legal obligations. To the extent that their responses to regulation and labor-management problems go beyond these minimum requirements, they show a strategic orientation. Island Creek, Consol, and Carter Oil all have shown such a strategic orientation in their responses. Carter Oil has the most elaborate response of the three.

Strategic Responses and States of Adaptation

In Chapter 2, three states of adaptation were identified and these were associated with three types of strategic responses. The strategic responses of the four coal companies do not fall neatly into the descriptive categories of Chapter 2. Nevertheless, there seem to be some clear patterns.

The response of NACCO broadly fits the label "avoidance." The company seeks to buffer itself from environmental uncertainty by confining its activities to the least uncertain segment. The utility market is the least ambiguous market segment for coal. Even here, NACCO has an overwhelming preference for long-term contracts, emphasizing those in which the customer and NACCO are engaged in a joint venture. These ventures tie the lifelong production of a mine to a utility customer. Bounded by long-term contracts with customers, long-term contracts with its miners, and mandates imposed by regulation, the management task at NACCO seems to be one of maximizing cost efficiency within these constraints. This is a viable strategy. However, it presumes the continued availability of profitable long-term contracts and customer financing. If this critical assumption should prove wrong, NACCO's survival may be threatened, given its current resources. NACCO's state of adaptation is closest to what was termed an unstable state.

As for Island Creek and Consol, their responses may be labeled "reaction." These companies do prefer the certainty of a long-term contract. But they also seem willing to play in the spot markets. However, both seem content to work only in those market segments that they know best. Industrial markets are largely ignored in their plans, and shelved for consideration at a more opportune time in the future. Likewise, their attitude to synthetics is best summarized by the comments of a Consol executive:[4] "If the nation eventually decides that it needs a synthetics industry, our company will have the coal and the expertise to lead in the development." The overall approach is not to ignore opportunities, and yet it is always in reaction to a definite environmental stimulus. The two companies also seem capable of sensing environmental trends. They have both gone beyond mere legal mandates on safety and environmental affairs and beyond contractual obligations with labor. Their strategies make them less vulnerable to changes in their product—market and regulatory environments and more capable of handling volatility in their labor relations. Both Island Creek and Consol are in a stable state of adaptation.

The adaptive response of Carter Oil would come closest to fitting the label "proactive." The company is about to set up the first commercial synthetics project by identifying a synthetic product and a market in which it can compete without artificial subsidies. The company lacks metallurgical-coal reserves, and yet it hopes to compete in that market segment if its joint experimentation on form coke with steel companies is a success. It could then divert some of its steam-coal reserves for conversion and sale to metallurgical-coal markets. Carter Oil's response is the only one in our study which has elements that can shape future business opportunities. The company's response to regulation has also been proactive. It has a very active public-affairs department that aims at informing the relevant public of Carter Oil's major moves. Carter Oil's management believes that if an industry has good communication with its community, problems can be solved without resorting to regulation. Where regulation exists, the company has adapted to the spirit of the legislation. Its effort at setting up industrywide training is a good example of the enlightened self-interest that guides Carter Oil's response—if training in the coal industry can be improved, companies like Carter Oil would not be one of the select few training facilities, which other coal companies would have to raid for their trained miners. The proactive stance of the company makes it closest among all coal companies to a neutral state of adaptation.

It must be emphasized that the state of adaptation has no clear relationship with profitability. While all three levels represent profitable operation in the steady state, it is possible for a company in an unstable state to be more profitable than one in a higher state of adaptation. This of course depends on the nature of the adaptive fit of the two companies. In fact, NACCO in this study shows a superior profitability to Carter Oil, which according to one estimate had initially been a losing proposition. NACCO is close to a condition of Unstable Fit, whereas Carter Oil is not adaptively fitted as yet. Carter Oil is, however, less vulnerable to challenges posed by the environment than NACCO. Carter Oil's level of adaptation is, therefore, higher.

The hierarchical arrangement of the states of adaptation of the four coal companies is in turn associated with distinctive adaptive abilities and adaptive processes. These will now be explored.

ADAPTIVE ABILITY

Adaptive ability was shown earlier to be determined by the Material Capacity (MATCAP) and the Organizational Capacity (ORGCAP) of a firm. The MATCAP and ORGCAP of the four coal companies varied significantly.

MATCAP

MATCAP of a firm was defined in Chapter 2 as the relative abundance of the firm's material resources and the latitude available to its managers for exploitation of these resources.

The two key material resources for a coal company are coal reserves and finances. Since most available private coal reserves in the United States have been acquired, and the rest are either under the federal government's lease moratorium or in the control of Indian tribes and state governments, coal reserves are not easily available for acquisition. The four coal companies in this study, fortunately, have rich coal reserves and are in fact among the top ten reserve holders in the industry. However, two factors, geographic distribution and extent of compliance-quality reserves, determine the flexibility offered by these reserves in strategic planning. Table 8−4 contrasts the steam-coal reserves of the four companies based on size and flexibility.

Table 8−4. A Contrast of the Steam-Coal Reserves of the Four Coal Companies as of 1977

	Size of steam-coal reserves	Percentage of steam-coal reserves of compliance quality in the East	Ratio of Eastern to Western steam-coal reserves
	Billion tons	%	Ratio
NACCO	5.1	—	10:90
Island Creek	2.4	11	90:10
Consol	12.4	—	45:55
Carter Oil	8.4	5	50:50

Carter Oil and Consol not only have sizable coal reserves, but they also have a balanced mix of holdings in both the East and West. Even if Western coal wins increasing favor, water scarcity in the West and other environmental considerations, together with the transportation crisis described in Chapter 3, will constrain the rapid development of Western coal. Consequently, an expansion strategy focused entirely in the West can be problematic. A balanced reserve holding offers the coal company access to both the Western and Eastern markets. The latter is a definite opportunity, especially if an economic stack-gas-scrubbing process can be found. At any rate, political forces will ensure that at least a modest demand obtains for Eastern coal.

Companies that have compliance-quality low-sulfur reserves in the East have several distinct advantages. Firstly, compliance-quality coal, as the name suggests, requires no scrubbing. Given the higher energy value of this coal as compared to Western coal, it has clear cost advantages. In Eastern markets such a coal can command premium prices because of the additional transportation-cost advantage. Even if scrubbing becomes mandatory, compliance-quality coal would have a tremendous market in the East as a blend fuel.

Whereas Island Creek has a much smaller reserve base than either Carter
Oil or Consol, it has a significant tonnage of low-sulfur reserves in the East.
This gives the company some unique advantages, as discussed above.

NACCO is the most constrained, given that its resources are largely in the
West, and its compliance-quality reserves in the East are virtually nil.

The financial capacity available to a manager is determined by the size of
the financial resources available to him and the latitude allowed in their use.
The financial resources of Carter Oil are the most enviable. Its parent Exxon
is one of the strongest corporations in the world. Lack of cash is certainly
not one of Exxon's problems.[5] In contrast, the financial resources available
to Island Creek, through Oxy, and Consol, through Conoco, are more modest. In the case of NACCO, raising additional finances will be difficult. As
discussed in Chapter 4, the company is not eager to expand its equity base.
While the company's borrowing capacity is good, its profitability is lower
than that of Island Creek and Consol. Additional interest burden may raise
the break-even point to an uncomfortable high, making the company's profitability very vulnerable. NACCO's current financing arrangement through
customer guarantees also faces an uncertain future (see Chapter 4). Besides
the extent of the financial resource available to a company, the latitude allowed in its use is also important.

Companies like NACCO depend one hundred percent on coal for their
profits. In contrast, a potential coal giant like Carter Oil may at best contribute 3 percent of its parent's (Exxon) profits in 1985. Profitability of coal
and coal-related products implies different levels of criticality for the overall
financial well-being of companies that own coal businesses. Consequently,
the latitude to experiment with strategies on coal varies from company to
company. Generally, companies that rely heavily on steam coal for their
overall profits in the short run are likely to avoid any risky strategies, especially when coal's conventional market as a fuel for utilities seems strong.
Even in the case of diversified companies, contribution from coal may be
critical to the overall profitability of the company.

Table 8–5 compares the contribution of coal to the profits of Oxy and
Conoco since their acquisitions of Island Creek and Consol, respectively.
Coal has been a major contributor to corporate profits after 1973 in both
companies. In fact, coal has since helped improve the overall profitability of
the two companies. Oxy and Conoco managements are, therefore, likely to
place at least modest financial expectations on coal in their near-term planning. While expansion in conventional coal markets will receive encouragement, the coal subsidiaries would get but limited latitude in experimenting
with risky strategies, especially in new markets.

In the case of Carter Oil there are no immediate profit expectations from

Table 8–5. Criticality of the Financial Performances of Consol and Island Creek for Their Parents

Year	Consol			Island Creek		
	Contribution to the profits* of Conoco %	Profitability of Conoco without Consol (%)	Profitability with Consol (%)	Contribution to the profits** of Oxy (%)	Profitability of Oxy without Island Creek (%)	Profitability (%) with Island Creek (%)
1967	16.7	5.7	6.0	—	—	—
1969	12.5	5.9	5.9	11.0	8.3	8.5
1971	6.7	3.8	3.6	4.3	4.8	4.5
1973	—	6.0	5.0	7.0	7.5	7.3
1975	42.9	2.9	4.3	58.0	2.7	5.6
1976	37.9	4.0	5.5	33.0	4.6	6.2

*Consol's profits refer to operating incomes after related income taxes but before extraordinary items and corporate credits and charges, such as interest and headquarters expenses. Contributions to net income from majority-owned subsidiaries are Conoco's equity in their net incomes.

**Island Creek's profits refer to income before gains from emergency fleet operations, interest income, interest and depreciation, income tax, extraordinary expenses, and unallocated corporate costs.

Source: Adopted from the Annual Reports of the two companies.

coal. As mentioned earlier, coal will at best contribute 3 percent of Exxon's profits in 1985. Exxon's interst in coal is in its potential substitutability for oil and gas. One should, therefore, expect to find in Carter Oil encouragement for innovative ideas on coal usage, despite the associated risks.

Summarizing the discussion in the previous pages, MATCAP of the four companies is distinguished in Table 8−6. While it is difficult to compress the classifications used in the table into one single measure of MATCAP, clearly Carter Oil has the richest MATCAP and NACCO the leanest. Island Creek and Consol have a moderate MATCAP. Table 2−6 pointed to how the richness of MATCAP is related to the state of adaptation that can be aspired for by a firm. In the earlier section, NACCO was shown to be in an unstable state of adaptation, Carter Oil was said to be in a neutral state of adaptation, and Island Creek and Consol in a stable state. The relative ranking of the MATCAP of the four companies matches the hierarchichal ranking of their states of adaptation.

Table 8−6. Distinguishing the MATCAP of the Four Firms

	Coal reserves		Financial resources	
Firms	Relative abundance	Flexibility in usage	Relative abundance	Latitude for experimentation
NACCO	Rich	Low	Modest	Low
Island Creek	Rich	Moderate	Rich	Moderate
Consol	Very rich	High	Rich	Moderate
Carter Oil	Very rich	High	Very rich	High

ORGCAP

ORGCAP is a measure of a firm's information-processing ability, determined by its level of differentiation and integration.

Differentiation was defined in Chapter 2 as the richness of the organization's communication links with the external environment. The more functional departments an organization supports, the more it opens itself to a variety of professional viewpoints. Though clearly not a precise measure, the variety of functions supported by an organization does present a crude measure of its differentiation. Table 8−7 contrasts the functional variety, both at the corporate and divisional levels in the four organizations. Table 8−8 provides a summary.

Carter Oil has the highest functional specialization among the four coal companies at both the corporate and divisional levels. NACCO has the lowest functional specialization at its corporate office. The most striking dis-

Table 8–7. A Comparison of the Functional Specialization of the Four Organizations in 1977

Functions	NACCO	Island Creek	Consol	Carter Oil
CORPORATE FUNCTIONS		Functional Heads		
Controller & Treasurer	VP & Treasurer	VP (Finance)	Exec. VP (Corporate Affairs)	Controller and Treasurer
Legal	Legal Counsel	Gen. Counsel	VP & Chief Counsel	*
Marketing	VP (Sales)	President (Island Creek Sales Company)	Exec. V.P. (Sales)	Marketing Manager
Purchasing	VP (Admin.)	General Manager (Purchases)	VP (Purchasing)	*
Resource Management	VP (Exploration)	Corporate Manager (Exploration & Mineral Acquisition)	VP (Exploration)	Resource Manager
Engineering	VP (Engineering)	VP (Engineering)	Exec. VP (Engineering)	Mining Manager
Planning	—	VP (Planning & Projects)	VP (Planning & Economics)	Planning Manager
Industrial, Employee and Public Relations	—	Exec. VP (Admin.)	Exec. VP (IR, ER & PR)	Administrative Coordinator
Industrial Engineering	—	Manager (IE)	Asst. to President	Manager (Planning)
Public Affairs	—	—	—	Manager (Public Affairs)

Table 8-7. A Comparison of the Functional Specialization of the Four Organizations in 1977 (Cont.)

Functions	NACCO	Island Creek	Consol	Carter Oil
Synthetics	—	—	—	Synthetics Operations Manager
DIVISIONAL FUNCTIONS				
Controller	—	Yes**	Yes	Yes
Regulatory Affairs	—	—	—	Yes
Purchasing	Yes	Yes	Yes	Yes
Engineering	Yes	Yes	Yes	Yes
Planning	—	—	—	Only at Monterey
Industrial Relations	Yes	Yes	Yes	Yes
Human Resources Development (incl. training)	Yes	Yes	Yes	Yes
Safety	Yes	Yes	Yes	Yes
Industrial Engineering	—	Yes	—	—
Environmental Affairs	Only at Western division	—	Yes	Yes

*Services provided by Exxon.

**Yes indicate that the company's divisions are organized for such a function

Table 8–8. Functional Variety in the Four Firms

	NACCO	Island Creek	Consol	Carter Oil
Corporate				
a. Number of functional departments headed by senior executives, i.e., VP or above	5	5	9	—
b. Other functional departments	1	4	—	9
c. Functional Departments at corporate headquarters	6	9	9	11*
Division				
d. Functional departments at the division	6	7	7	9

*Includes two functions performed by Exxon on behalf of Carter Oil.

tinction at the divisional level is the fact that unlike the other three companies, NACCO does not have a controller's department at its divisions. All divisional accounting data in NACCO are fed to the corporate controller's office by field staff, reporting directly to the corporate office.

Integration was defined in Chapter 2 as the richness of the organization's internal communication links. Lawrence and Lorsch (1967) suggest a hierarchy of integrative mechanisms, as listed below:

    i. Paperwork systems: Coordination is through exchange of information available in reports or through memoranda.

    ii. Management hierarchy: Coordination is through the first position in the hierarchy at which the two functions come under the same boss.

    iii. Direct management contact: Coordination is through formal or informal meetings between managers.

    iv. Temporary cross-functional teams. The coordination is achieved through the creation of temporary teams assigned a common goal.

The list is arranged to reflect higher integration as one goes down the list. The system of coordination used in the four coal companies between four common pairs of functions is contrasted in Table 8–9.

Operations, marketing, and personnel management are basic functions in most companies. Resource management is an important function in a coal company. The richness of the communication links between the resource-management, marketing, and operations functions indicates the extent to which the resource-management group is involved with the strategic deci-

Table 8–9. A Contrast of Coordination in the Four Companies

System of coordination	Coordination between			
	Operations and marketing	Operations and personnel management	Operations and resource management	Marketing and resource management
Paperwork systems			Island Creek	
Management hierarchy	NACCO Consol	Island Creek Consol	NACCO Consol	NACCO Island Creek Consol
Direct management contact	Island Creek Carter Oil (steam coal)	NACCO* Carter Oil		Carter Oil (steam coal)
Temporary cross-functional teams	Carter Oil (synthetics only)		Carter Oil	Carter Oil (synthetics only)

*Operations and personnel are decentralized functions at NACCO, falling fully within the jurisdiction of the divisional presidents.

sions of a coal company. It would seem that reserve acquisition and development would closely reflect market needs and operating realities, where such links are rich.

The variety of functions and the quality of coordination in the four coal companies jointly determine their ORGCAP. Table 8−10 summarizes the discussion on these two factors. On a relative scale, Carter Oil clearly has the best ORGCAP and NACCO the least. The distinction shown in the table is further corroborated by an analysis of other subsystems in the four companies, along the mechanistic−organic continuum described in Table 2−3.

Table 8−10. Distinguishing the ORGCAP of the Four Firms

Firms	Functional specialization	Level of integration
NACCO	Low	Moderate
Island Creek	Moderate	Moderate
Consol	Moderate	Moderate
Carter Oil	High	High

An Analysis of Various Subsystems of the Four Companies

Four of the important subsystems mentioned in Table 2−3 are discussed below.

Environmental Scanning: Each of the coal companies except NACCO has a formal planning department entrusted with the task of environmental scanning. In NACCO the President, Senior Vice-President, Vice-President (Sales), and Vice-President and Treasurer form the policy-making core. Their environmental-scanning effort is informal and unsystematic. In contrast, Island Creek and Consol both have a small staff group that make economic forecasts as a prelude to the yearly cycle of formal planning. In Carter Oil, the corporate-planning department puts out a yearly document that outlines assumptions about the long-term business environment and also suggests strategic scenarios appropriate to those assumptions. This document is frequently updated since the company's planning system is flexible and only loosely tied to the budgeting system.

Formal Organization: Chapters 4 through 7 described the formal organization of the four coal companies in some depth. All four organizations have well-specified tasks, functions, and roles. However, the top management at Carter Oil has a unique organization. The structure is flatter than in the other companies. This is because the President and the two Senior Vice-Presidents of Carter Oil together form a management committee to which all the departmental and divisional heads report. The two Senior Vice-Presidents have no specific functional charge. However, they act as "contact managers" for a set of functions, with the functions assigned changing regularly by rotation. This makes the organization a lot more open to expert ideas sponsored by the middle-level functional heads.

Authority in the four organizations has by and large been based on position. However, as mentioned above, at Carter Oil there is relatively better recognition of authority based on expertise because of its flat top-management structure.

Planning and Control: The planning-and-control systems of the four coal companies have interesting differences.

In NACCO the President makes all strategic decisions. He and his policy-making team of Senior Vice-President, Vice-President (Sales), and Vice-President and Treasurer decide on the projects to pursue, select customers, and determine shipment levels and prices. The capital expenditure required for the project is also decided at that level. As long as they meet these specifications, NACCO's divisional presidents have total authority to select appropriate means for achieving the goals. Divisional autonomy in NACCO, therefore, has relevance only to implementation. Revisions in plans to make up for shortfalls in implementation are, however, a divisional responsibility.

While Island Creek's planning system is also top-centered, attempts are being made to slant the planning process to cover as many levels of management as possible. The divisional presidents are being encouraged to propose plans, through the finalization of plans is still exclusively a corporate prerogative.

The planning process has become formalized at Consol since 1974. In fact, only in the last couple of years has the process of long-term planning and budgeting been given importance, with the tremendous personal backing of Consol's past Chairman, Ralph Bailey. The planning process at Consol is similar to that of Island Creek. The one difference is in the monitoring of plans. Consol works through a system of monthly review of divisional reports as opposed to Island Creek's formal monthly meetings. Meetings are arranged only when necessary. Variances against budgets are also reviewed with greater latitude. Budgets are looked at more as planning tools rather than definitive control devices. Consol also has a tradition of a yearly audit of each of its operations. The audit is carried out by a team of executives drawn from both Consol and Conoco.

In the case of Carter Oil, the individual subsidiaries have more autonomy in the preparation of plans. The corporate-planning department sends to both the subsidiaries a document "outlining assumptions about the long-term business environment and the suggested strategic scenarios that match the projected environment." This document defines the direction that Carter Oil's management committee has charted for the company. Within these guidelines, the subsidiaries are free to propose any plan. The corporate management committee acts as a sounding board for these plans. It exercises more of a vetoing authority than a decision-making authority in the planning process. Once the plans are finalized, monthly performances are reviewed as in other companies. But divisional performance is not merely tied down to budgets. For example, in the case of Carter Mining the progress in community-relations efforts is as important to its management as the development status of its mines. The divisional performance reports seem tailor-made to accommodate these differences.

Performance Appraisal and Reward Systems: NACCO's reward system is based largely on adherence to project parameters outlined for the divisional presidents. Financial performance is a key indicator. No special incentives other than the normal rewards of salary raises and promotions are offered. In the case of Island Creek, additional monetary incentives are offered for exceeding various targets in the operating budget. In order to ensure that safety is not traded for performance, minimum safety standards are laid down without the achievement of which the incentives would be inoperative. Incentives are payable to all levels of supervision up to and including the level of divisional presidents. Consol has a fairly flexible performance-appraisal system. Budgets are used more for planning purposes than for control. It also has an incentive scheme, but only for its executives. Carter Oil's system seems to reward the effort expended besides the results obtained. At all levels of management, there are three types of assessment made of an employee: (1) performance on the current job, (2) potential for the next higher job, and (3) training needs to help the manager make the transition. There is a career plan for each supervisor, with an approximate timetable for promotions. The individual's career aspirations are also documented, and an employee is offered maximum latitude to seek the most meaningful job available within the Exxon organization.

Leadership Style: The leadership style at NACCO is clearly top-down, with the President making most of the key decisions and handing them down for implementation. In contrast, in Carter Oil, the President allows his subordinates to make decisions. However, the President reserves the right to veto any decision that seems contrary to corporate interest. The leadership styles at Island Creek and Consol fall somewhere in between. There is participation in decision-making to the extent that subordinates are invited to present their proposals, but decision-making power rests with the President.

Summary: It seems from the above discussion that NACCO has more of a mechanistic arrangement, and Carter Oil is closest to having an organic arrangement. Island Creek and Consol fall somewhere in between. Table 8–11 provides a summary. As discussed in Chapter 2, the organic arrangement has the best capability for coping with a complex environment. Organizational capacity, therefore, increases from left to right in Table 8–11.

ADAPTIVE ABILITY AND STATES OF ADAPTATION

In the previous pages, the wide spectrum of adaptations shown by the four coal companies in this study were described. NACCO was shown to be in an unstable state of adaptation, Island Creek and Consol in a stable state, and Carter Oil in a neutral state. The adaptation of the four companies is also shown in Figure 8–2.

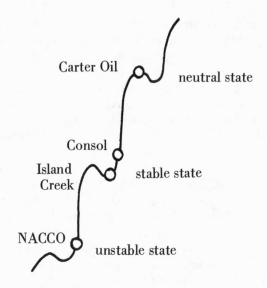

Figure 8–2. Adaptation of the Four Companies

The next question that was explored was whether the state of adaptation aspired to by a coal company was appropriate given the adaptive abilities of the four companies. MATCAP and ORGCAP were both considered. The

Table 8-11. Summarizing Various ORGCAP Attributes

	NACCO	Island Creek	Consol	Carter Oil
Environmental scanning	Unsystematic and informal	Systematic and formal	Systematic and formal	Flexible and formal
Formal organization	Position-based authority	Position-based authority	Position-based authority	Position- and some expert-based authority
Planning- and-control system	Top-down planning	Top-down (participative)	Top-down (participative)	Bottom-up
Performance appraisal	Strict financial measures of performance	Strict financial and non-financial measures of performance	Relatively loose measures of performance, financial and non-financial	Relatively loose measures of performance, financial and nonfinancial
	Based on financial performance	Based on operating budget	Not based only on performance against budget	Recognizes effort expended, in addition to output attained.
Reward system	Traditional promotions and raises	Added financial incentives	Traditional promotions and raises	Career development
Leadership style	President makes decision and announces them.	President presents challenge, invites suggestions, but makes decision, with a lot of staff support.	President presents challenge, invites decision, with a lot of	President permits subordinates to decide, but reserves right to veto their decisions.
Organizational arrangement	Boss-centered or mechanistic	Systems-centered or bureaucratic	Systems-centered or bureaucratic	Subordinate-centered or organic
ORGCAP	Lean	Moderate	Moderate	Rich

findings of this examination are summarized in Figure 8−3.

The four companies seem either in or very close to an adaptive fit, appropriate to their state of adaptation. NACCO is close to an Unstable Fit, Island Creek and Consol are practically in a Stable Fit, and Carter Oil is close to being in a Neutral Fit. Given that the adaptive ability of NACCO is rather poor, its defensive strategy—one of avoidance of the environment—seems most appropriate. Likewise, it is only because Carter Oil has superior endowments of ORGCAP and MATCAP that it can seek proactive strategies. Island Creek and Consol would need to increase their adaptive ability before seeking to be anything other than reactive in their strategies.

As was discussed in Chapter 2, companies can move from one level of adaptive fit to the next higher one. This would occur through two subprocesses: adaptive generalization and adaptive specialization. The former would help the company acquire better adaptive ability, and the latter would exploit such an ability to fit the company at a higher state of adaptation. These two adaptive processes will be discussed next.

ADAPTIVE PROCESSES

NACCO's Double Bind

The major challenge that NACCO faces is to move out of an unstable state of adaptation. It needs to improve both its material and organizational capacities to make such a transition. In the language of Chapter 2, it must focus on adaptive generalization. The company's financial resources were shown to be tight. Raising more equity or merging with a larger company might provide NACCO the much-needed financial resources. Additional finances will strengthen its bargaining power with utilities since it will then no longer be dependent on financial guarantees from utilities for the financing of its mines. Given the current preference of NACCO's majority shareholders, its management is unlikely to make any move that will dilute the ownership of the company. Without additional finances, the company also cannot acquire low-sulfur Eastern reserves and reduce its current overwhelming dependence on Western reserves for its expansion.

In response to this financial challenge, the company has instituted a very tight control system. All accounting information is fed directly to corporate headquarters, from where divisional financial reports are prepared. Top management keeps very close control on financial performance. A cost-conscious control system also finds favor with those utility companies that have signed cost-plus-management-fee contracts with NACCO. However, such a predominantly efficiency-oriented administrative focus has made NACCO's organizational capacity lean. The organization has no for-

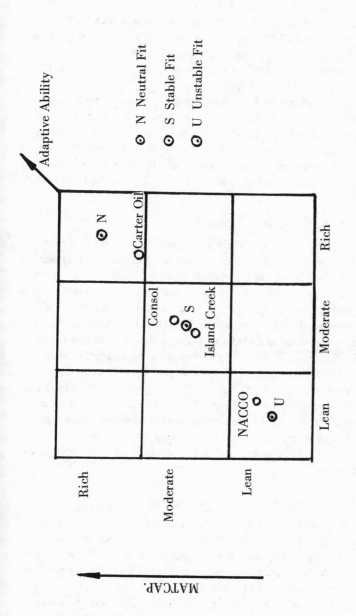

Figure 8–3. Adaptive Ability

Adaptive Ability

N Neutral Fit
S Stable Fit
U Unstable Fit

ORGCAP.

MATCAP.

Rich   Moderate   Lean

Lean   Moderate   Rich

N

Carter Oil

Consol
S
Island Creek

NACCO
U

mal market-surveillance capability. It is boss-centered, with strategic thinking concentrated at the very top. Finding new business niches is, therefore, the responsibility of NACCO's top management alone. Important strategic signals from the lower levels of management get ignored in such a setting. NACCO's Western coal reserves, for example, could have been of better grade if such signals had been recognized.

NACCO's top management is perhaps hesitant to merely expand organizational capacity unless it can back it up with increase in material capacity. Both are required for a transition from an unstable state of adaptation. The current administrative orientation in NACCO is to generate resources internally for improving material capacity, which in turn restricts the growth in organizational capacity. This double bind will keep pulling NACCO toward an Unstable Fit.

Defending the Status Quo at Island Creek

Island Creek is in a Stable Fit. There is no pressing need for it to move on to a Neutral Fit. Improvement in both material and organizational capacities would be required to make such a transition. Oxy, Island Creek's parent, obviously sees no need for Island Creek management to initiate such a change. Oxy has already established a separate subsidiary, the Sheridan Enterprises, to manage the development of Western coal. Likewise, the synthetics business would be attended to by Oxy's central research division. Thus, Island Creek is expected to cope only with the conventional steam-coal markets in the East. The adaptive process at Island Creek is, therefore, predominantly one of adaptive specialization. The management focus is predominantly efficiency-oriented, to keep it in its condition of fit. The market niches for Island Creek's coal have already been established. These are not expected to change dramatically, and even if they do, the company has the coal reserves and finances to respond to the changed circumstances at the appropriate time.

Consol and the Conoco Coal Development Company

Conoco's management realized that it could not manage a high-complexity business like synthetics within the same administrative arrangement used for managing the conventional coal businesses of its subsidiary, Consol. Conoco, therefore, created a new subsidiary called the Conoco Coal Development Company (CCDC) for managing the synthetics business.

In order to give it some clout in the organization, CCDC was placed under the direct charge of Conoco's Executive Vice-President for Corporate Planning. CCDC's charter included: (1) coordination of companywide R&D work on synthetics; (2) long-term planning for the synthetics business; and

(3) management of all synthetics projects, at least in their implementation stage.

CCDC could draw upon the expertise of both Consol and Conoco in the development of a synthetics project.

The creation of CCDC has certainly helped draw more top-management attention to the synthetics idea. However, the subunit seems to be performing more of a surveillance role, keeping management well informed on what is happening in the synthetics field. CCDC does not have within it the entrepreneurial ingredient to make it the nucleus of a synthetics division. In other words, CCDC represents Conoco's attempts at improving the technology component of its material capacity. It does not represent a full-fledged process of adaptive generalization.

The rest of the coal activities at Consol are managed through an arrangement that tends to be more mechanistic than organic. The company has an organizational structure that resembles a mechanistic arrangement. However, the planning-and-control systems, performance-appraisal system, and leadership style at Consol are not entirely mechanistic (see Table 8−11). The arrangement seems appropriate given that the conventional coal businesses need more of an efficiency orientation. Thus within Consol, like in Island Creek, there is no perceived pressing need for adaptive generalization.

The Process of Adaptation in Carter Oil

Carter Oil seems to have the material and organizational capacities required for a Neutral Fit, but it has not yet gotten to that level of fit. The company needs to reorient its administration from its current mode of adaptive generalization to one of adaptive specialization.

The managers of the two operating subsidiaries of Carter Oil have both attempted to incorporate Exxon's interdisciplinary approach to problem-solving in their administrative systems. Exxon has been able to transfer such a managerial style through careful recruitment of managers, and well-planned induction programs. The interdisciplinary approach cuts across organizational hierarchy and helps generate more innovative ideas. The impact is noticeable in a number of areas: (1) Carter Oil's vast coal reserves were acquired by a team which had no prior experience in coal; (2) its marketing effort was similarly organized without the benefit of any coal-industry experience; and (3) the synthetics project has gone through several iterations, the cross-functional team learning something new at each stage of iteration.

The company has learnt the coal business rather well in a short time, because of its administrative arrangement. However, its coal operations seem to be in the red. It is not surprising, therefore, to see the operating divisions of Carter Oil become increasingly efficiency conscious. The Monterey Coal

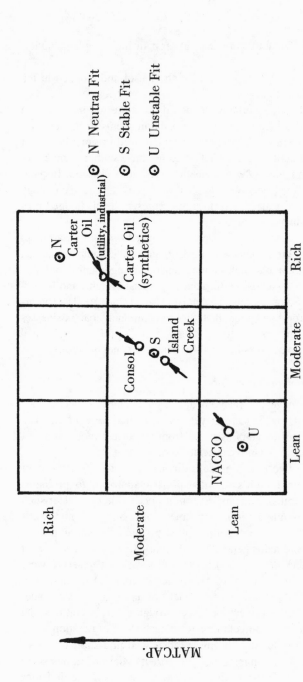

Figure 8—4. A Spectrum of Adaptations

Company has completed the design of its engineering systems, built with the experience brought in from a number of coal companies. These systems should help Monterey minimize delays, and guarantee the use of proper methods. Carter Mining has had a change in leadership reflective of the shift to a more efficiency-oriented administration.

The working groups, shaping the synthetics project, have brought it close to implementation. The administrative issue now facing Carter Oil's management is whether to help organize the synthetics business as a separate subsidiary under Exxon, U. S. A., or to organize it as an operating subsidiary of Carter Oil. There may be some advantages to retaining the synthetics activity within Carter Oil. Since coal would be its major raw material, the synthetics business would find synergies being associated with coal-mining subsidiaries. Whichever arrangement is chc,en, the synthetics business needs an organic administrative arrangement until such time as it matures. The synthetics technology is still open to a lot of development, and it is important for Carter Oil to remain open to these future developments and to maintain the momentum of its own research efforts.

SUMMARY

In this chapter the model of adaptation developed in Chapter 2 was used to illustrate the responses of four companies to the challenges posed by the coal industry.

The response of NACCO was shown to be defensive; that of Island Creek and Consol, reactive; and Carter Oil, proactive. These strategies were constrained to a large extent by the adaptive abilities of these companies. NACCO's management finds it difficult to improve the firm's material and organizational capacities and hence seems reconciled to an Unstable Fit. Island Creek and Consol seem content with the Stable Fit that they are in for the conventional coal businesses; their parents having created or assigned other organizational subunits to cope with the challenge of synthetics. As for Carter Oil, the company has adopted a highly subordinate-centered leadership style until recently. Such an administrative focus has helped the organization "learn" the coal business rather quickly. Its next administrative challenge is to improve its profitability. The company's operating subsidiaries are becoming more efficiency-oriented, and the synthetics business is likely to be formed into a separate organizational unit. Figure 8−4 sums up the discussion.

9. Broader Implications

The model of adaptation proposed in Chapter 2 provides a useful conceptual framework for understanding the strategic responses of firms in a single industry. As was illustrated in the previous chapter, the model not only helps distinguish the strategies of the four coal companies, but it also offers some explanations for these distinctions. The model proposes that there are three distinct strategies that a manager can choose for his firm, each of which will take the firm to a state of adaptation with its industry environment. Research done on other industries supports such a proposition (Miles & Snow, 1978). However, the model is by no means definitive and needs further development and validation.

The model describes three different states of adaptation arranged in a hierarchy, the transition from one state to the next higher one being constrained by the firm's adaptive ability and determined by the process of adaptation used in the firm (see Figure 9–1).

MANAGING ADAPTATION: THE GENERAL MANAGER'S JOB

The essence of general management is in fitting the firm more particularly for existence under the changing conditions of its environment. The process through which such an adaptation is achieved involves two important management processes: adaptive specialization and adaptive generalization. Adaptive specialization involves: (1) managing the choice of purpose for the firm, so as to exploit its adaptive ability, i.e., its material and human resources, optimally—the material resources of a firm include finances, technology, and key input materials; and (2) minimizing the misfit, if any, in the match between the chosen purpose and the firm's material and human

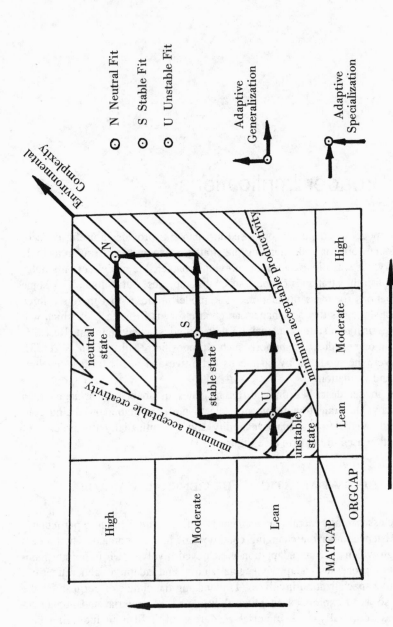

Figure 9–1. A Model of Adaptation

resources, by making appropriate improvements in either of the two resources or by revising the chosen purpose, or both.

In a state of fit, a firm generates a surplus called slack. Adaptive generalization requires the proper investment of slack. The process involves: (1)
investing in material resources and/or human resources of the firm, thus improving the adaptive ability of the firm; and (2) ensuring that in building
either resource the firm's efficiency and effectiveness are not lowered below
that required for survival.

Once the firm acquires a higher adaptive ability, adaptive specialization is
once again needed to improve the goodness of its adaptive fit. A general
manager can shape the evolution of the firm by his careful control over
adaptive generalization and adaptive specialization (see Figure 9−2).

The process of adaptive specialization is very similar to the process of
strategy formulation and implementation. If managed properly, both processes use the material and human resources of a firm optimally, by select-
ing a purpose that not only ensures the survival of a firm but also maximizes
returns to its stakeholders. This process has been discussed extensively in
the business-policy literature (e.g., Christensen, Andrews, & Bower, 1973).

As this study has demonstrated, adaptive specialization is, however, but
one aspect of strategic management. The other, adaptive generalization, is
scarcely addressed in policy literature. Ansoff (1979) voices a similar concern: "Practically all of literature has focused on strategies of action in the
external environment. Concepts of 'strategy of structure' now need to be
developed." The latter strategy addresses the question: "How do we config-
ure the resources of the firm for effective response to unanticipated sur-
prises?" (pp. 31, 44). In the pages that follow some useful concepts for
managing adaptation are explored.

MANAGING ADAPTATION: SOME USEFUL CONCEPTS

A general manager can help shape the strategy of his firm by skillfully
manipulating the administrative levers available to him, thus exploiting its
adaptive ability. Such a process has been referred to as "managing the decision premises" (Simon, 1945) or "managing the structural context"
(Bower, 1970). The same administrative levers if operated differently can
help the firm improve its adaptive ability. The important administrative levers available to a general manager are organizational structure, planning-
and-control systems, reward systems, resource-allocation systems, and
leadership style. Each of these will be discussed briefly to highlight how it
can be used in managing the process of adaptation.

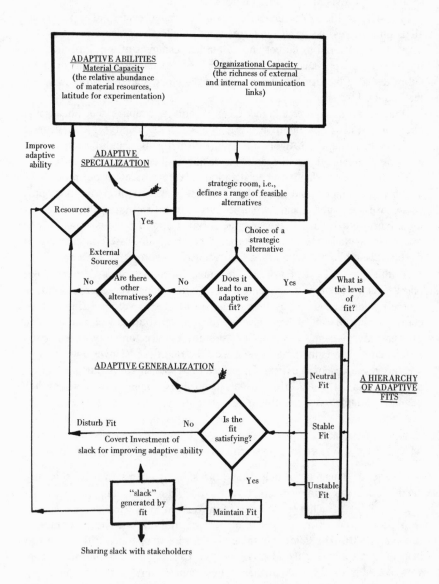

Figure 9-2. Managing Adaptation

Organizational Structure

It is possible to design two distinct organizational units: one for generating slack, with which the adaptive ability of a firm can be enhanced, and the other for investing slack so as to exploit the adaptive ability of the firm. In a divisionalized firm, for example, some divisions can be assigned products that characteristically generate large amounts of cash—far more than what these divisions can profitably reinvest. Such divisions typically operate in mature slow growth markets but enjoy high market shares. In contrast, other divisions can be assigned products that need a net investment of cash for exploiting their full profit potential. These products are typically associated with high growth markets in which the firm wants to build and hold a high market share. In the terminology of the Boston Consulting Group,[1] the first set of divisions may be called "cash cows" and the second "stars." The cash cows produce slack, which can be invested in improving the material and organizational capacities of stars. A star is the nucleus for a major new strategy. By carefully managing the portfolio of cash cows and stars, it is possible to ensure the continued growth in material and organizational capacities of a firm (see Figure 9–3).

The advantage of distinguishing divisions that generate slack from those that consume it is that a consistent set of administrative arrangements can be prescribed for each. A cash cow division is typically managed for productivity, and a star division is managed for creativity. As was discussed in Chapter 2, an organic arrangement is best suited to support creativity and a mechanistic arrangement more appropriate for improving productivity.

If planned carefully a portfolio approach to adaptation can be very effective. However, it must be remembered that whereas the overall firm is assured of growth and survival, it is through the conscious sacrifice of cash cows that stars may be fed. The adaptive ability of cash cows is in fact intentionally curtailed or even diminished. The real administrative challenge in this mode of adaptation is to ensure a delicate balance between creativity and productivity, by managing the portfolio of stars and cash cows, respectively. Such a balance between creativity and productivity can also be achieved within the same organizational unit, by managing other administrative systems suitably.

Planning-and-Control Systems

A formal planning system can be designed either for more "practicality" or for more "creativity" by fine-tuning the linkage between the planning and budgeting subsystems (Shank, Niblock, & Sandalls, Jr., 1973). Plans and budgets are linked in three distinct ways: (1) Content linkage relates to the correspondence between the data presented in the plan document and that

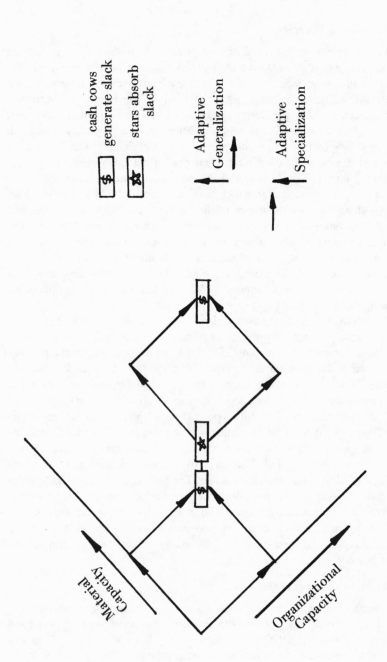

Figure 9-3. A Portfolio Concept of Adaptation

presented in the budget; (2) organizational linkage focuses on the relationship between the units responsible for planning and budgeting; and (3) timing linkage is concerned with the sequencing of the annual planning and budgeting cycles.

The tighter the linkages, the more productivity-oriented the planning system becomes. Conversely, the looser the linkages, the more creativity-supportive the planning system is. Table 9−1 provides a brief summary of the administrative devices available to a manager to make the linkages either tight or loose.

Table 9−1. **Managing the Linkages between Planning and Budgeting**

Type of linkage	Administrative arrangement	Nature of linkage
1. Content	Level of financial details in the plan.	Tight, if comparable to that in budget.
	Level of rounding in the plan.	Tight, if same as that of the budget.
	Conformity between plan and budget numbers for those years which are common to both documents.	Tight, if high conformity.
	Structure of the content.	Tight, if structured by organizational units.
2. Organizational	Relationship between the organizational units responsible for planning and budgeting processes.	Tightest, if the two functions are combined in one department; and loosest if they report to different top-level executives.
3. Timing	Sequencing of the planning and budgeting cycles.	Tight, if budgeting cycle completed first, with minimal elapsed time.
	Time horizon for planning.	Tight, if horizon is short.

Source: Shank, Niblock, & Sandalls, Jr., 1973.

By manipulating the linkages between the planning and budgeting systems, the general manager can either ensure a heavier emphasis on short term efficiency or strongly encourage the shaping of strategies useful for the long run. A constant emphasis on one can compromise the other. An alternating emphasis on both productivity and creativity is required for adaptation.

Reward Systems

It is difficult to influence the process of adaptation through the reward system per se. However, in concert with other administrative systems, a reward system can help strike a healthly balance between a managerial orientation that only exploits the material and human resources of a firm for current performance and an orientation that also builds resources for future use. Most reward systems encourage only the former orientation. Some try to inculcate a long-term orientation through a stock-option plan.

An alternate design that seems effective is to clearly identify two types of managerial performances: (1) efficient implementation of short-term goals, and (2) creative development of long-term opportunities. Texas Instruments (TI), for example, uses such a design for performance measurement (see Figure 9–4). The two performances are distinguished and both are factored in for deciding rewards. The key to ensure the long-term survival of an organization is to distinguish, measure, and reward efforts of executives that shape future strategies for the firm.

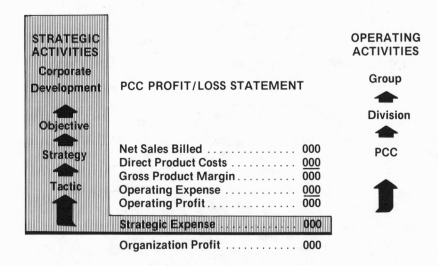

Source: "Texas Instruments Incorporated: Management Systems." ICCH 9–172–054

Figure 9–4. A Reporting System on Dual Measures of Performance

Resource-Allocation Systems

The process of adaptation is really one of managing resources. The resource-allocation system performs the important role of allocating material resources of the firm. When a firm reaches a condition of fit, it starts earning steady profits. The financial well-being that results has to be shared in part with the various stakeholders. Dividends may be raised, employee and managerial compensation improved, prices of products dropped, suppliers offered better terms, etc. (see Table 9–2). The cooperation of all stakeholders is essential for the survival of an organization (Barnard, 1938). However, after having ensured the continued contribution of all stakeholders, the general manager must invest the surplus or slack (Cyert & March, 1963) so as to improve the adaptive ability of the firm. This investment again may be made overtly or covertly. The profit-and-loss statements of companies hide a number of activities that refer to future development (Vancil, 1972). A new organizational unit may have been created to generate future ideas. This certainly increases the employee and managerial compensation in a reporting period without bringing in matching revenues. In fact, building organizational capacity involves a good deal of such expenditures. The statement may also hide efforts to improve technological capacity. A number of R&D projects may be expensed away in a single year, though the ensuing benefits may come much later. It is very important to be cognizant of these "invest-

Table 9–2. Sharing with Stakeholders

Expected revenue	R − ΔR shared with customers through lower prices
Expected costs	
Material	M + ΔM shared with suppliers through better terms
Employee and managerial compensation	C + ΔC shared with employees and managers through higher compensation
Other costs and taxes	0
	‾‾‾‾‾
Profits after tax	P − ΔP
Dividends	D + ΔD shared with stockholders through higher dividend
	‾‾‾‾‾
Retained earnings	E − ΔE reduction in resources for further investment

ments.'' Being revenue expenditures they have first charge on the financial resources of a firm, and it is only the residue left after such expenditures that is available for capital expenditures. Managing these covert investments is as important as managing the more overt capital expenditures.

One effective capital expenditure system is the Objectives, Strategies, and Tactics system (OST) used by Texas Instruments. The company instituted the system to avoid diversion of resources toward short-term crises, and to help focus on ''larger opportunities to solve problems of the right scale for the whole corporation.''[2] The OST is a resource-allocation system overlayed on the organization structure in a matrix fashion, thereby casting most TI managers in two modes: the operating mode and the strategic mode (see Jelinek, 1979, for details of the system). The essential features of the system are:

1. An operating manager who has an idea which can contribute to a new tactic, strategy, or objective somewhere in the TI organization can seek funding for that idea in the OST system. The idea may or may not be related to his immediate operating environment.

2. In his strategic mode, that manager can choose to spend his OST funds anywhere in TI (not just his department or group) to get the skills and resources which he needs.

3. The OST system is supported by a reporting system that separates operating performance from progress toward strategic goals (see Figure 9–4). This ensures that both short-term and long-term activities get the proper attention of managers.

4. The system is also supported by other management systems which encourage performance in both the operating and strategic modes.

The OST system per se may be tailor-made to TI's needs. However, the essential concepts of the system are transferable in other contexts.

Leadership Style

There is no single leadership style that is best suited to managing adaptation. In fact, the required leadership style would depend on the firm's state of adaptation, and the nature of the industry environment. Moreover, leadership style can often be changed only with a change in the leader. Therefore, unlike other administrative levers discussed above, change in leadership style is not an option often available in managing adaptation. However, it is useful to recognize that some leaders are good entrepreneurs, while others are good consolidators. The former encourage creativity and help in the building of resources—in short, they are supportive of adaptive generalization. The latter are efficiency conscious and more suited to exploiting resources—in short, they are more adept at adaptive specialization. The kind of leader a firm has can, therefore, significantly influence its process of adaptation.

Successful firms have had, either by conscious design or accident, a healthy balance of both types of leadership. In General Motors, for example, William Durant created the resources for Alfred Sloan to exploit (Sloan, 1972). Sloan identifies three simultaneous patterns in the way Durant set up General Motors: (1) variety in cars for a variety of tastes and economic levels; (2) diversification, calculated to cover the many possibilities in the engineering future of the automobile, in search of a high-average result instead of an all-or-none proposition; and (3) integration through the manufacture of the parts and accessories that make up the anatomy of the motorcar. Though the financial performance of General Motors under Durant's leadership was dismal, he had provided the resources that Sloan could build on. Sloan, on the other hand, provided the administrative genius required to exploit the vast potential of General Motors. His controlled decentralization of the company put it firmly on the road to growth and profitability. Distinct as the Durant and Sloan styles of management were, both were crucial to the adaptation of General Motors.

Summary

Managing adaptation requires the skillful manipulation of the various administrative levers described above. There seem to be two broad administrative choices that are open:

The first is to create two separate types of organizational units, one aimed at adaptive specialization and the other at adaptive generalization. The former type of unit is designed to operate in the more mature segments of the industry, whereas the latter is designed to operate in the growth segments of the industry. The former helps generate slack for the firm, while the latter helps the firm shape new strategies. Such an administrative arrangement has been popular among some coal companies. The mature utility segment of the business is managed by organizational units that are oriented toward productivity. In contrast, the emerging synthetics business is designed to be handled by a separate organizational unit, as for example the Conoco Coal Development Company in the case of Consol. Once such an organizational cleavage is made, it is easy to associate a consistent arrangement of administrative systems with each unit. A mechanistic arrangement may be associated with the "cash cow" type of organizational unit, and an organic arrangement with the "star" type organizational unit. The process of adaptation requires the juggling of the portfolio of cash cows and stars (see Table 9−3).

Table 9–3. Balancing the Portfolio

	Source of resources	Use of resource
Internal		
Cash cows	Generates financial surplus	No net usage
Stars	Generates a surplus of *good ideas* for new products, processes, or markets	Uses resources both covertly and overtly for building: organizational capacity, technological expertise, and physical facilities
External	Transfer/external sourcing of finances Transfer/external recruitment of skilled personnel Transfer/external sourcing of technology	—
	Sources =	Uses

Carter Oil, for example, used "external" financial, personnel, and technology sources to build its coal-mining subsidiaries and the synthetics work force. The coal-mining subsidiaries are now being given more of a mechanistic orientation, so that they can start providing surpluses to build the synthetics business. A company with strong external resources, obviously, would have an easier job of managing its business portfolio than a company like NACCO, which has no significant external sources. If in such a company the internal sources are also poor, the question of considering new business segments does not arise. NACCO, for example, cannot afford to venture into the synthetics business.

The second broad administrative choice is to alternate emphasis on productivity and creativity. If an industry cannot be segmented meaningfully or if a firm chooses not to have multiple organizational units functioning within an industry, adaptation can be managed by manipulating the administrative systems of the firm to provide such an alternating emphasis (see Table 9–4). The dilemma of how much productivity and creativity an organization should have is a serious one. Companies have a natural tendency to follow the productivity route (Abernathy, 1978). A manager must consciously counterbalance such a tendency with an occasional creativity orientation, if he wants his firm to remain adapted with its environment.

Table 9–4. Manipulating the Administrative Levers

Administrative system	Productivity orientation	Creativity orientation
Planning system	Tight linkages with the budgeting system.	Loose linkages with the budgeting system.
Reward system	Mostly short-term performance.	Short- and long-term performance.
Resource allocation	Minimize covert investments in organizational capacity and technology.	Manage covert investments.
	Conventional capital-expenditure system.	A system of capital expenditure like the OST.
Leadership style	Exploit ideas.	Generate ideas.

The process of building a firm's resources is a consciously managed process, characterized by three key activities: (1) identifying and managing covert investments of a firm's slack in organizational and technological capacities; (2) managing the capital expenditure system of the firm in a way that encourages proposals which explore and define future strategies, in addition to proposals that implement chosen strategies; and (3) aligning the administrative systems to provide a healthy blend of creativity and productivity orientations to the firm.

Crucial as adaptive generalization is to the long term survival of the firm, it is a process that receives little encouragement or reward. Adaptive generalization is aimed at making the firm more effective, and in so doing efficiency may sometimes have to be compromised. The financial performance of the firm may consequently not be very strong in the short run. Unfortunately, evaluation of managerial performance does not often distinguish between being misfitted with a purpose and being misfitted by default. A firm cannot move to a higher level of adaptive fit without disturbing its old fit and progressing in the interim through several regions of misfits (see Figure 9–1). Such a process of transition should be distinguished from a firm that has fallen from its market niche and is rapidly headed for disaster. The first firm is building its adaptive ability, while the second is rapidly losing its adaptive ability. A general manager must be rewarded for building a firm's adaptive ability, just as he is for exploiting its adaptive ability. Both are required for adaptation.

MANAGING COAL

This study has implications for the management of coal at two levels: (1) managing a coal company, and (2) public policy on coal.

Implications for Coal-Company Managers

This study provides a comprehensive conceptual scheme for understanding the various forces that shape the strategy of a coal company. It is clearly addressed to managers of large coal companies, those that are or aspire to be among the top twenty[3]producers of coal for energy markets. Small coal companies were not considered for the study, as they are projected to assume a very minor role in the industry.[4]

Since the four coal companies were carefully chosen to be representative of the industry, the case studies and their analysis should provide insights to managers on how coal can be managed. It seems that the adaptive abilities required to exploit all the new opportunities for coal can be found only in some coal companies. In many cases, either the lack of proper coal reserves or the unwillingness to experiment when financial risk is high, i.e., inadequate material capacity, seems to be the immediate constraint. Whereas large oil companies operating in the coal industry may not find it difficult to improve their material capacities, organizational capacities must be concurrently improved in these companies if the new opportunities are to be successfully exploited. A coal-company manager must make a careful audit of his firm's adaptive ability and choose either adaptive specialization or adaptive generalization as is relevant to the firm's context. Figure 9-2 provides a flow chart useful for this purpose.

Administering a coal company is becoming very challenging because of the broad spectrum of product–market complexities that seem to be emerging in the industry. Better administrative skills are also required for a more proactive response to the human-resource-management problem and for coping with new regulations. Not only must labor-management practices be improved in the industry, but better control must also be exercised on transportation of coal, if reliability of coal supply is to be assured. In short, management practices in the coal industry must be upgraded in a number of areas if coal is to be an important source of energy.

Implications for Public Policy

Coal has drawn much recent attention from energy planners in the government. Expanded use of coal is foreseen, both in its conventional form as a solid fuel as well as in its converted form as a synthetic gas or liquid. Governmental intervention is proposed to help double the demand for coal. Governmental intervention, however, often tends to be fragmented, lacking a comprehensive framework for action (Abernathy & Chakravarthy, 1979). In the case of coal, there already is accumulated evidence of such disjointed legislation. The scrubber controversy, the proposed market protection for coal, and synthetics are three examples.

The Clean Air Act of 1970 proposed minimum air-quality standards for utilities, giving them the choice of either burning low-sulfur coal (predominantly found in the West) or installing stack-gas scrubbers to clean up the flue gases discharged by the utility's coal-fired power plants. Just when utilities were ready to make that trade-off, the Clean Air Act was amended in 1977, barring the Envionmental Protection Agency from discriminating against high-sulfur Eastern coal in favor of low-sulfur Western coal. The Agency further proposed in September 1978 that all new coal-fired power plants be equipped with scrubbers. The proposal clearly neutralized the low-sulfur advantage of Western coal. The pollution issue has since been the cause of a major political battle among coal-state senators.[5] The inability of the federal government to clearly resolve conflicting priorities in energy and environmental protection has also been an aggravating factor. The net result has been to force utilities into deferring their capital-investment decisions. Thus a primary market for coal has been thrown into disarray.

Market protection for coal should normally have been welcomed by coal companies. And yet, the National Coal Association has criticized the government for its attempts to create additional markets for coal through legislation, prohibiting the burning of oil and gas in new boilers and forcibly converting other such existing facilities as have capabilities to burn coal.[6] The NCA's stand is partly to show support for coal's best customers—the utility companies. Beyond that, there is a real fear among some coal-company managers that by accepting such governmental protection the coal industry makes itself vulnerable to eventual price regulation.

In the case of synthetics, the major thrust of governmental support has been to provide funding for industry-sponsored R&D projects. If the pattern represents an intent to help early commercialization of coal-liquefaction and -gasification technologies, industry experts would argue for more market incentives in addition to support for developmental research. Consol's Eric Reichl suggests that the government could mandate, for example, the mixing of a certain percentage of nonpetroleum-based fuels with gasoline. If the amount of synthetics mixed is small, the cost of the mixture would not hurt customers badly. Besides, such a mandate would make cost of producing synthetics a competitive dimension. This market pressure will help early commercialization and support several innovative processing technologies.

Besides the fragmented approach to coal in federal energy plans, there is a real danger in the apparent monolithic view of the industry that prevails among public-policy makers.

This study has clearly shown that the coal industry accommodates a wide spectrum of adaptations. The adaptive posture of a coal company determines the product–market complexity that it can handle. Clearly, many coal companies are limited by their adaptive abilities and adaptive processes from participating in all the markets that are available to coal. These firm-centered limitations, when aggregated, shape the industry's response to the coal challenge; perhaps more so than the governmental carrot-and-stick. Thus, for example, a coal company in an unstable state of adaptation cannot be interested in industrial markets for coal or the synthetics business. A planning matrix such as in Figure 9–5 can be prepared for the coal industry. The goals for each market segment should be compared with the likely production for that segment. Either more realistic goals should be established for coal through such an exercise, or alternatively appropriate incentives should

Type of Coal Co.	Nature of Adaptation		MARKET SEGMENTS			Expected Contribution by Industry Segment
	MATCAP & ORGCAP	State	Utility	Industrial	synthetics	
Independent	Lean	unstable	P_{uu}	—	—	P_{uu}
Acquisitive Diversifier (incl. few oil cos.)	Moderate	stable	P_{su}	P_{si}	—	$P_{su} + P_{si}$
De novo entrant (large oil cos.)	Rich	neutral	P_{nu}	P_{ni}	P_{ns}	$P_{nu} + P_{ni} + P_{ns}$
Expected contribution by market segment			$P_{uu} + P_{su} + P_{nu}$	$P_{si} + P_{ni}$	P_{ns}	P PLANNING GAP G
NATIONAL GOAL			G_u	G_i	G_s	

Figure 9–5. The Planning Matrix

be targeted at select coal companies. It is in the latter context that the proposed Horizontal Divestiture bill needs review.

The Horizontal Divestiture bill is aimed at large petroleum companies that have entered the coal industry. Proponents of the bill argue that: (1) Oil/natural gas and coal are substitutes in the production of electricity. It could be in the interest of the oil companies to withhold their coal from utilities in order to increase the value of their oil holdings, including increasing the value of oil production and reserves; (2) Oil/natural gas and coal are part of a larger energy market. The acquisition of coal by companies who are also in the petroleum business raises the level of concentration and lowers the level of competition in this energy market. It could be possible, therefore, for oil companies to increase their market power by acquiring coal companies.

Others point out that the competition in the coal industry will not be adversely affected by the entry of large petroleum companies.[8] In fact, their entry can provide the vast financial, technical, and managerial resources required to establish the synthetics business. Most petroleum companies have the capability of reaching a neutral state of adaptation (Figure 9–5), and, therefore, can actively participate in all three market segments for coal. The Horizontal Divestiture bill, if passed, would seriously compromise the national goal for coal; the voids in supply left by the departure of oil companies may not all be filled up by other coal companies. Industrial markets and synthetics would certainly suffer. Not many coal companies have the material and organizational resources to compete in these segments.

Federal policy on coal needs a thorough review to make it consistent and comprehensive. This study demonstrates the need to factor in the varying adaptive abilities of coal companies in any such policy revision.

Appendix: Coal and Coal Mining

The purpose of this appendix is to provide the reader with a short introduction to coal and the technology of coal mining.

WHAT IS COAL?

Coal was formed from organic matter subjected to millions of years of heat and to the pressure of succeeding layers of sedimentary deposits. These processes progressively reduced the content of volatile matter and moisture and increased the percentage of fixed carbon in coal. This carbon, when burnt in air, generates heat.

The depth of burial and the time of compaction of the coal generally determine its ranking. There are essentially four ranks commonly used for coal:

Lignite coal is the youngest on the coal scale. Brown to black in color, it shrinks and crumbles when exposed to air. It has a low energy value[1] compared to older coals and is noncoking.[2]

Subbituminous coal is black in color with a higher heating value than lignite coal, but it is subject to spontaneous combustion. It is also noncoking.

Bituminous coal or soft coal is considered the most important solid fuel for both domestic use and industrial purposes. Black in color, it weathers slowly or not at all. Certain varieties also have good coking qualities.

Anthracite coal or hard coal is the oldest in geological history. With the highest percentage of carbon, it burns easily and smokelessly and is, therefore, most valuable for heating purposes. It is, however, also noncoking.

Lignite has the least fixed carbon, approximately 30 percent. Volatile matter and moisture constitute the rest of the volume. In contrast, the highest-ranking meta-anthracite has close to 90 percent fixed carbon.[3]

Coal is further classified by grade, which is a way of expressing the quality of the coal. Although the quality of the extracted coal is affected by its content of sulfur, ash, and other constituents, steam-coal resources are categorized primarily in terms of their sulfur content. Sulfur is an undesirable element in coal. It lowers the quality of coal used for metallurgical purposes. It also leads to the formation of corrosive and toxic oxides of sulfur when sulfurous coal is burnt in power plants. The oxides of sulfur condense to corrode boiler tubes, and the uncondensed oxides enter the atmosphere causing air pollution.

U.S. COAL

The United States is estimated to have between one-fifth and one-third of the world's coal resources.[4] Some 400 billion tons of these resources have been carefully measured and assessed as being exploitable under local economic conditions and available technology. Geologists estimate that the total U.S. resources of coal are in the region of 3.2 trillion tons.[5] Even if liberal mining allowances are given, the coal reserves of the United States are estimated to be far larger than the known oil deposits in the Middle East. Figure A–1 shows the U.S. coal reserves by regions. The regions are broadly divided by the 100° 0' longitudinal meridian, or more commonly the Mississippi River. Coal lying on the west of the divider is called Western coal and on the east of the divider Eastern coal. Western coal is predominantly better-grade, i.e., it has a sulfur content of 1 percent or less, but is also lower-rank, i.e., it has a lower energy value. However, given the size of the Western reserves, 63 percent of the country's potential coal energy (on the basis of energy equivalent in bituminous coal) is located in the West.[6]

OPERATION OF A COAL MINE

The methods used to extract coal depend on the conditions prevailing at the site of the seam. Some of the factors which affect the methods used are: the depth of the coalbed, the size (height) and flow of the coal seam, the structural conditions of the earth between the seam and the surface, and the general surface terrain.

There are essentially three types of coal mines: undergound mines, auger mines, and strip or surface mines. The depth of the coalbed is the principal determinant in the choice of a mining method. Since 1945, the coal output from surface mines in the United States has nearly doubled (see Figure A–2). In comparison to underground mines, formerly the predominant source of coal, surface mines are three times as productive and involve fewer potential hazards for the miners.

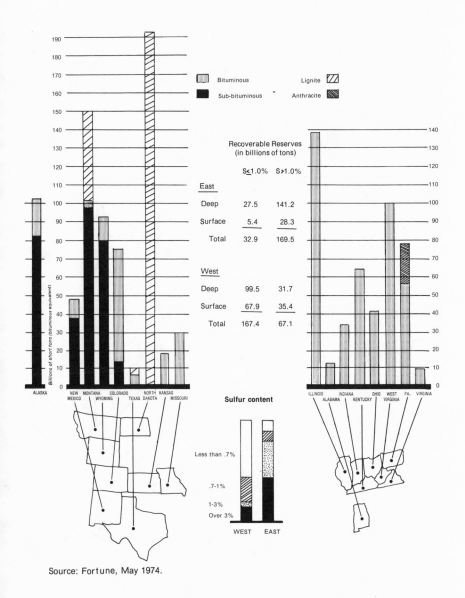

Recoverable Reserves
(in billions of tons)

	S≤1.0%	S>1.0%
East		
Deep	27.5	141.2
Surface	5.4	28.3
Total	32.9	169.5
West		
Deep	99.5	31.7
Surface	67.9	35.4
Total	167.4	67.1

Bituminous

Sub-bituminous

Lignite

Anthracite

Billions of short tons (bituminous equivalent)

ALASKA

NEW MEXICO · MONTANA WYOMING · COLORADO TEXAS · NORTH DAKOTA · KANSAS MISSOURI

ILLINOIS ALABAMA · INDIANA KENTUCKY · OHIO · WEST VIRGINIA · PA. VIRGINIA

Sulfur content

Less than .7%

.7-1%

1-3%

Over 3%

WEST   EAST

Source: Fortune, May 1974.

Figure A–1. East and West, There's Fuel for Centuries

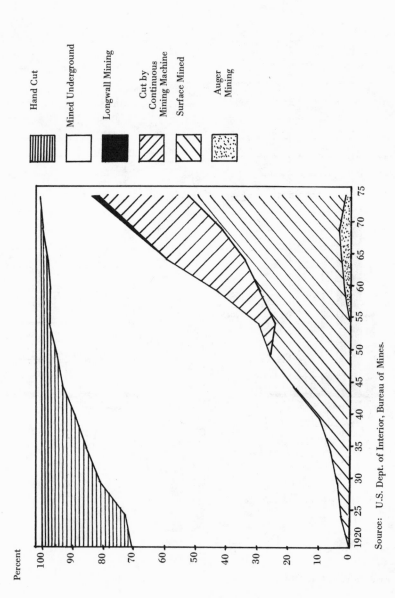

Source: U.S. Dept. of Interior, Bureau of Mines.

Figure A–2. Trends in Bituminous-Coal Mining in Underground and Surface Mines, 1920–1973

Underground Mining

Planning and development of today's sophisticated underground mining systems is complex. Mines are usually planned in terms of rolling five-year engineering plans which outline the schedule of extraction and plot routes of haulage, drainage, ventilation, supply, and personnel movement. The care necessary in planning and constructing the initial air, haulage, and travel routes is underscored by the mines' expected life of up to sixty years.

There are three types of underground mines (see Figure A−3) depending on the depth of the coalbed. If the coal can be reached horizontally from the side of the hill, the mine is called a drift mine. If, however, the coal must be approached from a perceptible angle, the mine is called a slope mine. When the coal seam is located deep beneath the earth's surface, requiring the use of shafts, the mine is referred to as a deep-shaft mine.

There are basically two distinct techniques used in underground mining: the room-and-pillar method and the longwall method.

Room-and-Pillar Mining: In this technique only part of the coal is extracted, with pillars of coal being left to support the roof and prevent cave-ins. The amount of coal recovered of the total coal found in the seam averages about 50 percent. Economic pressures have induced the industry to seek methods to increase the recovery factor for this technique. One such method is to systematically rob the pillars after an area's initial working. This method allows the roof to collapse and has increased recovery to as high as 80−85 percent.

The specific mining plan will vary with the local conditions encountered, but the general procedure is to drive a main entry along the seam from one or both sides. Side entries are then cut, forming a crosshatch of tunnels at right angles. As coal is removed, these side entries eventually become large rooms. The entries are spaced far enough apart to leave a pillar of coal between rooms of sufficient size to adequately support the roof. The size of the rooms and pillars depends primarily on the character of the coal and the amount of roof pressure.

Ventilation is provided by air forced down the main entry, distributed through the various rooms, and exhausted through an auxiliary entry. It is critical that air be provided at all times to each working face of the mine to sweep away the highly explosive methane gas released by the coal.

The *conventional method* of mining by the room-and-pillar technique consists of the following steps. First, a machine is brought up to the working face—like a vertical wall at the end of a corridor—and a deep slot is cut in the coal to help the wall shatter when blasted. A mobile drill is then moved into position to bore holes in the coal face for sparkproof explosives or cyl-

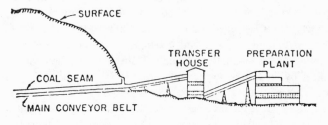

DRIFT MINE

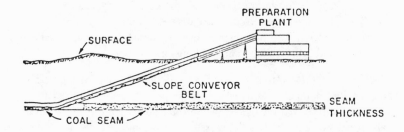

SLOPE MINE

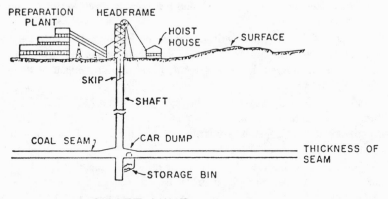

SHAFT MINE

Source: S. M. Cassidy, Ed., Elements of Practical Coal Mining.

Figure A−3. Principal Types of Underground Mines

inders of compressed air. The machines are removed and then everyone takes cover while the face is detonated. A loading machine is brought in and sweeps the coal onto a conveyor which transports it to the shuttle cars. Once the coal is removed, a roof bolter is moved into position to secure the roof structure.

The *continuous miner*, introduced in the early 1950s, mechanized the steps in conventional mining. In one operation it tears coal from the seam with revolving steel teeth and loads it for transport to the mine opening.

Longwall Mining: This technique was borrowed from Europe and introduced in the United States in 1966. It removes the coal from a large face ranging in length from 300 to 650 feet by a shearing machine which planes back and forth across the face allowing the roof to gently cave in behind it. The principal advantage of this method is its ability to recover 85 percent of the coal in a seam in one operation. Whereas continuous miners yield 200 to 400 tons per crew shift, the longwall technique can average 700 tons per crew shift. In ideal seams with thicknesses of about four feet, yields of 2,000 tons per shift have been achieved. Cost savings from longwalling result not only from higher productivity levels but also from major reductions in certain auxiliary costs. Most significant of these are the savings achieved by the elimination of roof bolting which ordinarily absorbs 15−20 percent of the manpower in a mine. Other savings are derived from easier supervision, simpler ventilation, and simplified service operations. In addition, the system is the only one suitable when weak roof conditions exist.

Strip Mining

At least one-fifth of the nation's best coal deposits are well suited for strip mining (also called surface mining), for they lie within one hundred feet of the surface. The use of strip mining in the United States has been accelerating due to rapid cost increases in underground mining. Approximately half of the industry's coal output in 1974 was produced by surface mining. Surface mines can be opened faster than underground mines, generally have fewer labor difficulties, and are safer to operate. In addition, 80−90 percent of the coal can be recovered, and the average production rates per man-day average three times those achieved in underground mines. In the West where thick coal seams exist, production costs per ton are so low that the coal can be economically competitive despite its reduced heat value and high reclamation and transportation costs.

In its simpler form, strip mining consists of the following steps: (1) removing and placing aside the earth and rock above the seam (commonly referred to as the overburden); (2) breaking up the exposed coal and hauling it from the mine by truck; and (3) replacing the overburden, grading it to its original contour, and replanting the vegetation. The equipment used in strip mining ranges in size from ordinary bulldozers and front end loaders to immense power shovels and draglines. The power shovels and draglines used to remove the overburden constitute the largest mobile machines in the world and must be erected on-site.

Auger Mining

Auger mining is a method that relies on the use of large drills up to sixty inches in diameter to recover coal that has too much overburden to strip mine economically. Because the nature of the earth covering seams of coal varies considerably, it is often impractical to exhaust a coal supply close to the surface by stripping alone. As the coal supply accessible to stripping is exhausted, walls around the uncovered area remain. Augers are driven into these open wall faces to recover the remaining coal in the seam, which lies beneath the heavier overburden. Introduced in 1945, auger mining now accounts for approximately 3 percent of the nation's coal production.

Coal Processing

Once the raw coal is out of the mine, further processing prior to delivery to the customer is required. In a preparation plant located near the mine, the raw coal is subjected to a complex sequence of sizing, wasting, and blending operations which remove the coal's impurities and bring it in line with customer specifications. After the coal is processed, it is usually stored in silos to await shipment.

Notes

CHAPTER 1

[1]World Energy Conference Survey of Energy Resources, 1974; as reported in *Coal Facts: 1974–1975*, National Coal Association, Washington, D.C.

[2]Major oil companies involved with coal.

[3]Other entrants besides Exxon include such big names in the oil industry as Texaco, Tenneco, Sunoco, Shell, Kerr-McGee, Mobil, Atlantic Richfield, Phillips. While none of these is among the top ten producers or reserve holders, most of them have over 1 billion tons of coal reserves.

[4]The Carter Oil Company was renamed Exxon Coal, U.S.A. on January 1, 1980.

[5]The Appendix describes briefly the distribution of U.S. coal reserves.

[6]Throughout this study Western coal refers to coal found west of the 100°0' longitudinal meridian, or approximately west of the Mississippi. Eastern coal refers to coal found east of the Mississippi. Western coal is predominantly better-grade, i.e., it has a sulfur content of 1 percent and less, but is also lower in rank than Eastern coals, i.e., it has a lower energy value.

[7]L. G. Evans, Executive Vice-President, Island Creek Coal Company (See Chapter 5).

[8]See Appendix for a brief discussion of the size, location, rank, and grade of U.S. coals.

[9]See Appendix for a brief description of coal-mining technologies in use.

CHAPTER 2

[1]Ashby demonstrates how every system has certain "essential variables" that must be kept within assigned limits in order to ensure the survival of the system. The essential variables of a business organization are "effectiveness" and "efficiency."

230   **Notes**

CHAPTER 3

[1]The National Coal Association (NCA) is a national trade association of coal-producing companies which represent its members in legislative matters and in the promotion of coal utilization.

[2]The Bituminous Coal Operators Association, Inc., (BCOA) is a national association of coal-producing companies which represents its members in collective bargaining with their employees on matters of wages, hours, and working conditions, and is engaged in the promotion of better mine health and safety methods.

[3]NCA and BCOA, "Federal Coal Mine Health and Safety Act of 1969. A Constructive Analysis with Recommendations for Improvement," 1977.

[4]"Confrontation," *Forbes*, November 15, 1972.

[5]"The Gloom in Coal," *Business Week*, November 28, 1977.

[6]J. Le Roy Balzer and R. E. Nelson, "Establishing an Environmental Department," AMC 1975 Mining Convention.

[7]In the case of Carter Oil, for example, even the most optimistic scenario for coal would show a contribution of less than 3 percent of Exxon's projected earnings in 1985 (see James Flanigan, "Does Exxon Have a Future?," *Forbes*, August 15, 1977).

[8]General Accounting Office, "The State of Competition in the Coal Industry," December 30, 1977.

[9]Martin B. Zimmerman, "Estimating a Policy Model of U.S. Coal Supply," WorkingPaper No. MIT-EL-77-042WP, Massachusetts Institute of Technology, December 1977.

[10]Dick Kirschten, "Watch Out! The Great Coal Rush Has Started," *National Journal*, October 29, 1977.

[11]Ibid.

[12]"Confrontation," *Forbes*, November 15, 1972.

[13]"Coal Transporters Face Challenge," *Keystone Coal Industry Manual*, 1977.

[14]"Coal Transporters Face Challenge," Ibid.

[15]Mel Horwitch, "Uncontrolled Growth and Unfocused Growth: Unsuccessful Life Cycles of Large Scale, Public-Private, Technological Enterprises," Symposium on the Management of Science and Technology, Rio de Janeiro, June 22−23, 1978.

[16]All these processes are described briefly in "New Processes Brighten Prospects of Synthetic Fuels from Coal," *Coal Age*, April 1974.

[17]George Getschow, "Coal Miners are Living 'Good Life' as Wages Soar with Oil Prices," *Wall Street Journal,* November 10, 1978.

[18]U.S. Department of Labor, *Technology Change and Productivity in the Bituminous Coal Industry 1920−60*, November 1961.

[19]"A New Harmony at the UMW," *Business Week*, December 24, 1979.

[20]John A. Patton, "The Foreman: Most Misused Person in Industry," *Management Review*, November 1979.

[21]Bob Arnold, "The Coal Boss," *The Wall Street Journal,* November 6, 1975.

[22]John A. Patton, op. cit.

[23]Edmond Faltermeyer, "Clearing the Way for the New Age of Coal," *Fortune*, May 1974, pp. 215−338.

CHAPTER 4

[1]Annual Report, 1947.
[2]Annual Report, 1953.
[3]Annual Report, 1964.
[4]"NACCO Aims for Doubling of Output," *Coal Age*, October 1977.
[5]Stripping ratio is the ratio of depth of overburden to the depth of the coal seam.

CHAPTER 5

[1]*Fortune*, March 1938.
[2]Ibid.
[3]In "The Making of a Giant, the History of Island Creek Coal Company," *Oxy Today and Yesterday*, No. 9, 1977, p. 13.
[4]Excerpts from "Background Notes and Comments on 'The Individuals Count' Theme," Island Creek, 1976. The reference is to younger miners.
[5]Ibid.
[6]Ibid.
[7]See Section (C)(1) of the contract between the UMW and BCOA, March 1978. J. E. Katlic was one of the industry negotiators. He considers this addition a most important one.
[8]Stonie Barker, Jr., "The Making of a Giant, The History of Island Creek Coal Company," *Oxy Today and Yesterday*, No. 9, 1977, p. 13.

CHAPTER 6

[1]Continental Oil Company, *Conoco, The First One Hundred Years* (New York: Dell, 1975), p. 205.
[2]"Unlocking Noble County's Troublesome Treasure," *Conoco 77*, Vol. 2, p. 19.
[3]Ralph E. Bailey, Chairman and Chief Executive Officer, Consol, "Coal Operating Environment and Strategies," *Strategies and Outlook,* May 1, 1977, p. 47.
[4]Ibid.
[5]"Up in Smoke," *Forbes*, December 1975.
[6]Ralph E. Bailey, *Strategies and Outlook*, p. 50.
[7]Ibid.
[8]Ralph E. Bailey, *Strategies and Outlook*.
[9]See Appendix for an explanation of longwall mining.
[10]"The Development of Consolidation Coal Company's Centralized Management Development Program," Consol, August 1977.
[11]Compliance quality refers to approximately 0.5 percent sulfur in Western coals and 0.7 percent sulfur in Eastern coals, by weight (equivalent to 1.2 pounds SO_2 per million BTU and applicable to plants built in 1972–78). The difference in percentages is because of the lower heating value of Western coals. Western coals have approximately 70 percent of the heating value, in BTU/lb, of that of Eastern coals (10–12,000 BTU/lb).

[12]*Coal Facts*: 1974—*1975,* National Coal Association, Washington, D.C., p. 76.

[13]As of 1973, Consol had approximately 10 billion tons of reserves, which would last nearly 200 years at Consol's then rate of production. Over 75 percent of these reserves had not been assigned to a specific project or contract.

[14]Roger Haynes was the Conoco officer transferred to Consol in 1966 to help in its recruitment efforts. He was in charge of employee relations in 1975.

[15]In late 1977, B. R. Brown was elected President of Consol. R. E. Samples became the Chairman of Consol on Ralph Bailey's promotion to President of Conoco; Brown continued to hold temporary charge of the industrial-, employee- and public-relations functions; and Samples held temporary charge of the sales function.

CHAPTER 7

[1]"History of the Carter Oil Company," a company report, 1977.

[2]All the marketing executives at Carter Oil have come from Exxon.

[3]"History of the Carter Oil Company," a company report, 1977.

[4]"Coal, America's Ace in the Hole," *Exxon USA*, Fourth Quarter, 1976.

[5]Also called Substitute Natural Gas.

[6]Co-op programs are programs run cooperatively by the company and an educational or vocational training school. The latter provides formal classroom instruction and the company provides complementary practical training.

[7]Carter Mining Company was not unionized.

[8]James Flanigan, "Does Exxon Have a Future?" *Forbes*, August 15, 1977.

[9]Reactivity refers to the chemical activity of coal in the gasification process.

[10]A "contact executive" is a management committee member who is responsible for providing policy guidance to those organizations for which he is the contact. He stays well informed about the plans of those organizations and the problems they face. The organizations consult him on any matter they expect to review with the management committee. On many matters, he himself has the final say.

[11]However, one of the former senior vice-presidents, R. H. Quenan, had considerable experience in the coal industry prior to joining Exxon.

CHAPTER 8

[1]"The Outlook for Coal Demand and Supply," National Coal Association, October 12, 1977.

[2]The Synthetic Fuels Corporation, established by the federal government, is projected to provide incentives for a capacity of 2 million barrels per day of synthetic liquid and gas by 1985. This converts to approximately 188 million tons of coal per year. The program includes biomass conversion, oil-shale retorting, recovery from tar sand, etc.—other processes besides coal gasification and liquefaction. The projection for coal should be lower than 188 million tons.

[3]B. R. Brown, the then executive vice-president, industrial, employee and public relations (see Chapter 6).

[4]Eric Reichl, President of the Conoco Coal Development Company (see Chapter 6).

[5]James Flanigan, "Does Exxon Have a Future?" *Forbes* August 15, 1977.

CHAPTER 9

[1]See "A Note on the Boston Consulting Group Concept of Competitive Analyses and Corporate Strategy," Intercollegiate Case Clearing House, No. 9–175–175, 1975, for a summary description of the BCG approach.

[2]"Texas Instruments Incorporated," ICCH 9–172–054, Intercollegiate Case Clearing House, Harvard Business School, Boston, 1972.

[3]The top twenty coal companies currently contribute over 50 percent of the industry's production.

[4]"The Oil Majors Bet on Coal," *Business Week*, September 24, 1979, p. 104.

[5]"Coal-state Senators, Environmentalists Waging Political Battle Over EPA Levels," *Wall Street Journal,* May 7, 1979.

[6]Telegram sent on April 26, 1977, by Carl E. Bagge, President, National Coal Association to President Jimmy Carter.

[7]General Accounting Office, "The State of Competition in the Coal Industry," December 30, 1977.

APPENDIX

[1]The energy value of coal is measured in various units, e.g., British Thermal Unit (BTU), calorie. The BTU is commonly used in the United States and represents the heat required to raise the temperature of a pound of water by one degree Fahrenheit.

[2]Coking is the process by which volatile matter is removed from coal, leaving a material of high carbon content called coke which is used in steel-making as well as for special fuel purposes. Coking coal or coal used in the production of steel is commonly referred to as metallurgical coal. This appendix will not deal with coking coals.

[3]*Coal Resources of the United States* (A Progress Report, *October 1, 1953*), Geological Survey Circular 293, U.S. Department of Interior, p. 8.

[4]*Coal Facts: 1974–1975*, National Coal Association, Washington, D.C. p. 72.

[5]Ibid.

[6]Edmund Faltermeyer, "Clearing the Way for the New Age of Coal," *Fortune,* May 1974.

Bibliography

Abernathy, William J. *The Productivity Dilemma: Roadblock to Innovation in the Automobile Industry*. Baltimore, Maryland: Johns Hopkins University Press, 1978.

Abernathy, William J., & Chakravarthy, B. S. Government Intervention and Innovation in Industry: A Policy Framework. *Sloan Management Review*, Spring 1979.

Andrews, Kenneth R. *The Concept of Corporate Strategy*. Homewood, Illinois: Dow Jones–Irwin, 1971.

Ansoff, H. Igor. The Changing Shape of the Strategic Problem. In Schendel, Dan E., & Hofer, C.W. (Eds). *Strategic Management: A New View of Business Policy and Planning*. Boston: Little, Brown, 1979.

Ashby, W. Ross. *An Introduction to Cybernetics*. London: Chapman & Hall, Ltd., and University Paperbacks, 1971.

Barnard, Chester I. *The Functions of the Executive*. Cambridge, Massachusetts.: Harvard University Press, 1938.

Bower, Joseph L. *Managing the Resource Allocation Process: A Study of Corporate Planning and Investment*. Boston, Massachusetts.: Graduate School of Business Administration, Harvard University, 1970.

Burns, Tom, & Stalker, G.M. *The Management of Innovation*. London: Tavistock Publications, 1961.

Chakravarthy, Balaji S. Adapting to Changes in the Coal Industry: A Managerial Perspective. Doctoral dissertation, Harvard University, 1978

Chandler, Alfred D. *Strategy and Structure: Chapters in the History of the American Industrial Enterprise*. Cambridge, Massachusetts.: MIT Press, 1962.

Christensen, C. Roland, Andrews, K.R. & Bower, J.L. *Business Policy: Text and Cases*. Homewood, Illinois.: Richard D. Irwin, 1973.

Christensen, C. Roland, Berg, N. A., & Salter, M. S. *Policy Formulation and Administration: A Casebook of Top-Management Problems in Business*. Homewood, Ill.: Richard D. Irwin, 1976.

Christenson, Charles J. The "Contingency Theory" of Organization: A Methodological Analysis. Working Paper HBS 73–36, Graduate School of Business Administration, Harvard University, 1973.

Cyert, Richard M., & March, James G. *A Behavioral Theory of the Firm*. Englewood Cliffs, New Jersey.: Prentice-Hall, 1963.

Dunn, Edgar S., Jr. *Economic and Social Development: A Process of Social Learning*. Baltimore, Maryland.: Johns Hopkins University Press, 1971.

Galbraith, Jay R. *Designing Complex Organizations*. Reading, Mass.: Addison-Wesley, 1973.

Greiner, Larry E. Evolution and Revolution as Organizations Grow, *Harvard Business Review*, July–August 1972.

Jelinek, Mariann. *Institutionalizing Innovation: A Study of Organizational Learning Systems*. New York, New York.: Praeger, 1979.

Kast, Fremont E., & Rosenzweig, J. E., *Contingency Views of Organization and Management*. Chicago, Illinois.: Science Research Associates, 1973.

Lawrence, Paul R., & Lorsch, J. W. *Organization and Environment: Managing Differentiation and Integration*. Boston, Massachusetts.: Graduate School of Business, Harvard University, 1967.

Learned, Edmund P., Christensen, C. R., & Andrews, K. R. *Problems of General Management*. Homewood, Ill.: Richard D. Irwin, 1961.

Learned, Edmund P., Christensen, C. R., Andrews, K. R., & Guth, W. D. *Business Policy: Text and Cases*. Homewood, Ill.: Richard D. Irwin, 1969.

Levitt, Theodore. Marketing Myopia, *Harvard Business Review*, September–October 1975.

Miles, Robert H., & Cameron, K. S. Coffin Nails and Corporate Strategies, Working paper No. 3, School of Organization and Management, Yale University, 1977.

Miles, Raymond E., & Snow, C. C. *Organizational Strategy, Structure and Process*. New York, New York.: McGraw-Hill, 1978.

Normann, Richard, *Management and Statesmanship*. Stockholm: Scandinavian Institute for Administrative Research, 1976.

Roethlisberger, Fritz J. *The Elusive Phonomena: An Autobiographical Account of My Work in the Field of Organizational Behavior at the Harvard Business School*, Cambridge, Mass.: Harvard University Press, 1978.

Rumelt, Richard P. *Strategy, Structure, and Economic Performance*. Boston, Massachusetts.: Graduate School of Business Administration, Harvard University, 1974.

Salter, Malcolm S. Stages of Corporate Development, *Journal of Business Policy 1*, *1*, 1970.

Schendel, Dan E., & Hofer, C. W. *Strategic Management: A New View of Business Policy and Planning*, Boston, Massachusetts.: Little, Brown, 1979.

Scott, Bruce R. Stages of Corporate Development. Harvard Business School, Intercollegiate Case Clearing House, ICCH No. 9–371–294, 1971.

Shank, John K., Niblock, E. G. & Sandalls, W. T., Jr. Balance "Creativity" and "Practicality" in Formal Planning, *Harvard Business Review,* January–February, 1973.

Simon, Herbert A. *Administrative Behavior: A Study of Decision-Making Processes in Administrative Organization.* New York, New York: Macmillan, 1945.

Simon, Herbert A. *The Sciences of the Artificial.* Cambridge, Mass.: MIT Press, 1969.

Sloan, Alfred P., Jr. *My Years with General Motors.* Garden City, N.Y.: Doubleday, 1972.

Stobaugh, Robert, & Yergin, D. (Eds.). *Energy Future.* New York: Random House, 1979.

Vancil, Richard R. Better Management of Corporate Development, *Harvard Business Review*, September–October, 1972.

Wilson, Carroll L. *Coal: Bridge to the Future.* Cambridge, Mass.: Ballinger, 1980.

Woodward, Joan. *Industrial Organization: Theory and Practice.* London: Oxford University Press, 1965.

Wrigley, Leonard. Divisional Autonomy and Diversification. Doctoral dissertation, Harvard University, 1970.

Index

United States Coal and Oil Company, 86
United States Oil Company, 85
United Thacker Coal Company, 86
Unit train, 55
Unstable Fit, discussion of, 27. *See* Adaptive fit, unstable
Unstable state, discussion of, 20. *See* Adaptation, unstable state of
Utah International, 48
Utility markets, 41, 53, 171, 172, 173, 174, 217; strengthening of, 2; and NACCO, 69; and Island Creek, 87; and Consol, 111; and Carter Oil, 160

Vancil, Richard R., 211

Virginia Pocahontas Division, Island Creek, 95

Western Region, Consol, 125
West Kentucky Coal Company, 87
White hat function, 91, 92
Wilson, Carroll L., 1
Winkler, synthetics technology, 10, 57, 138, 142
Woodward, Joan, 16
Working conditions, in mines, 37
World War I, impact on coal industry, 106, 170
World War II, impact on coal industry, 37, 68, 86, 106, 169
Wrigley, Leonard, 15